D0823322

DISCARDED
From Nashville Public Library

The Main Street of America Cookbook

66

A Culinary Journey Down Route 66

by Marian Clark

COUNCIL OAK BOOKS

TULSA AND SAN FRANCISCO

ALSO BY MARIAN CLARK:

THE ROUTE 66 COOKBOOK

THE SOUTHWESTERN HERITAGE COOKBOOK

COUNCIL OAK BOOKS

TULSA, OK 74120

USA

©1997 BY MARIAN CLARK

ALL RIGHTS RESERVED

FIRST EDITION 1997

01 00 99 98 97   6 5 4 3 2 1

DESIGNED BY CAROL HARALSON

ISBN 1-57178-024-6

LIBRARY OF CONGRESS CATALOGING-IN-PUBLICATION DATA

Clark, Marian, 1934—
    Main street of America cookbook / by Marian Clark. -- 1st ed.
        p.   cm.
    "A Route 66 culinary adventure."
    Includes bibliographical references (p.   ) and index.
    ISBN 1-57178-024-6 (pbk, : alk. paper)
        1. Cookery, American. 2. Restaurants—United States—Guidebooks.
3. United States—Guidebooks. 4. United States Highway 66.
I. Title.
TX715.C577797   1997
641.5973—dc21   97-28528
                                            CIP

PHOTO CREDITS

BY DAN HARLOW: Halftitle page ("Coffee 10¢"), cover photo ("Rose City Diner"), and cover photo detail shown above contents on page 7 ©Dan Harlow, Orange, California.

BY SHELLEE GRAHAM: Frontispiece ("Rio Bravo"), title page ("Time to Eat"), contents spread (detail of "City Diner Sign"), and illustration for preface, pages 8-9 (detail of "Trucking on 66") ©Shellee Graham, Bridgeton, Missouri.

Postcard images pages 17, 71, 107, 115, 181, 207, 237, 267 from the collection of Michael Wallis and Suzanne Fitzgerald Wallis, Tulsa, Oklahoma.

FOR REBECCA AND MEGAN

WHO CONSTANTLY CHALLENGE ME
WITH THEIR OWN SPIRIT
OF ADVENTURE

C O N T E N T S

Preface

"66 IS THE MOTHER ROAD. . . "

JOHN STEINBECK

WHAT CAN WE EXPECT to find along Route 66 today?" This question, or one similar to it, has been repeated often as I have traveled America's most famous highway the last few years. *The Main Street of America Cookbook* is my response to that question.

Food in a cultural context remains one of my passions. The recipes in this book reflect today's lifestyle. The food is a unique expression of who we are.

I began this new search along Route 66 in Chicago where Navy Pier is the city's amazing gift to the world. The pier offers a sensory experience both monumental and overpowering, a lasting tribute to man's creative ability.

At the western terminus of the highway, busy Santa Monica Pier bustles with energy, satisfying a whole new generation with excitement, opportunity, and the promise of vistas yet to be explored.

Between the two, I rediscovered Route 66 communities that have taken on new life in the 90s. Some bustle with the pride of Main Street renewal programs. Others are quiet and sleepy. But the 1926 images are gone forever. Inevitable changes have turned each toward the future.

In every town I moved away from Route 66, a few blocks and sometimes a few miles, to explore new areas. I met exciting young chefs who are determined to serve the best of today's cuisine. And I found classic remains—those comfortable and homespun cafes where locals exchange news and renew friendships.

"FOOD HAS NEVER TAKEN A BACK SEAT ON ROUTE 66. IT NEVER WILL. IF YOU FANCY YOURSELF A TRUE 'ROAD WARRIOR,' AND SAVOR HOT FOOD AND COLD DRINK, YOU WILL UNDERSTAND THAT MEAL STOPS ARE STILL THE BEST WAY TO MARK YOUR TRAIL WHEN TRAVELING THIS COUNTRY'S MOST FAMOUS HIGHWAY."

MICHAEL WALLIS

". . . 66 DID
INDEED SPAN
THE NATION,
GAVE BIRTH TO
THE MOTEL AGE,
AND THE WINDS
THAT BLEW UP
ITS DUST ALSO
BLEW UP
FUNDAMENTAL
CHANGES IN
AMERICA."

JENKIN LLOYD JONES

"THE MOST
AMERICAN THING
IN AMERICA IS
U.S. ROUTE 66—
IT PUTS THE ACT
OF GOING ABOVE
THE ACT OF
ARRIVING."

THE NEW REPUBLIC

"LOADING UP ON
LOCAL
SPECIALTIES IS
THE ONLY WAY
TO GET THE TRUE
FLAVOR OF THE
PLACES YOU
VISIT."

JOHN MARIANI

I also met a host of wonderful hometown cooks who still prepare the mouth-watering dishes remembered from childhood. They willingly shared favorite recipes, happy to showcase their ethnic favorites and creative adaptations. I found those good cooks in many places—working in libraries, volunteering with 4-H Clubs, operating bed and breakfasts, entering food competitions at community fairs, and gathering recipes for church cookbooks. Their recipes reflect a yeasty mix of cultures, gleaned from people who form the heart and soul of our country. From Navy Pier to Santa Monica Pier, Route 66 communities offer amazing variety. Travelers today can sample mouth-watering cornbread at a fun-filled dutch oven cookoff in New Mexico, eat an enormous country breakfast spread under the never-ending Texas sky, and enjoy perfectly fried catfish served with pride in a Missouri cave.

All along the Main Street of America there remain opportunities to savor delicious bites of history. Have dinner in a bank-turned-restaurant that was once robbed by Jesse James and Cole Younger, eat breakfast at El Tovar surrounded by the ghosts of Harvey girls who helped tame the West, and marvel at a tree inside a 1934 cedar building where good food is still served to weary guests.

The sometimes quirky culture of the 90s is also evident. A life size, neon-trimmed yellow submarine bursts forth from a mall storefront in California featuring (what else?) submarine sandwiches. And a great cafe with the unconventional title of Yippee Yi Yo is housed inside a busy 1910 grocery store in Oklahoma.

Community festivals and fairs all along Route 66 showcase local creativity. Participants can sample a piece of the world's largest onion burger in El Reno, Oklahoma, compete for

10

honors in preparing the best horseradish jelly in Collinsville, Illinois, or join others in an old-fashioned California grape stomp in Rancho Cucamonga, California. All these things shape community identity and add to a sense of pride.

Of course, many Route 66 road giants remain—-places like Ted Drewes in St. Louis, the Big Texan in Amarillo, and the El Rancho Hotel in Gallup—-places to be revisited, refueling the soul and satisfying a need to remember the past.

In the sidebars that accompany the recipes, I made suggestions of "What to see," "Where to eat," and "Where to stay." There was no attempt to rate or rank. Suggestions listed under "What to see" are the places that fascinated me.

Eateries that are mentioned range from the elegant to the smallest of diners. In no way did I try to make a "complete" list. I'm sure I missed a number of great places. But I did visit all but a handful of the restaurants listed, not always to eat, but to go in, absorb the atmosphere, and talk with cooks, guests, chefs, or owners. A few places were recommended by trusted friends. A few may no longer be in business by the time you begin your own search. Ownership changes unexpectedly. A restaurant that offers great food one week may not meet expectations at another time. I chalk this up to experience. For me, searching for the great one-of-a-kind stops beats eating generic food at chains every time.

Bed and breakfasts along the highway offer a new perspective for travelers. Always warm and comfortable, with a host and hostess who invariably enjoy people, we found them to be terrific places to learn about each area. Bed and breakfasts weren't included on my list unless I made personal contact. But like

"A STOP IN ONE OF THE SMALL TOWNS MOST ANYWHERE ALONG OLD ROUTE 66 OFFERS EVIDENCE THAT LIFE BEGINS AT THE OFFRAMP. AWAY FROM THE SUPERSLAB, YOU CAN STILL ORDER A PIECE OF PIE FROM THE PERSON WHO BAKED IT, STILL GET YOUR CHANGE RIGHT FROM THE SHOP OWNER, STILL TAKE A MOMENT TO CARE AND BE CARED ABOUT, A LONG WAY FROM HOME."

TOM SYNDER

"ROUTE 66 IS A
GIANT CHUTE
DOWN WHICH
THE REST OF THE
NATION IS
SLIDING INTO
SOUTHERN
CALIFORNIA."

FRANK LLOYD WRIGHT

"ROUTE 66. THE
NAME IS MAGIC.
ROUTE 66. IT
WILL ALWAYS
MEAN GOING
SOMEWHERE."

MICHAEL WALLIS

restaurant owners, those operating bed and breakfasts tire, change management, close, and reopen with new enthusiasm. We live in a dynamic society—nothing remains the same forever. New opportunities always remain. We will journey again.

I want this cookbook to salute all the wonderful cooks who welcomed me into their kitchens and their lives. This book is as much their story as it is the story of Route 66 today. The collection encompasses a wide range of dishes. Some purely regional, some traditional American, some with European or Asian roots, but all with the personal touch of proven favorites. The whole has blended together as a somewhat uncommon cookbook, one that I hope you can take along as you travel Route 66 in order to meet the people and enjoy the opportunities available in each area.

Traveling through Route 66 communities today is still one of the best ways to see our country. Europe has the Orient Express, China has the Great Wall, and America has Route 66. The Main Street of America continues to capture the imagination and essence of our nation. The highway offers an eight-state culinary adventure!

My suggestion is to travel short segments of the old road at one time. Drive Main Streets, explore, and examine what each community considers worthwhile. Don't hurry. Eat at the one-of-a-kind stops. Visit and ask questions, search for the unexpected, and add to your own collection of special treasures. You will be richly rewarded. I can guarantee that you will leave each town as I did, with fresh impressions and new enthusiasm!

MARIAN CLARK

TULSA, OKLAHOMA 1997

ACKNOWLEDGMENTS

WONDERFUL PEOPLE all along Route 66 shared their time, their stories, and their cherished recipes to make this book possible. I have been enriched by each person and feel very fortunate to have made new friends I will always treasure.

My husband, Ken, was invaluable in the search. He offered counsel and support, traveled countless miles, helped clear up computer problems, sampled many, many recipes, and never complained when we missed meals or I took off on a new expedition.

The rest of my family was wonderful, too. A cousin, Donna Lea, traveled with me to Chicago as photographer, driver, and record keeper. My sister-in-law and her husband, Mary and Bob Fair, tested recipes, took photographs, traveled the highway, and reconfirmed information. My daughter, Rebecca tested recipes and did proofreading and my son, Kevin, helped solve computer problems.

Special thanks to Ann Arwood, my friend and fellow home economist who carefully tested many of the recipes. And my thanks to her husband, J.P., who also tested and sampled the results.

Chuck Tegeler solved computer problems, helped when I needed answers and made hardware and software problems go away. His help was invaluable.

Liz Medley proofread. Mary Gubser shared ideas and wisdom from her own publishing experience. Ethel Riggin traveled with me and helped locate several of the people whose

ROUTE 66 STATE ASSOCIATIONS, NATIONAL FEDERATION AND ROUTE 66 MAGAZINE

ROUTE 66 ASSOCIATION OF ILLINOIS 2743 Veterans Parkway, Suite 166, Springfield, Illinois 62704

ROUTE 66 ASSOCIATION OF MISSOURI P.O. Box 8117, St. Louis, Missouri 63156

KANSAS HISTORIC ROUTE 66 ASSOCIATION P.O. Box 169, Riverton, Kansas 66770

OKLAHOMA ROUTE 66 ASSOCIATION P.O. Box 21382, Oklahoma City, Oklahoma 73156

OLD ROUTE 66 ASSOCIATION OF TEXAS P.O. Box 66, McLean, Texas 79057

NEW MEXICO ROUTE 66 ASSOCIATION 1415 Central NE, Albuquerque, New Mexico 87106

HISTORIC ROUTE 66 ASSOCIATION OF ARIZONA P.O. Box 66, Kingman, Arizona 86402

CALIFORNIA HISTORIC
ROUTE 66 ASSOCIATION
2127 Foothill Boulevard,
#66, LaVerne, California
91750

*There are also Route 66
Associations in Belgium,
Canada, Japan, France,
and the Netherlands.*

NATIONAL HISTORIC
ROUTE 66 FEDERATION
"Working nationwide to
save the legendary high-
way." P.O. Box 423,
Tujunga, California 91043-
0423

ROUTE 66 MAGAZINE
326 West Route 66,
Williams, Arizona 86046

recipes are included. Glaida Funk was particularly helpful in locating several homemakers whose contributions enriched the Illinois segment. Cheryl Grace, my husband's office manager, provided help and support. Michael and Suzanne Wallis shared their support, enthusiasm, and "Pretty Boy's Apple Pie."

And to countless librarians, newspaper office personnel, Chamber of Commerce employees, and other community supporters all along the highway, my thanks for being so kind in answering questions! Route 66 Association members in every state gave me wonderful help as well.

I would also like to express my special appreciation to each of the following people for their special contributions.

ILLINOIS

Marilynn Kelly, Assistant Director of Public Relations, Navy Pier, Chicago; James Sheahan, Mayor's Office of Special Events, Taste of Chicago Festival; Kathy Hedrich, Chicago; Karen McFarland, Chicago; John Curran, Chicago; Dolly Johnson, Volunteer Services Dept., Northwestern Memorial Hospital, Chicago; Harvey and Jackie Dunn, La Grange; Mark Dunn, La Grange; Helen Bryan, Wilmington; Amy Gantzert, Morris; Mayreta Webber and Juanita Tews, Chenoa Library; Tom Knudsen, Bloomington; Tom Teague, Springfield; Beverly Lessen, Lincoln; Staff at the Edwardsville Public Library; Sallie Jo Burtin, Collinsville Convention and Visitors Bureau; Judy McCann, Collinsville.

MISSOURI

Pat Biggs, Webster Groves; Lisa Nouss, Mary Lou Koelkebeck, Susan Barley, Diane Gombaro, Cheryl Behan, Elene L. Ginsburg, and June Sadler, all of St. Louis; Lori Murray, Kirkwood; Pat Walker, Springfield; Virginia Krietmeyer, Tulsa; Barbara Poage, Springfield Convention and Visitors Bureau; Crista Shaler and Sherry Cook, Springfield.

KANSAS

Dorotha Senter, Galena; Gena Shockley, Galena; Scott Nelson, Riverton; Forrest Nelson, Riverton; Carolyn Nichols, Baxter Springs; Mary Ellen Lee, Baxter Springs; Sheryll Vogel, Riverton.

OKLAHOMA

Staff at the Tulsa City/County Library; Micky Johnson, Quapaw; Jana Logan and Vicki Crawford, Commerce; Jill Fitzgibbon, J-M Farms, Inc., Miami; Peggy Angle, First National Bank of Miami; Beverly McLain, Oklahoma Tourist Information Center, Vinita; Mike and Steve Kennon, Chouteau; Jeanie Norman, Grand Lake Chamber of Commerce; Sherry McKay, Afton; Marilyn Peterson, Tulsa; Suzanne Holloway, Tulsa; Randy Reynolds, Tulsa; Laurie Quinnelly, Lifestyle Editor, *Sapulpa Daily Herald*; Jim Hubbard, Sapulpa Historical Museum; Myra Kemp, Bristow; Joann Smith, Stroud Library; Carol Smaglinski, *Edmond Evening Sun*; Mary Ellen Flanagan, Oklahoma City; Margie Snowden North, Erick; Eunice Gamble, Erick; Kay Atkins, Texola.

TEXAS

Delbert and Ruth Trew, Alanreed; Gladys Breedlove, Amarillo; Kay Kennedy, Amarillo; Betty Farrell, Amarillo; Joann Harwell, Vega; Melba Rook, Landergin; Robert and Priscilla Jacobson, Adrian; Fran Houser, Adrian.

NEW MEXICO

Carolyn Lee, Santa Fe; David and Rebecca Steel, Albuquerque; Martha Heard, Albuquerque; Jake Lovato, Bernalillo; Ethel E. Hill, Gallup; Suzy McComb, Moriarty Chamber of Commerce.

ARIZONA

John Erwin and the staff at Flagstaff City-Coconino County Public Library; Staff at Flagstaff Visitors Bureau; Valerie Rodenbaugh, Tulsa and Winslow; Holbrook Chamber of Commerce; Vilma Delgadillo, Seligman, Jackie Rowland, Oatman.

CALIFORNIA

Dan Harlow, Director of Victorville Route 66 Museum, Orange; Bob and Mary Fair, Medford, Oregon; Mike Fair, Colorado Springs, Colorado; Sally Gilmore, Pasadena; David and Mary Lou Knudson, Tujunga; June Hart, Azuza; the staff at Monrovia Public Library; Russell Barnard and Mitch Cohen, Santa Monica Pier.

Route 66, The Main Street of America, was launched from Grant Park in the heart of Chicago in 1926. The highway with a thousand echoes snaked south and westward to the Pacific Ocean. Those echoes still resound throughout Illinois. Some call them tradition. Others say Illinois natives evolve from strong roots, but whatever the term, a fierce pride remains in this anchor state where Route 66 began its journey.

Always a leader in the cattle, hog, corn, and wheat industries, it is only natural that Illinois offers culinary treasures yet to be discovered.

Begin by feeding your body as well as your soul at Widow Newton's on Navy Pier, then reminisce in the old Pump Room seats at Wolf's Head Inn or dine at a table where Eleanor Roosevelt visited with her friends in Bloomington. Sample the smoothest caramels in Illinois, attend a festival to celebrate horseradish, and experience the best of good home cooking shared by prairie cooks in communities from Chicago to the Mississippi. Illinois along Route 66 offers entertainment, variety, charm, history, and hundreds of satisfying culinary experiences!

Chicago

2.8 million residents, more than 8 million in the metroplex

WHAT TO SEE:

NAVY PIER Spend time at Navy Pier to discover food and fun for the whole family. Grand Ave. at Lakeshore Dr. (800) 595-PIER

TASTE OF CHICAGO Visit the "Taste of Chicago Festival," the biggest and most popular summer festival in the city. Grant Park on Lake Michigan, 10 days surrounding the 4th of July each year. (312) 744-3370

ARCHITECTURAL TOURS Take one of more than 50 tours sponsored by the Chicago Architecture Foundation. (312) 922-TOUR

CYCLING Cycle along Lake Michigan, May through October. 435 E. Illinois. (312) 923-0100

ART INSTITUTE Visit the Art Institute of Chicago, Michigan Ave. at Adams St., to see the world's greatest collection of Impressionist paintings and much more. (312) 443-3600

MERCHANDISE MART Tour the Merchandise Mart, one of the largest buildings in America. 200 World Trade Center. (312) 644-4664

GOOD FOOD IN CHICAGO:

The city of Chicago caters to those who love to eat. More than 6,000 restaurants offer an eclectic presence and provide the public with a smorgasbord of taste treats. Hearty steaks, Chicago-style pizza, Italian sausages, and German beer are only a few of the favorites. Other culinary hits from Chicagoland that have become a part of our American culture include Cracker Jacks, Butterfingers, Hostess Twinkies, Fannie May chocolates, cafeterias, and McDonald's restaurants.

Begin your journey at Navy Pier, just a few blocks from Grant Park. The powerful presence of the new Navy Pier has dominated the Lake Michigan waterfront since renovation was completed in 1995. Over 50 acres of promenades, gardens, shops, restaurants, and entertainment attractions offer unique opportunities in this magnificent city.

Navy Pier is a proud city's redevelopment miracle that will challenge the imagination of both young and old for years to come. The 15-story Ferris wheel provides a magnificent view of the city. The Chicago Children's Museum, IMAX Theater, and a host of dinner cruise boats contribute their own unique set of opportunities.

Over 15 vibrant restaurants are scattered along the pier offering visitors a mouth-watering array of culinary delights. These three fine eateries exemplify the variety and quality of the dining experience at Navy Pier.

Crystal Garden Cafe can be found under a canopy of geodesic lights inside a one-acre botanical park. The six-story glass atrium houses more than 70 palm trees along with evergreens, flowering anthuriums, ivy, and over 200 seasonal flowers.

This year-round tropical paradise also includes dramatic fountains and plenty of seating for visitors to enjoy the spectacular scenery.

At night, thousands of chains of miniature lights reflect from the glass dome, creating a year round Christmas fairyland.

Crystal Garden Cafe offers casual dining on one side of the atrium. When the weather is fine, sliding glass doors provide extra space on an outer deck. Patrons can absorb the Chicago skyline, glide with sailboats on Lake Michigan, and soar with the landmark Ferris wheel that rises 150 feet overhead.

The menu at this unique cafe offers a variety of moderately priced creative dishes prepared with the help of sous'chef Tim Hurley, who shared this recipe for stuffed jalapeños, a Crystal Garden favorite.

CRYSTAL GARDEN CAFE
Stuffed Jalapeños

For each order, serve 5 medium-sized jalapeños, cleaned, seeded, and stemmed. Combine equal quantities of cream cheese, cottage cheese and ricotta cheese. Blend well. Stuff each pepper with the mixture.

Dip jalapeños in beaten eggs, then flour, then again in beaten eggs, and finally dip in fine bread crumbs combined with chile powder and paprika. Deep fry in canola oil heated to 350° until jalapeños are lightly browned. Serve accompanied with sour cream, lemon slices, and tomatillo sauce.

TOMATILLO SAUCE:

5 TOMATILLOS
1 LARGE CLOVE GARLIC, UNPEELED
1 SMALL JALAPEÑO, STEMMED AND SEEDED

ZOO Visit Lincoln Park Zoo, 2200 N. Cannon Dr. (312) 742-2000

SEARS TOWER Climb to the skydeck of the world's second tallest building, Sears Tower, 1,454 feet high, 233 S. Wacker Dr. (312) 875-9696

MAGNIFICENT MILE Shop along the Magnificent Mile—Michigan Ave.—or buy famous Frango Mints at Marshall Fields, the ultimate world-class department store at 111 North State St.

WHERE TO EAT:

AT THE NAVY PIER Widow Newton's Tavern, Crystal Garden Cafe, and Charlie's Ale House, all at 600 E. Grand Ave.

THE BERGHOFF 17 W. Adams St.

ELI'S CHICAGO'S FINEST, INC. 6510 W. Dakin St.

ZINFANDEL 59 W. Grand Ave.

POLKA SAUSAGE AND DELI 8753 S. Commercial Ave.

LOU MITCHELL'S Jackson and Canal

PIZZERIA UNO 29 E. Ohio St. Dished up its first pie in 1943 and considered the mother of all deep-dish pizza places.

CHESDAN'S RESTAURANT AND PIZZERIA 4465 S. Archer Ave. A good stop for Chicago-style pizza since 1948.

THE PARTHENON 314 S. Halstead for good Greek food.

WHERE TO STAY:

These two great American classics made up a part of the Chicago skyline even before Route 66 existed:

THE PALMER HOUSE 17 E. Monroe St.

THE BLACKSTONE HOTEL 636 S. Michigan Blvd.

1 SMALL ONION, CHOPPED
1/2 CUP CILANTRO
PINCH OF SALT

Husk and wash tomatillos. Roast the tomatillos, garlic, jalapeño and onion in a heavy skillet, stirring constantly until barely softened. Peel garlic and remove any blackened portions. Place in a blender or food processor with cilantro and coarsely chop. Add salt. Serve warm or chilled as an accompaniment to stuffed jalapeños. Makes 1-1/2 cups sauce.

At Widow Newton's Tavern, guests savor American cuisine among rare European antiques. This spirited Old English style roadhouse highlights open-hearth cookery and a full-service bar. Here is a place to pamper the palate, let your imagination run wild, become immersed in astrology, and enjoy the history of elaborate antiques including a fine collection of rare books, Frederick Hart sculptures, James Tissot art, and ceiling murals based on myth and astrology by Cindy and Jorge Simes.

Widow Newton's Tavern combines a sensitive integration of fine cuisine, image, and theme. A broad range of professional skill is evident. This is a place guests will not soon forget. Carl Sandburg called Chicago the "hog butcher to the world" so it seems very appropriate to include this sage-rubbed rack of pork on the menu. The pork recipe was created to serve from the large rotisserie oven at the tavern. A regular kitchen oven and roasting pan will achieve the same delicious results.

WIDOW NEWTON'S TAVERN

Sage-Rubbed Rack of Pork with Maple Whipped Sweet Potatoes

FOR THE PORK:

1 BONE-IN, CENTER-CUT PORK LOIN
1/4 CUP HONEY
1/2 CUP OLIVE OR VEGETABLE OIL
1/2 CUP CHOPPED FRESH SAGE
SALT AND FRESHLY GROUND PEPPER TO TASTE

FOR THE MAPLE WHIPPED SWEET POTATOES:

10 MEDIUM-SIZED SWEET POTATOES
1 CUP HIGH QUALITY MAPLE SYRUP
1/2 CUP BROWN SUGAR
CINNAMON TO TASTE
SALT AND PEPPER TO TASTE

In a mixing bowl combine honey, olive oil and sage. Brush mix over pork loin and marinate overnight. Roast pork in a preheated 350° oven for approximately 1-1/2 hours or until the internal temperature reaches 155°. Let meat stand for 15 minutes before carving.

Roast sweet potatoes in same oven until soft. Let cool for approximately 5 minutes but do not allow them to get cold. Remove skins. Place in a mixer with a paddle and whip until creamy. Add syrup, brown sugar, and cinnamon. Serve with the pork. 6 to 8 servings.

Charlie's Ale House, Navy Pier, is similar in style to the original Charlie's Ale House in Lincoln Park. Traditional tavern food is served here along with good down-home cooking. Homestyle pot roast, chicken pot pie, and meatloaf dinners are always on the menu. Desserts are simple but luscious—warm apple cobbler and chocolate mud pie. More than 40 different beers are available.

The atmosphere at Charlie's Ale House lends itself to light-hearted fun. There is seating for 80 inside, and an even larger crowd can be accommodated on the comfortable outdoor deck where customers can watch the crowds and take in some of the Chicago skyline.

Navy Pier employees gather here after hours to relax and swap stories. It's a great stop for visitors as well!

CHARLIE'S ALE HOUSE
Meat Loaf

1/2 MEDIUM-SIZED ONION, FINELY CHOPPED

1/2 SMALL RED BELL PEPPER, FINELY CHOPPED

2 CLOVES GARLIC, MINCED

1 TABLESPOON OIL

2 POUNDS GROUND BEEF

1 CUP BREAD CRUMBS

4 EGGS

6 TABLESPOONS PARMESAN CHEESE

1/2 CUP CHOPPED FRESH PARSLEY

2 TABLESPOONS WORCESTERSHIRE SAUCE

1-1/2 TEASPOONS BLACK PEPPER

1 TEASPOON SALT

1/4 CUP KETCHUP

Sauté onion, pepper, and garlic in oil until translucent. Let cool.

Mix remaining ingredients except ketchup and combine with the sautéed vegetables. Place mixture in loaf pan. Pour ketchup over meat loaf and bake in a preheated 375° oven for 1 hour. 8 to 10 servings.

The Taste of Chicago Festival, held each year in Grant Park, is the country's largest outdoor food. The annual week-long festivities surround the 4th of July and attract crowds estimated at more than 2-1/2 million. At this "American Celebration," taste-tempting dishes from around the world are served from dozens of gaily decorated tents and a special gourmet pavilion. Participants also have an opportunity to see food demonstrations by nationally known personalities.

The TASTE OF CHICAGO COOKBOOK *features many of the recipes served at the festival. Here is one fine example.*

CHESDAN'S RESTAURANT AND PIZZERIA

Toasted Ravioli

40 TO 50 MEAT OR CHEESE RAVIOLI
   (AVAILABLE IN GROCERY STORES)
1 CUP FLOUR
1/2 CUP PANCAKE MIX
1/2 TEASPOON SALT
1/4 TEASPOON PEPPER
1 CUP WATER, OR ENOUGH TO MAKE THICK
   BATTER
1-1/2 CUPS ITALIAN BREAD CRUMBS
VEGETABLE OIL FOR FRYING
1/2 POUND SLICED PROVOLONE CHEESE

Combine the flour, pancake mix, salt and pepper with just enough water to make the consistency of a thick batter. Dip ravioli into batter and let excess drip off, then dip into bread crumbs to coat. Fry ravioli in 350° vegetable oil for 2 to 3 minutes, or until golden brown. Top each ravioli with a small slice of Provolone cheese. Place in toaster oven until cheese begins to melt. Serve with meat or marinara sauce. 8 to 10 servings.

Chicago's large Greek community celebrates each August at the Greek Town Festival held on Halstead Street between Monroe and Van Buren. Chefs from over fifteen Greek restaurants prepare a wide array of traditional food. Entertainment includes dancing, ancestral and contemporary Greek music, fortune telling, games for children, and spectacular food booths.

KEFTETHES

Greek Meatballs

1 POUND GROUND BEEF

2 EGGS

3 SLICES DRY BREAD, CRUMBLED

1 ONION, FINELY CHOPPED

3 TABLESPOONS DRY MINT, CRUMBLED

1 TEASPOON SALT

1/4 TEASPOON PEPPER

FLOUR FOR COATING

OIL FOR FRYING

Mix the ingredients well. The mixture should be soft. With wet hands, roll into cocktail-sized meatballs, using about 1 level tablespoon of the mixture for each. Roll each lightly in flour and deep fry for 2 to 3 minutes.

Instead of frying, these may be baked in the oven at 325° for about 5 minutes, then turned and baked 5 more minutes. Approximately 36 meatballs.

This hearty Chicago recipe is both delicious and wholesome. It appeared in FIRST THERE MUST BE FOOD, a fund-raising cookbook published by the Volunteer Service Department at Chicago's Northwestern Memorial Hospital. The cookbook is filled with taste-tempting favorites from the many hospital volunteers.

FIRST THERE MUST BE FOOD

Beef and Lentil Soup

3 TABLESPOONS ALL-PURPOSE FLOUR

2 TEASPOONS SALT

1/4 TEASPOON PEPPER

2 POUNDS BEEF FOR STEWING, CUT INTO
   1/2 INCH CUBES

3 TABLESPOONS VEGETABLE OIL

5 TO 6 CUPS WATER

5 MEDIUM CARROTS, SCRAPED AND THINLY
   SLICED

2 CUPS SLICED CELERY

2 LARGE ONIONS, CHOPPED

1 CUP DRIED LENTILS, WASHED AND SORTED

1 TABLESPOON LEMON JUICE

1-1/2 TEASPOONS SALT

1 TEASPOON DRIED WHOLE THYME

Combine flour, salt, and pepper in a
medium bowl; dredge beef in flour mixture.

Heat oil in a large Dutch oven. Add beef
and cook until browned on all sides. Add
water; cover and simmer 45 minutes. Skim off
any fat. Stir in carrots, celery, onion, lentils,
lemon juice, salt, and thyme. Cover and
simmer 1 hour or until meat and vegetables
are tender, stirring occasionally. 3 quarts.

GOOD FOOD IN CICERO:

*The popularity of Chicago-style pizza has
spread across the country. Here is one version that
showcases homegrown tomatoes and features three
types of cheese. For ease in preparation, use a
commercially prepared pizza crust that can be
found on the bread aisle or specialty food section at
most supermarkets.*

Cicero

population 68,000

WHAT TO SEE:

RACE TRACK Sportsman's
Park Race Track and
Hawthorne Racecourse.
(708) 780-3700

DRIVE-IN GIANT Bunyon
Drive-In giant, 20 feet tall,
carrying a huge hot dog.

WHERE TO EAT:

BUNYON DRIVE-IN 6150
Ogden Ave.

Berwyn

population 46,000

WHAT TO SEE:

ZOO Brookfield Zoo, 1st
Ave. and 31st St. between
Berwyn and LaGrange.

WHERE TO EAT:

NOVI'S 6746 Ogden Ave.
Great Italian sausage and
beef!

WHITE CASTLE 7155
Ogden Ave. The famous
chain began in St. Louis in
1921.

THE DUMPLING HOUSE
4109 Harlem (corner of Old
66 and Harlem). A local
favorite for quality
Bohemian food and fresh
home-cooked meals since
the 1950s.

Countryside

population 6,000

WHERE TO EAT:

RT. 66 CAFE AND GRILL
6201 Joliet Rd. (between
294 and 45)

WILLIAM TELL 6201 Joliet
Rd.

**LITTLE JOE'S (SINCE
1969)** 20 E. Plainfield Rd. A
local favorite for Italian beef
and sausage. Locals ask for
"combos" with sweet and
hot peppers.

Indian Head Park

population 3,600

WHERE TO EAT:

WOLF'S HEAD INN
Corner of Joliet Rd. and
Wolf Rd. The interior offers
surprising memorabilia
including former seats from
Chicago's Pump Room
along with collectibles from
Al Capone and ***Gone with
the Wind.***

Triple Cheese Pizza

1 READY-MADE BAKED PIZZA CRUST (16
  OUNCES)
6 TABLESPOONS PESTO SAUCE
1 CUP GRATED FONTINA CHEESE (ABOUT 4
  OUNCES)
5 TO 6 PLUM TOMATOES, SEEDED AND
  THINLY SLICED
1 TABLESPOON DRIED, CRUMBLED OREGANO
1/2 TEASPOON DRIED BASIL
BLACK PEPPER TO TASTE
1/2 CUP FRESHLY GRATED MOZZARELLA
  CHEESE (ABOUT 2 OUNCES)
1/3 CUP FRESHLY GRATED PARMESAN
  CHEESE

Preheat oven to 450°. Place pizza crust on
large baking sheet. Spread with pesto.
Sprinkle evenly with Fontina cheese.
  Arrange tomatoes over pizza. Season with
oregano, basil, and black pepper. Add
mozzarella and Parmesan cheese. Bake until
crust is golden and topping is bubbly, about
10 minutes. 4 servings.

GOOD FOOD FROM COUNTRYSIDE/LAGRANGE:

*Jackie and Harvey Dunn shared their
expertise as I searched for good food on or near
Route 66 through the busy Chicago metroplex.
Thanks to their help, I discovered several
outstanding one-of-a-kind stops including Little
Joe's and The Dumpling House. Both eateries offer
giant doses of local flavor. Jackie is a good cook
who loves to serve fresh fish available at local
markets. She found this favorite recipe several years
ago in a Lake Erie cookbook. It is always popular
with guests.*

Jackie Dunn's Baked Walleye á la Orange

1 CUP ORANGE JUICE

1/4 CUP SOY SAUCE

2 POUNDS WALLEYE FILLETS

1/2 TEASPOON SALT

1 CUP LOW FAT SOUR CREAM

2 TABLESPOONS GRATED ORANGE PEEL

1/2 CUP GRATED PARMESAN CHEESE

1/2 CUP BREAD CRUMBS

2 TABLESPOONS BUTTER OR MARGARINE, MELTED

1 ORANGE, THINLY SLICED

Combine orange juice and soy sauce in a shallow bowl. Add fillets. Cover and place in refrigerator for 2 to 3 hours. Remove fillets and place in a greased, 9 x 13 baking dish. Combine salt, sour cream, grated peel, and half the cheese. Spread over fish.

Mix remaining cheese, bread crumbs, and melted butter and sprinkle over the top. Bake in a preheated 350° oven for 30 minutes. Garnish with orange slices and serve. 6 servings.

GOOD FOOD FROM LEMONT/ROMEOVILLE:

White Fence Farm recipes remain a closely guarded secret. Even Duncan Hines, who recommended the restaurant for many years, never included a recipe. However, a few secrets are shared. The restaurant's hallmark chicken is baked thoroughly before being flash fried for three minutes. It arrives at the table hot, golden, and crispy.

Willowbrook

population 8,900

WHERE TO EAT:

DELL RHEA'S CHICKEN BASKET 645 Joliet, (Illinois 83 and I-55)—a Route 66 classic stop.

Lemont/ Romeoville

Romeoville population 14,000

WHAT TO SEE:

MUSEUM Romeoville, Isle a la Cache Museum, 501 Romeo Rd. (815) 886-1467

ANTIQUES Antique Association of Lemont. Quality shops on Main, Stephen, and Canal. (708) 257-1318

LOCKPORT Lockport, 1 mile east of Route 66 on Route 7.

PIONEER SETTLEMENT See the Pioneer Settlement on the shores of the Illinois and Michigan Canal. Great stop! (815) 835-5080

WHITE FENCE FARM
Joliet Rd. (take Exit 269
from I-55). Open Tuesday—
Saturday 5:00-8:30; Sunday
12:00-7:30. Call for reservations. Free museum, fried
chicken a specialty. (708)
739-1720

Side dishes include pickled beets, exceptionally crisp coleslaw, kidney bean salad, small, slightly sweet corn fritters, and cottage cheese. Among the desserts is a delicious ice cream called Brandy Ice.

Since opening in the early 1920s, the restaurant has grown to the current 12 dining rooms serving 1000 people. Crowds who throng to the popular stop attest to quality and good service. These recipes did not come from White Fence Farm but are similar to the very popular dishes.

Corn Fritters

I CUP CREAM-STYLE CORN

I CUP CRACKER CRUMBS, FINELY GROUND

I CUP FLOUR

2 TABLESPOONS SUGAR

I/2 TEASPOON SALT

I/2 CUP MILK

I TEASPOON BAKING POWDER

2 EGGS

VEGETABLE OIL FOR FRYING

Combine all ingredients except the oil and mix thoroughly. Drop spoonfuls into deep hot fat, about 375°. Brown fritters on both sides. Drain and keep warm in oven until served. Just before serving, sprinkle lightly with powdered sugar. 6 servings.

Brandy Ice

I QUART RICH FRENCH VANILLA ICE CREAM

4 TABLESPOONS BRANDY

Soften ice cream and stir in brandy. Quickly spoon into individual serving dishes and return to freezer until ready to serve. Remove from freezer 5 minutes before serving to allow ice cream to soften slightly. 8 servings, 1/2 cup each.

At Mia Figliai and Company the ambiance is almost as appealing as the good food. The restaurant is located in an 1891 restored auditorium. Extraordinary tin ceilings, brick walls, hardwood floors, and limestone columns were revealed when the historic building was brought to life again only a few years ago.

Now an enthusiastic young culinary team combines classic techniques with current trends to provide diners with the best of different cuisines. Fresh fish and grilled meats are specialties. Those enjoying vegetarian fare will also find creative and satisfying combinations of pasta, mixed grains, and beans. Executive chef Peggy Gerdes shares this popular entree.

Mia Figliai
Chicken Marsala

1 POUND BONELESS, SKINLESS CHICKEN
   BREAST
2 CUPS SLICED WILD MUSHROOMS (CRIMINI,
   PORTABELLAS, OR SHIITAKE)
1 MEDIUM RED ONION, MINCED
1 CUP CHICKEN BROTH
3/4 CUP MARSALA WINE
1 TABLESPOON CORNSTARCH
1 TABLESPOON WATER
SALT AND FRESH BLACK PEPPER TO TASTE
HOT COOKED PASTA

Cut chicken breasts into strips. Sauté chicken with mushrooms and onion until almost cooked through. Add chicken broth and wine. Reduce slightly and add cornstarch that has been mixed with water.

Joliet
population 76,800

WHAT TO SEE:

GAMING CAPITAL OF THE MIDWEST Empress Casino, 2300 Empress Dr. (708) 345-6789 for reservations; Harrah's Joliet Casino, 151 N. Joliet St.

THEATER Rialto Square Theater is an elegantly restored 1926 vaudeville movie palace. Tours, dinner packages available. 102 N. Chicago St. A must-see experience! (815) 726-7171 for information or (815) 726-6600 for performances.

PARK Will Joliet Bicentennial Park, the original commercial center of Joliet.

MURALS Murals at Union Station and on other historic buildings.

HISTORIC WALK Historic Bluff Street Walk and Fall Color Cruises. For information call (815) 740-2344.

JACOB HENRY MANSION Tours by appointment, occasional dinner theater and meal packages, 20 S. Eastern Ave. (815) 722-3936 or (815) 722-1420

PATRICK C. HALEY MANSION Open for special dinners and banquets. 17 S. Center St. (815) 726-6800

HERITAGE CORRIDOR
Canal National Heritage
Corridor—the first navigable
route from Lake Michigan
to the Mississippi River

WHERE TO EAT:

MIA FIGLIAI & COMPANY
158 N. Chicago St.

THE KEG RESTAURANT
AND PUB 20 W. Jackson.
(708) 257-1318

Simmer until thickened. Add freshly ground black pepper and salt to taste.

Serve on a bed of freshly cooked hot pasta. 4 servings.

Joliet is often referred to as the city of steel and stone. It was settled by Irish, Italian, and Eastern Europeans who worked the river corridor between Lake Michigan and the Mississippi River. Food here is rich and hearty. The pride of ethnic heritage is strong.

Irish soda bread is the classic peasant bread found on the dining room table of every Irish home. The bread is crusty and is most often served while still warm. Traditional loaves had no shortening but today, many housewives add a small amount of shortening as well as oats, sugar, or currants to enrich this family favorite.

Traditional Irish Soda Bread

3 CUPS ALL-PURPOSE FLOUR

1 TABLESPOON BAKING POWDER

1 TEASPOON BAKING SODA

1 TEASPOON SALT

1-1/4 CUPS BUTTERMILK

Lightly coat a baking sheet with vegetable spray. Sift flour, baking powder, soda, and salt into large mixing bowl of heavy duty mixer with paddle attachment or into workbowl of a heavy duty food processor. Gradually add buttermilk to form a slightly moist dough. Turn out onto a lightly floured work surface and knead until smooth, about 1 minute. Do not overwork or the dough will be tough.

Form dough into ball and transfer to baking sheet. Flatten into a 7-inch diameter round. Using a sharp knife, cut crisscross lines 1/4 inch deep into top of dough to form an X. Bake bread in a preheated 400° oven for 35 to 40 minutes until bread is brown and crusty. Wrap warm bread in a clean kitchen towel to cool. Slice and serve while warm. 1 loaf.

Irish coffee, an American traditional after-dinner drink may or may not have gotten its start in Ireland. Regardless of its origin, the popularity of this beverage continues. This is one way it is served in Joliet.

Irish Coffee

1/2 CUP WHIPPING CREAM

2 TEASPOONS POWDERED SUGAR

1 TEASPOON VANILLA

8 OUNCES IRISH WHISKEY OR BRANDY

8 TEASPOONS BROWN SUGAR

8 CUPS STRONG, HOT COFFEE

Whip cream with powdered sugar and vanilla. Place 1 ounce (2 tablespoons) whiskey and 1 teaspoon brown sugar into each heatproof mug; stir. Pour hot coffee into mugs; top with whipped cream and serve immediately. 8 cups.

Wilmington

population 4400

WHAT TO SEE:

CONSERVATION AREA
Des Plaines Conservation area including 80-acre tall-grass prairie.

ANTIQUES Antique shops near IL 53 and Water St.

GEMINI GIANT In front of the Launching Pad Cafe (20 feet tall and 500 pounds).

WHERE TO EAT:

LAUNCHING PAD CAFE
Try their 66 burgers, orange dream shakes, and hot wings!

Braidwood

population 4400

WHAT TO SEE:

WILDLIFE AREA Mazonia State Fish and Wildlife Area.

DEPOT See the brightly painted old train depot.

WHERE TO EAT:

GOLDEN MINE FAMILY RESTAURANT IL 53 (Route 66) and IL 113.

KEVIN'S KORNER

Godley

population 350

Once a thriving mining town, Godley is almost gone today.

Many of Braidwood's early settlers were of Italian and Bohemian descent. Lu Ann Bolatto, like many of her friends, prepares bunya caulda, a popular Eastern European dish that is thick as porridge and served like a dip with Italian bread or with vegetables like celery, cabbage, zucchini, or peppers.

The Italian version of this dip is called Bagna Cauda, a specialty of the Piedmont region of Italy, where raw vegetables are dipped into a blend of olive oil, butter, garlic and anchovies.

Bunya Caulda

1 POUND REAL BUTTER

14 HEADS OF GARLIC, CLEANED AND MINCED

7 CANS OF ANCHOVIES, DRAINED

7 PINTS HALF-AND-HALF

1 PINT WHIPPING CREAM

Melt the butter and sauté the garlic and anchovies.

Continue cooking very slowly until anchovies are so soft the mixture becomes smooth. Add the half-and-half and whipping cream and bring mixture to a boil, stirring constantly. Reduce heat and simmer for 3-1/2 to 4 hours. Stir carefully to prevent burning. Mixture will be thick like a porridge. Serve as a dip with crusty Italian bread and raw vegetables. About 4 quarts.

Rich and Linda Henry's Farmer's Delight

1-1/2 POUNDS GROUND BEEF
2 CANS (15-1/2 OUNCES EACH) CORN,
    DRAINED OR THE EQUIVALENT AMOUNT OF
    CORN CUT FROM THE COB
2 CUPS (OR MORE) MASHED POTATOES
SALT AND PEPPER TO TASTE

Brown the beef, season to taste, and place in a 8-1/2 x 11 baking dish. Pour corn evenly over the meat and top with cold mashed potatoes (a great way to use leftovers). Bake in a preheated 350° oven for 30 minutes or until potatoes are lightly browned. 6 servings.

GOOD FOOD IN HAMEL:

Rickey Miller of Hamel published KITCHEN MEMORIES FROM MY CHILDHOOD in 1994 in honor of her father's 90th birthday. The booklet is a tribute to her family as well as other pioneers of German descent who settled the Hamel area. Many of the recipes in the book reflect the practical and thrifty lifestyle of the good cooks in this small community. Miller points out that she enjoyed learning to cook as a child because the stories that went with the food made each dish special.

KITCHEN MEMORIES
Spoon Bread

1 CUP HOT WATER
1 CUP CORNMEAL
2 TABLESPOONS SHORTENING
1 TEASPOON SALT
1 TABLESPOON SUGAR
1/2 TEASPOON SODA
1 CUP BUTTERMILK
2 EGGS

Hamel
population 550

WHAT TO SEE:

CHURCHES St. Paul's Church, the Church of the Neon Cross.

66 SIGNS Wilton Rinkel Farm southwest of town.

WHERE TO EAT:

EARNIE'S RESTAURANT An old roadhouse. See the conductors still on the building across the street from a time when a streetcar ran from St. Louis to Chicago. Route 157 at Route 140. Open at 11:00 a.m. daily, closed Sundays.

Edwardsville

population 14,600

WHAT TO SEE:

MUSEUM Madison County Historical Museum, 715 W. Main.

SOUTHERN ILLINOIS UNIVERSITY

TWO HISTORIC DISTRICTS St. Louis Street Historic District and LeClaire Historic District. A walking tour guide is available at the Chamber of Commerce.

WHERE TO EAT:

A & W DRIVE-IN RESTAURANT (SINCE 1954) Carhops still serve you here! 604 St. Louis.

HONEY BEE INN 454 E. Vandella

PK'S Over 30 years in Edwardsville. 202 South Buchanan St.

YUM-YUM SHOPPE 5 Ginger Creek Parkway

Mix water and cornmeal together. Add shortening, salt, and sugar. Dissolve soda in buttermilk and add to mixture. Add well-beaten eggs last. Bake in an iron skillet or greased baking pan in a preheated 375° oven for 30 to 40 minutes. Spoon from hot pan to serve. 5 to 6 servings.

GOOD FOOD FROM EDWARDSVILLE:

The Italian influence can be felt in many of the dishes prepared in this southern Illinois community. Toasted ravioli first became popular in nearby St. Louis and many residents prepare their own version of mostaccioli, sometimes referred to as ziti. Pork steaks and gooey butter cakes are two other traditional staples along this segment of Route 66. Barb Driesner, who is a member of the staff at the Edwardsville Library, says her mostaccioli recipe is very typical.

Barb Driesner's Mostaccioli

1 POUND HAMBURGER
1 POUND ITALIAN SAUSAGE
1 ONION, DICED
1 BOX (16 OUNCES) RIGATONI OR MOSTACCIOLI NOODLES
1 JAR (28-OUNCES) ITALIAN PASTA SAUCE
8 OUNCES MOZZARELLA CHEESE, GRATED
1 TEASPOON GARLIC POWDER

Brown the hamburger and sausage with the onion. Drain thoroughly. Add sauce and garlic powder. Meanwhile, cook the rigatoni noodles. Layer 1/2 of the meat mixture in the bottom of a 9 x 13 inch baking dish. Cover with the noodles and half of the cheese. Repeat with remaining meat. Sprinkle remaining cheese on top. Bake uncovered in a preheated 350° oven for 30 minutes until mostaccioli is hot and bubbly. Add more pasta sauce if desired. 8 servings.

Members of the Edwardsville Garden Club recently published RECIPES OLD AND NEW, in honor of the 55th anniversary of their group. The collection is filled with delicious recipes reflecting the best from this lovely southern Illinois community.

RECIPES OLD AND NEW
Jean Elliott's Salad of Asparagus, Pears, and Walnuts with Honey Mustard Dressing

4 CUPS MIXED RED AND GREEN LEAF
   LETTUCE
1 SMALL CONTAINER ALFALFA SPROUTS
1 LARGE RIPE BOSC PEAR
1 CUP ENGLISH WALNUTS
12 QUALITY ASPARAGUS STALKS
LEMON JUICE

Arrange cleaned, trimmed lettuce in a large glass bowl. Toss spouts with lettuce. Poach asparagus until barely tender, drain and flash cool in freezer for 15 minutes. Cut stalks in half lengthwise as well as across the girth. Cut lower halves into bite sized pieces and toss with greens. Arrange top split stalks on greens and add thinly sliced pears that have been peeled and treated with lemon juice. Sprinkle with walnuts and serve with honey mustard dressing. 8 servings.

1/3 CUP HONEY

2 TABLESPOONS YELLOW MUSTARD

1 GREEN ONION

3 TABLESPOONS TARRAGON VINEGAR

3/4 CUP VEGETABLE OIL

Combine all ingredients in food processor. Blend until smooth. Store tightly covered in refrigerator.

RECIPES OLD AND NEW

Jean Foehrkolb's Cinnamon-Orange Pork Tenderloin

1/2 CUP CORN FLAKES

1 TABLESPOON BROWN SUGAR

2 TEASPOONS GRATED ORANGE RIND

2 TEASPOONS GROUND CINNAMON

2 PORK TENDERLOINS (1/2 POUND EACH)

1-1/2 TABLESPOONS PLAIN NONFAT YOGURT

1-1/2 TABLESPOONS ORANGE JUICE

VEGETABLE COOKING SPRAY

Position knife blade in food processor bowl; add corn flakes, brown sugar, orange rind, and ground cinnamon. Process mixture until cereal is crushed. Set mixture aside. Trim fat from tenderloins. Combine yogurt and orange juice in a small bowl; brush over tenderloins. Dredge tenderloins in cereal mixture. Place meat on a rack in a roasting pan coated with cooking spray. Insert meat thermometer into thickest part of tenderloin if desired. Bake in a preheated 350° oven for 45 to 50 minutes or until meat thermometer registers 160°. Transfer to serving platter. Allow to stand 10 minutes; slice meat diagonally across grain into thin slices. 4 servings.

Jean Elliott's
Yeast Waffles

Collinsville

population 23,000

2 CUPS MILK

1 PACKAGE ACTIVE DRY YEAST

1/2 CUP WARM WATER

1/3 CUP MELTED BUTTER

1 TEASPOON SALT

1 TEASPOON SUGAR

3 CUPS SIFTED FLOUR

2 EGGS, BEATEN

1/2 TEASPOON BAKING SODA

Scald milk; cool to lukewarm. Sprinkle yeast on warm water in a large bowl; stir to dissolve. Add milk, butter, salt, sugar, and flour to yeast. Mix thoroughly until smooth. Cover and let stand at room temperature overnight. When ready to bake, add eggs and baking soda. Beat well. Bake in a preheated waffle iron. 6 to 8 waffles.

GOOD FOOD IN COLLINSVILLE:

Collinsville is the Horseradish Capitol of the World. Over 60 percent of the world's supply of the spicy herb is grown in the bottomlands around the town. So naturally, many of the favorite dishes prepared by the good cooks around here include horseradish. This tasty recipe for chicken wings was shared for the McLean, Texas recipe book, CRUISINE DOWN OLD ROUTE 66, *first published in 1990.*

WHAT TO SEE:

70-FOOT CATSUP BOTTLE
Atop a 100-foot tower, recently restored tribute to Brooks Catsup. One mile south of downtown on Highway 159.

JUNE HORSERADISH FESTIVAL

SEPTEMBER ITALIAN FESTIVAL

CAHOKIA MOUNDS WORLD HERITAGE SITE (618) 345-4300

MINER'S THEATER ON MAIN STREET Main Street with renewed ghosted signs, antique and collectible shops, a history museum in the library, and good places to eat.

Granite City / Mitchell / East St. Louis

WHAT TO SEE:

CHAIN OF ROCKS BRIDGE Closed now, at Mitchell.

GRANITE CITY LOCKS The navigational locks at Granite City are the largest in the western hemisphere.

CASINO QUEEN RIVERBOAT Exit I-55 at 3rd St. and turn right on River Park Dr.

CRUISINE DOWN OLD ROUTE 66

Jean Linden's Missiszippy Wings

4 POUNDS CHICKEN WINGS

1/2 CUP PREPARED HORSERADISH

1/2 CUP KETCHUP

1/4 CUP SUGAR

1/3 CUP LEMON-LIME SODA

1/4 CUP WATER

2 TABLESPOONS COOKING OIL

1/2 TEASPOON GARLIC SALT

1/4 TEASPOON PEPPER

Wash then remove and discard tip sections of 4 pounds of chicken wings. Pour mixture over wings in bowl small enough that all are covered. Cover bowl and refrigerate overnight. Remove wings and place on foil lined shallow baking pan. Bake in preheated 350° oven for one hour or until wings are well done and crispy. Turning and basting after 1/2 hour assures more even crispness. About 24 wings.

The easiest and safest recommended way to continue is to take I-55 across the Mississippi into St. Louis. Head west and enjoy!

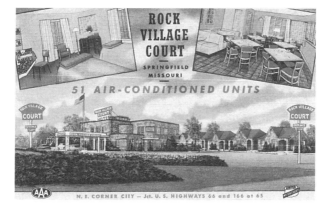

Cross the fabled Mississippi, magnificent in its grandeur and power, to enjoy St. Louis, a city that has moved into the future by restoring its past. The riverfront with its warehouse district and the Union Railroad Station is buzzing with activity and crammed full of inviting new restaurants.

This is a state where the southern influence is obvious on its bountiful tables. Superb food springs from steamboat chefs, farmers who sell fruits and vegetables from their rich lowland crops, and hardworking immigrants who started wineries, breweries, and packing houses. All add a special culinary authority. Begin the Missouri experience with with a famous "concrete" at Ted Drewes Frozen Custard. Admire the tree that helps hold up the ceiling in the most famous restaurant in Pacific. Feast on chocolate fudge and French onion soup. Sample the best wine in Missouri. Then spend the night at a bed and breakfast located on an historic Civil War site. "Dine with the Dinosaurs" in Dance Hall Cave, and visit the home of "throwed rolls" in Springfield. And finally, absorb a giant dose of nostalgia with Lowell Davis at Red Oak II. Take time to appreciate the variety along Route 66 in Missouri!

St. Louis

WHAT TO SEE:

GATEWAY ARCH Eero Saarinen's shining stainless-steel rainbow, Riverfront at Market St. **(314) 425-4465**

FOREST PARK Site of the 1904 World's Fair. Includes St. Louis Art Museum, the History Museum, St. Louis Zoological Park, the Jewel Box, and more. Bounded by I- 64, Lindell, Skinker and Kingshighway Boulevards.

MISSISSIPPI RIVER Tom Sawyer, Huck Finn, and Becky Thatcher Cruises depart four times daily from the base of the Gateway Arch, weather permitting.

LACLEDE'S LANDING Riverfront between Eads and Martin Luther King Bridges for exciting shops and restaurants. **(314) 241-5875**

MISSOURI BOTANICAL GARDENS 4344 Shaw Blvd. **(314) 577-5100**

ST. LOUIS UNION STATION Filled with specialty shops and good restaurants. 18th and Market Streets. **(314) 421-4314**

GOOD FOOD IN ST. LOUIS:

The city was host to the 1904 Louisiana Purchase Centennial Exposition and World's Fair where ice cream cones and hot dogs were introduced. Iced tea and Dr. Pepper also gained popularity at this great exposition. Busch Beer, Vess Beverages, and Ted Drewes Frozen Custard characterize the city today.

Lafayette House Bed and Breakfast is a lovely 6,000 square foot home built in 1876 by James Eads, the builder of the Eads Bridge, as a wedding gift to his daughter. Builders of the Queen Anne Victorian mansion used the finest materials available including walnut woodwork and staircases, and 14-foot ceilings. Located across the street from Lafayette Park, it is near shops and restaurants and five minutes from the historic city center.

The home has been a bed and breakfast since 1985. In 1995, Nancy Buhr and Annalise Millet became the new owners. Annalise, a former pastry chef, delights in preparing gourmet breakfasts.

LAFAYETTE HOUSE
Pumpkin Chocolate Chip Muffins

1 CUP SLICED ALMONDS

3-1/2 CUPS FLOUR

2 CUPS SUGAR

2 TABLESPOONS PUMPKIN PIE SPICE

2 TEASPOONS SODA

1/2 TEASPOON BAKING POWDER

1/2 TEASPOON SALT

4 EGGS

1 CAN (16 OUNCES) PUMPKIN

1/2 POUND BUTTER, MELTED

3/4 CUP CHOCOLATE CHIPS

Combine dry ingredients in large mixing bowl. Beat together the eggs, pumpkin, and butter. Pour liquid into the center of the dry ingredients and stir until barely blended. Stir in the chocolate chips. Bake muffins in lightly greased 2-1/2 inch tins in a preheated 350° oven for 25 minutes. These muffins freeze well. 2 to 2-1/2 dozen muffins.

For travelers who want a giant dose of history with their bed-and-breakfast stay, Geandaugh House offers the perfect stop.

This cozy "Prairie House" is one of the oldest in the city; some say it dates to the 1700's. Elizabeth Kennerly, a cousin to William Clark, is listed as an early owner. Perhaps both he and Meriwether Lewis were among early visitors. The house is both early French Colonial and early Federal.

Gea and Wayne Popp offer a memorable stay with memorable food for breakfast.

GEANDAUGH HOUSE
Yogurt Breakfast Sundae

1/4 CUP SLICED ORANGE
1/4 CUP SLICED PEACH
1/4 CUP APPLE
4 TO 5 GRAPES
2 TABLESPOONS VANILLA YOGURT
CHOPPED PECANS TO TASTE

Combine fruit in a sherbet dish. Drop yogurt on top of fruit. Sprinkle with pecans. Substitute other fruit if desired. 1 serving.

SOULARD MARKET A traditional city market with all its sounds and smells. 7th and Lafayette. (314) 622-4180

GRANT'S FARM 10501 Gravois Rd. (314) 577-2626

ANHEUSER-BUSCH BREWERY TOUR I-55 at Arsenal St. (314) 577-2626

WHERE TO EAT:

TED DREWES FROZEN CUSTARD The classic Route 66 stops for the best custard in America! 6726 Chippewa or 4224 S. Grand.

GATEWAY RIVERBOAT DINNER CRUISES 500 L.K. Sullivan Blvd. (314) 621-4040

BEVO MILL German cuisine, 4749 Gravois.

BISSELL MANSION DINNER THEATRE 4426 Randall Pl.

BLUEBERRY HILLS CAFE Among many other awards, voted home of Best Hamburgers, Best Restroom Graffiti and Best Jukebox in America. 6504 Delmar Ave.

JAKE'S STEAKS AT LACLEDE'S LANDING 707 Clamorgan

TONY'S World-famous Italian food. 410 Market St.

SCHNEITHORST'S HOFAMBERG INN Just south of I-40 at Lindberg Blvd. —the best of German cuisine! 1600 S. Lindberg.

BUSCH'S GROVE An interesting old place with bungalows. 9160 Clayton Rd.

YACOVELLI'S RESTAURANT 407 Dunn Rd. (I-270 at Graham Rd.)

UNION STATION Union Station eateries all under one roof. (Try Dierdorf & Hart.)

WHERE TO STAY:

LAFAYETTE HOUSE BED-AND-BREAKFAST 2156 Lafayette Ave. (314) 772-4429

GEANDEAUGH HOUSE BED-AND-BREAKFAST INN 3835 S. Broadway. (314) 771-5447

LEMP MANSION INN AND RESTAURANT 3322 DeMenil Pl. (314) 664-8024

THE WINTER HOUSE 3522 Arsenal St. (314) 664-4399

WITH HANDS & HEART COOKBOOK was published in 1990 by the St. Louis Bethesda Hospital Women's Board and includes superb recipes from outstanding local women as well as great dishes from chefs at some of the best restaurants and clubs in St. Louis. Try this delicious sample!

WITH HANDS & HEART
Toasty Cheese Crackers

2 CUPS SHREDDED CHEDDAR CHEESE

1/2 CUP GRATED PARMESAN CHEESE

1/2 CUP BUTTER OR MARGARINE, SOFTENED

3 TABLESPOONS WATER

1 CUP FLOUR

1/4 TEASPOON SALT

1 CUP UNCOOKED OATMEAL

Beat cheeses, butter, and water until smooth. Add flour and salt, mix well. Stir in oatmeal until blended. Shape dough to form two 12-inch rolls. Wrap securely and refrigerate four hours. Cut into 1/8 to 1/4 inch slices. Flatten slightly and bake at 400° on greased cookie sheet until edges are lightly browned, approximately 10 to 12 minutes. The recipe is easy and can be done ahead. 100 or more bite-sized crackers.

USO'S SALUTE TO THE TROOPS COOKBOOK was compiled from the Volunteers and Friends of the James S. McDonnell USO at Lambert-St.Louis International Airport. There are over 250 tasty recipes in this collection from the largest airport USO in the world.

USO's Salute to the Troops

Gail's Cheesy Broccoli Soup

3/4 CUP CHOPPED ONION

2 TABLESPOONS MARGARINE

5 CUPS WATER

6 CHICKEN BOUILLON CUBES

8 OUNCES FINE EGG NOODLES

1 TEASPOON SALT

2 PACKAGES (10 OUNCES EACH) FROZEN
   CHOPPED BROCCOLI

1/2 TEASPOON GARLIC POWDER

4 CUPS MILK

1 POUND VELVEETA CHEESE, CUBED

1 TEASPOON PEPPER

Saute onion in margarine. In large pot, combine water and bouillon cubes. Bring to boil. Add noodles and salt. Cook for 3 to 4 minutes until noodles are tender. Remove from heat and stop boiling. Add onions, broccoli, and garlic powder.

Cook until broccoli is just tender then remove from heat again. Add milk, cheese, and pepper. Stir until cheese melts. Serve hot. Can be made ahead and frozen for one month. Approximately 12 generous servings.

St. Ambrose Parish ON THE HILL COOKBOOK is a great tribute to the Italian cooks of St. Ambrose Parish in St. Louis. The book features the authentic art of Italian cooking.

St. Ambrose Parish On the Hill

Green Pasta Salad with Crabmeat and Roasted Bell Pepper Vinaigrette

4 RED BELL PEPPERS

2 TABLESPOONS RED WINE VINEGAR

1 TEASPOON SUGAR

PINCH CAYENNE

2 TABLESPOONS OLIVE OIL

1 POUND GREEN PASTA (FLAVORED WITH
BASIL, IF AVAILABLE)

1/4 POUND CRABMEAT, FRESH COOKED
(LOBSTER OR SCALLOPS MAY BE USED)

FRESH BASIL FOR GARNISH

Roast bell peppers over open flame or under broiler till blackened. Peel skin off under cold running water. Remove seeds. Blend peppers, vinegar, sugar, cayenne, and olive oil in food processor or blender until completely pureed.

Bring four quarts water to boil; cook pasta. Drain and rinse with cold water.

To serve, pour vinaigrette on individual plates, arrange pasta on top, and garnish with crab and basil. 6 servings.

GATEWAYS is a treasury of 296 tested recipes published by the Friends of St. Louis Children's Hospital. This lovely hardbound, full-color cookbook features an extensive entertaining guide and double-tested recipes.

GATEWAYS

Cashew Shrimp Salad

1 PACKAGE (10 OUNCES) TINY FROZEN PEAS

1 POUND SHRIMP, STEAMED, PEELED,
DEVEINED, AND CUT INTO BITE-SIZED
PIECES

2 CUPS CHOPPED CELERY

1 CUP LOW-FAT MAYONNAISE

1 TABLESPOON FRESH LEMON JUICE

1 TEASPOON CURRY POWDER

GARLIC SALT TO TASTE

1 CUP UNSALTED CASHEWS

1 CAN (5 OUNCES) CHOW MEIN NOODLES

Combine the first seven ingredients in a large bowl and toss well. Cover and chill at least 30 minutes. Add cashews and noodles and toss again. Serve on lettuce leaves. 6 to 8 servings.

COOKING IN CLOVER, published by the Jewish Hospital Auxiliary in support of Barnes-Jewish Hospital, has sold over 30,000 copies since it was first printed in 1977. A second book, COOKING IN CLOVER II, is now available.

COOKING IN CLOVER
Italian Stuffed Tomatoes

8 MEDIUM TOMATOES
SALT
3 TABLESPOONS OLIVE OIL
6 GREEN ONIONS, FINELY SLICED
1 PINT FRESH MUSHROOMS, FINELY SLICED
1 CAN (8 1/2 OUNCES) ARTICHOKES,
　　DRAINED AND COARSELY CHOPPED
2 CLOVES GARLIC, MINCED
1 TEASPOON ITALIAN SEASONING
1 TEASPOON BASIL
1 TEASPOON SOY SAUCE
1/2 TEASPOON SUGAR
1/4 CUP DRY BREAD CRUMBS
1/4 CUP GRATED PARMESAN CHEESE

Slice off tops of tomatoes. Scoop out pulp, drain and reserve.

Lightly salt the tomato cups and drain on paper towels for 30 minutes.

In a large skillet heat olive oil to medium-high heat. Add green onions, reserved tomato pulp, mushrooms, artichokes, and garlic and sauté 3 to 4 minutes. Add Italian seasoning, basil, soy sauce, salt, and sugar and continue to sauté until liquid evaporates.

Spoon vegetable mixture into drained tomato cups. Top with combined bread crumbs and Parmesan cheese. Bake in preheated 400° oven for 10 minutes or until tomatoes are hot and bubbly. 8 servings.

THE TASTY PALATTE COOK BOOK was published by the South County Art Association and includes specialties from the many ethnic groups living in the St. Louis area. The association has had a scholarship program for many years and encourages the very young with awards at their annual art festival.

THE TASTY PALATTE
Plum or Peach Buckle

1 STICK BUTTER
1/2 CUP SUGAR
1 CUP FLOUR
1-1/2 TEASPOONS BAKING POWDER
PINCH OF SALT
3/4 CUP MILK
12 PRUNE PLUMS, PITTED AND HALVED OR 2
    CUPS SLICED PEACHES
1/4 TEASPOON CINNAMON
1/2 CUP SUGAR
GRATED ORANGE OR LEMON RIND

Melt butter in 8-inch round or square baking pan. In bowl, mix sugar, flour, baking powder, salt, and milk. Pour butter over flour mixture slowly and evenly and do not stir. Arrange plums or peaches on top of mixture. Sprinkle fruit with mixed sugar and cinnamon, and rind. Bake in preheated 350° oven for 40 to 50 minutes. Batter will rise to top and form a crust. Serve with whipped cream if desired. 6 servings.

Kirkwood

population 27,500

Eastlake Inn offers the charm and elegance of a 1920s colonial home in the heart of this attractive bedroom community. The Inn can be found just 5 blocks south of Manchester Road, the 1926–1932 alignment of Route 66 through Kirkwood. Lori Murray has been the innkeeper since 1992 and her love for the home and surrounding tree-covered yard is evident in the comfortable yet relaxed atmosphere. Enjoy a delicious breakfast in the dining room or sunporch before seeing the many nearby attractions. Lori, a member of the Chamber of Commerce, can direct guests to all of the interesting stops.

WHAT TO SEE:

TRANSPORT MUSEUM
The National Museum of Transport on Barrett Station Rd. (314) 965-7998

WORLDWAYS CHILDREN'S MUSEUM
100 W. Country Center

THE MAGIC HOUSE
(314) 822-8900

ST LOUIS CHILDREN'S MUSEUM 516 S. Kirkwood. (314) 822-8900

EASTLAKE INN
Orange-Glazed Cranberry Pumpkin Bread

3 1/2 CUPS ALL-PURPOSE FLOUR

1 2/3 CUPS SUGAR

2 TEASPOONS BAKING SODA

2 TEASPOONS PUMPKIN PIE SPICE

3/4 TEASPOON SALT

1 TEASPOON BAKING POWDER

16 OUNCES WHOLE CRANBERRY SAUCE

16 OUNCES SOLID PACK PUMPKIN

3/4 CUP CHOPPED PECANS

3/4 CUP VEGETABLE OIL

4 EGGS

GLAZE:

1 CUP POWDERED SUGAR

1/4 CUP UNDILUTED ORANGE JUICE

1/4 TEASPOON GROUND ALLSPICE

In a large bowl mix the flour, sugar, baking soda, pumpkin pie spice, salt, and baking powder. In a second bowl stir together

WHERE TO STAY:

THE EASTLAKE INN BED AND BREAKFAST 703 N. Kirkwood Rd. (314) 965-0066

WHERE TO EAT:

CAFE VICTORIAN 142 W. Monroe

JEREMIAH'S 131 W. Argon

CAFE PARADISO
N. Kirkwood and Jefferson

MASSA'S 210 N. Kirkwood

JOSEPH'S ITALIAN CAFE
451 S. Kirkwood

CITIZEN KANE'S STEAKHOUSE 133 W. Clinton Pl.

Eureka
population 4800

WHAT TO SEE:

Quaint town of antique and craft shops.

SIX FLAGS OVER MID-AMERICA

Pacific
population 4,400

WHERE TO EAT:

RED CEDAR INN
1047 E. Osage

the remaining ingredients until well mixed. Add pumpkin mixture to flour mixture and stir until moistened. Pour batter into two 9 x 5 x 3 greased loaf pans. Bake in preheated 350° oven for 65 minutes. Cool in pans for 10 minutes then remove to cooling racks.

Mix glaze ingredients together and stir until smooth. Completely cool bread then drizzle glaze over top and sides. 2 loaves.

GOOD FOOD IN PACIFIC:

Ginger Gallagher at the Red Cedar Inn delights in serving her customers the good food they have grown to expect from this Route 66 historic location that first opened in 1934. Don't forget to locate the tree that helps support the ceiling in this eatery that is filled with so many memories.

RED CEDAR INN
Bread Pudding

- 1 DOZEN RAISED DONUTS
- 1 CUP SUGAR, OR ADJUST TO TASTE
- 1 QUART MILK
- 1 TEASPOON NUTMEG
- 1 TEASPOON CINNAMON
- 6 EGGS, BEATEN
- 1/2 CUP RAISINS (OPTIONAL)

Crumble donuts in a 2-quart baking dish. Combine sugar, milk, nutmeg, and cinnamon and stir to dissolve sugar. Add eggs and beat until mixture is well blended and smooth. Sprinkle raisins over doughnuts then pour egg mixture over both. Place in a preheated 350° oven and bake for 1 hour. Serve while warm or allow to cool if desired. 10 to 12 servings.

GOOD FOOD IN ST. CLAIR:

Betty Huff lives just off Springfield Road (Old 66) in St. Clair and has traveled the historic highway more times than she can count. Her family compiled a cookbook in 1996 and called it DINING WITH KINGS. The collection of good food comes from the descendants of William and Ethel King who lived in Franklin County, Missouri, during the early part of the 20th century. Betty is one of their granddaughters. This good cake is also called a Depression Cake as it was first made in the 1930s.

DINING WITH KINGS
Betty Huff's Boiled Raisin Cake

1 BOX (15 OUNCES) RAISINS
2 CUPS SUGAR
2 CUPS WATER
2 TABLESPOONS SHORTENING
1 TEASPOON SALT
1 TEASPOON BAKING SODA
1 TEASPOON CINNAMON
1 TEASPOON GROUND CLOVES
3 CUPS FLOUR
1 CUP CHOPPED NUTS

CARAMEL ICING

1 CUP BROWN SUGAR
1/2 CUP WATER
1 HEAPING TEASPOON BUTTER
1 HEAPING TEASPOON FLOUR
1 HEAPING TEASPOON WHITE SUGAR

Boil raisins, sugar, water, and shortening for 5 minutes. Allow to cool. Add remaining ingredients to the raisin mixture. Spray a 9 x 11 baking pan with nonstick spray. This cake was originally baked in a heavy greased and floured iron skillet. Pour batter into pan and bake for 45 minutes in a preheated 350° oven.

St. Clair
population 4200

WHAT TO SEE:

OLD INTERNATIONAL SHOE FACTORY ANTIQUE MALL Located in the old St. Louis Shoe Factory at 160 N. Main St.

ST. CLAIR HISTORICAL MUSEUM Hibbard St.

WHERE TO EAT:

LEWIS CAFE Good home cooking in a cafe that has been in the same family since 1938. 145 S. Main St.

For the icing, mix flour and white sugar; then add other ingredients. Stir together until smooth. Bring to boil and spread over cake while warm. 12 servings

Betty Huff's
Half Hour Apple Butter

2 CUPS UNSWEETENED APPLESAUCE

1/2 CUP SUGAR

1 TEASPOON CINNAMON

1/2 TEASPOON ALLSPICE

1/8 TEASPOON GINGER

1/8 TEASPOON GROUND CLOVES

Combine all ingredients in saucepan. Mix well. Bring to boil. Cook for 30 minutes on low heat, stirring frequently. 1-3/4 cups.

Jean King Runge shared this Funnel Cake recipe that had been given to her by Virginia Burt. Funnel Cakes can be found at most fairs and festivals throughout this part of the country.

Jean King Runge's Funnel Cake

2 EGGS, WELL BEATEN

1-1/2 CUPS MILK

2 CUPS FLOUR

1/2 TEASPOON SALT

1 TEASPOON BAKING POWDER

Mix all ingredients until smooth. Heat 2 cups oil until hot (375°F.). Pour mixture from a pitcher in a lacy pattern over the hot oil. Brown on each side. Remove from oil and drain on paper towels. Sprinkle with powdered sugar on both sides. 6 to 8 funnel cakes.

Among other lush garden produce, Stanton residents often grow small red potatoes. The flavor is terrific and the potatoes are used quickly since they don't keep well. This recipe is typical of low-fat recipes that are so popular today. It makes a great addition for picnics, perhaps to Meramec Caverns and the nearby park.

Creamy Potato Salad

1-1/4 POUNDS SMALL RED POTATOES
1 CUP PLAIN LOW-FAT YOGURT
2 TABLESPOONS DIJON MUSTARD
2 TABLESPOONS FINELY CHOPPED FRESH TARRAGON
1/2 SMALL RED PEPPER CUT IN MATCHSTICK STRIPS
1/3 CUP DICED GREEN ONION
1/3 CUP DIAGONALLY SLICED CELERY
SALT AND PEPPER TO TASTE

Cook potatoes whole in boiling salted water until tender, about 25 minutes. Drain and cool. Cut potatoes into bite sized pieces.

Stir yogurt, mustard, and tarragon in large bowl until blended. Add potatoes, red pepper, onion, and celery. Toss to blend. Season with salt and pepper to taste, cover, and chill before serving. 5 servings.

GOOD FOOD IN SULLIVAN:

"A break from reality, stay with us and enjoy," says Robert Seal, innkeeper at the Sleepy Seal Bed and Breakfast. The Fisher-Seal House, built in 1884, was once home to J. Henry Fisher, a Sullivan banker. He and his brother Leo were among the largest land holders in Southeast Missouri.

Stanton

population 500

WHAT TO SEE:

MERAMEC CAVERNS Five levels of unusual formations. You're here! The barn signs paid off! 3 miles south of town. (573) 468-3166

JESSE JAMES WAX MUSEUM From I-44 take exit 230. (573) 927-5233

ANTIQUE TOY MUSEUM From I-44 take Exit 230.

WHERE TO EAT:

CAVERN CITY HIDEOUT A local favorite for good food. 2379 S. Service Rd., on Old 66. (573) 927-5213

Sullivan

population 5700

WHAT TO SEE:

**MERAMEC STATE PARK,
MERAMEC STATE FOREST**
Daniel Boone traveled here
in the 1880s. 4 miles east on
SR 185. (573) 468-6072

SHOPS An abundance of
antique stores. Enjoy the
shops along Main St.

WHERE TO EAT:

**HOMER'S HICKORY
SMOKED BBQ** Locals say
this the best barbecue in the
area. 693 Fisher.

DU KUM INN 101 Grande
Center

WHITE HOUSE GRILL
960 E. Springfield

**WHERE TO
STAY:**

**THE SLEEPY SEAL BED
AND BREAKFAST** (Fisher-
Seal House) 52 Hughes
Ford Rd. (573) 468-7585

*The home's porch columns were salvaged
from the 1904 World's Fair. A review in the ST.
LOUIS POST DISPATCH says, "The whole home is
brimming with quirky charm not likely to be
appreciated by the staid." The porch and first floor
are filled with antiques and collectables including
a delightful village of gnomes.*

*Seal makes creamy fudge for his guests and
ships candy across the country. He always
demonstrates his candy making skill at Sullivan's
Annual Spring Thing and Fall Fling. Seal is also
a master baker who prepares scrumptious
cinnamon rolls for guests who have enjoyed one of
the three cozy rooms at the Sleepy Seal Bed and
Breakfast.*

*Don't even think about calories if you decide
to prepare Robert's Hunka Hunka Fudge Sundae.
Robert says he bakes a smoked Ozark ham with
sliced pineapples and cherries, then slathers the
ham with honey and brown sugar. When the ham
is ready to serve, he reserves the rich pineapple and
cherries to add to each sundae. If you're not baking
a ham, just follow the directions in the recipe
below and enjoy!*

SLEEPY SEAL BED AND BREAKFAST
Hunka Hunka Fudge Sundae

1 CAN (15 OUNCES) SLICED PINEAPPLE
8 MARASCHINO CHERRIES
HONEY, BUTTER, BROWN SUGAR, AND CIN-
    NAMON
1 POUND SLEEPY SEAL CHOCOLATE FUDGE
    (OR ANOTHER BRAND OF HIGH QUALITY
    FUDGE)
2 TABLESPOONS QUALITY PEANUT BUTTER
1 TEASPOON MILK
4 SMALL BANANAS SLICED LENGTHWISE
1 QUART FRENCH VANILLA ICE CREAM
1/2 PINT CREAM, WHIPPED

Sauté the fruit, in a mixture of honey, butter, a touch of cinnamon, and brown sugar.

Using a double boiler or the microwave, melt the candy with peanut butter and milk. Place a sliced banana in the bottom of each sundae dish, top with ice cream and the fruit. Pour melted chocolate over each dish and top with real whipping cream and a final cherry. 4 large sundaes.

GOOD FOOD IN CUBA:

The Franklin Street Food Company is a relatively new stop on Route 66 that shouldn't be missed. It is presided over by chef/owner Cort Bick who left St. Louis to establish his outstanding restaurant in a quieter, more relaxed atmosphere. He says this soup has become a staple. At first he served it only at lunch, but due to customer demand he has added it to the evening menu. The recipe is fashioned after a soup from the Famous and Barr Department Store in St. Louis years ago.

FRANKLIN STREET FOOD COMPANY
French Onion Soup

- 3 POUNDS YELLOW ONIONS, PEELED AND TRIMMED
- 1-1/2 STICKS UNSALTED BUTTER
- 2 TABLESPOONS PAPRIKA
- 4 BAY LEAVES
- 1 TEASPOON SALT (ELIMINATE IF USING SALTED BUTTER, ABOVE)
- 2 TEASPOONS BLACK PEPPER, COARSE GRIND OR CRACKED
- 1 CUP FLOUR
- 3 QUARTS RICH BEEF STOCK
- 12 SLICES GOOD FRENCH BREAD (1-INCH THICK)
- SHREDDED NATURAL SWISS CHEESE

Bourbon

population 1200

WHAT TO SEE:

ONONDAGA CAVE On the Meramec River near Leasburg. (573) 245-6576

DILLARD MILL Picturesque restored red mill on the banks of Huzzah Creek. (573) 244-3120

LOCAL AMUSEMENTS Area wineries , antique shops, auctions, and fairs, plus canoe trips, rafting, horseback riding, and rodeos

Cuba

population 2500

WHERE TO EAT:

FRANKLIN STREET FOOD COMPANY 617 Franklin St.

WHERE TO STAY:

WAGON WHEEL MOTEL Well-maintained example of the glory days along Route 66.

St. James

population 3500

WHAT TO SEE:

ST. JAMES WINERY 540 Sydney St. (573) 265-6200

MERAMEC SPRING PARK East on Highway 8. First iron works east of Mississippi. (573) 265-7124

WHERE TO EAT:

HICKORY TREE SAUSAGE FARM AND PASTRIES Don't miss this outstanding stop! 541 Highway B. (573) 265-8246

JESSE JAMES HIDEOUT St. James exit to north access road of I-44 between St. James and Rolla.

WHERE TO STAY:

THE PAINTED LADY BED AND BREAKFAST 1127 Jefferson St. (573) 265-5008

Cut onions in half from top to bottom, (with the grain), lay cut side down and cut 1/4 inch slices again with the grain.

Melt butter in a gallon pot. Add onions and slowly cook until tender, 20 to 30 minutes.

Add paprika, bay leaves, salt and pepper. Stir well.

Slowly add flour a little at a time, stirring well to incorporate after each addition. Simmer for 5 minutes.

Bring stock to a boil and add to onion mixture in small amounts stirring well after each addition. Simmer very slowly for 30 minutes. This soup is best if made the day before.

To assemble, select ovenproof crock or soup bowls. Place on jelly roll pan and fill almost to top with hot soup. Cut and place 2-inch croutons of French bread on top. Mound generously with shredded Swiss cheese.

Place under broiler until cheese is melted and slightly browned. Meanwhile, brush slices of French bread with extra virgin olive oil; toast. Serve with soup. Enjoy! 12 servings.

GOOD FOOD IN ST. JAMES:

As travelers drive up to The Painted Lady Bed and Breakfast, they will feel certain the home is a turn-of-the-century Victorian mansion with many years of hidden secrets behind the gaily painted exterior. In reality, creative innkeepers Sandy and Wanda Zinn built and decorated the home themselves. They opened their attractive bed and breakfast in 1995. Guests awaken in the morning to the aroma of coffee and a full country breakfast. These bran muffins are exceptionally good!

THE PAINTED LADY BED AND BREAKFAST

Raisin Bran Muffins

5 CUPS SIFTED FLOUR

3 CUPS SUGAR

1 BOX (12 OUNCES) RAISIN BRAN CEREAL

5 TEASPOONS BAKING SODA

2 TEASPOONS SALT

1 TEASPOON CINNAMON

1/2 TEASPOON ALLSPICE

4 EGGS, WELL BEATEN

1 QUART BUTTERMILK

1 CUP COOKING OIL

Mix dry ingredients together. Add eggs, buttermilk and oil.

Stir well. Bake as many muffins as desired in a preheated 350° oven for approximately 25 minutes. This batter keeps well in the refrigerator for up to 4 weeks. Use as needed.

Note: When baking from chilled dough, let dough rise at room temperature for 1 hour before baking. Approximately 4 dozen muffins.

The St. James Winery is operated by Pat Hoffhur and her sons, John and Andrew. The winery is recognized across the country. BON APPETIT MAGAZINE in January of 1995 selected the St. James Winery Seyval Blanc 1993 as one of the 50 Best Wines of 1994. Tours of St. James Winery are offered daily and a gift shop tempts all who stop. Pat is a home economist who loves to incorporate her wines in good food. She is currently preparing her own cookbook and graciously shared several of her favorite recipes.

Golden Punch

1 BOTTLE SCHOOL HOUSE WHITE WINE
   (SEMI-DRY WHITE, VERY FRUITY)
3 CUPS CANNED PINEAPPLE JUICE, CHILLED
1 CUP ORANGE JUICE
1/2 CUP LEMON JUICE
JUICE OF ONE FRESH GRAPEFRUIT
1 CUP STRONG TEA
1-1/2 CUPS SUGAR
1/4 TEASPOON POWDERED GINGER
ICE
FRESH OR CANNED GRAPES
1 BOTTLE ST. JAMES CHAMPAGNE

In a punch bowl, combine the white wine, pineapple, orange, lemon, and grapefruit juices and tea. Mix sugar and ginger; add to punch bowl and stir until dissolved. Add ice cubes and just before serving add grapes and Champagne. 35 servings, 4 ounces each.

Chicken and Rice in Wine

1/3 CUP CHOPPED GREEN PEPPER
1/3 CUP CHOPPED ONION
1 TABLESPOON BUTTER OR MARGARINE
3/4 CUP UNCOOKED RICE
1 CAN (14-1/2 OUNCES) CHICKEN BROTH
2 CUPS DICED, COOKED CHICKEN
1 CAN (10-3/4 OUNCES) MUSHROOM SOUP
3/4 CUP ST. JAMES COUNTRY WHITE WINE
   (SEMI-DRY WITH MILD FRUITY TASTE)
2/3 CUP DRAINED, SLICED WATER CHEST-
   NUTS (5 OUNCE CAN)
1 CAN (7 OUNCES) DRAINED FRENCH-STYLE
   GREEN BEANS (OPTIONAL)
SALT AND PEPPER TO TASTE
1/2 CUP TOASTED BREAD CRUMBS
PARSLEY FOR TOPPING

Sauté the pepper and onion in butter or margarine. Cook rice in chicken broth. Add pepper and onion to rice mixture. Stir in chicken, soup, wine, water chestnuts, and green beans. Pour mixture into a 9 x 11 casserole that has been sprayed with oil. Sprinkle crumbs on top. Bake in a preheated 350° oven for 40 minutes. Garnish with parsley. 6 to 8 servings.

GOOD FOOD IN ROLLA

Classic dishes don't have to have long, complicated names. Great regional American food can be simple yet exciting when prepared with fresh ingredients and served with a dash of creativity. This wonderful salad came straight from a Rolla garden and proved again that simple, wholesome dishes are hard to beat.

Wilted Greens with Country Ham

1/4 CUP OLIVE OIL
1 CUP THINLY SLICED RED ONION
1/2 CUP BROKEN PECANS
1/2 CUP SLIVERED COUNTRY HAM
2 TABLESPOONS BALSAMIC VINEGAR
2 TABLESPOONS MAPLE SYRUP
8 CUPS MIXED FRESH GARDEN GREENS
    (KALE, SPINACH, PURPLE LETTUCE, ARUGU-
    LA, CLEANED AND DRIED)
SALT AND PEPPER TO TASTE

Heat olive oil in a large skillet. Add onions and sauté, stirring constantly for about 5 minutes. Add nuts and continue cooking another two minutes. Stir in ham, continue cooking until ham is warm. Add vinegar and maple syrup. Stir and remove from heat.

Rolla

population 14,500

WHAT TO SEE:

ROUTE 66 MOTORS AND GENERAL STORE Owners Wayne and Pat Bales are Missouri Route 66 officers and road enthusiasts.

MEMORYVILLE USA A lavish classic car museum and antique stop. Exit 184 from I-44 (I-44 and 63 Junction). (573) 364-1810

PHELPS COUNTY JAIL AND DILLON CABIN MUSEUM Jail housed civil war prisoners and museum includes area artifacts and Civil War history. Third and Park.

MID-CONTINENT MAPPING CENTER US Geological Survey. 1400 Independence Road .Tours Monday—Friday. (573) 341-0811

STONEHENGE Partial replica, University of Missouri at Rolla campus. An official North American triangulation point.

BURMA SHAVE SIGNS Recreated by American Safety Razor Company / Reminisce.

JESSE JAMES HIDEOUT
Highway V exit to North
access road between Rolla
and St. James, then County
Road RA off north access of
I-44.

**ZENO'S STEAK HOUSE AT
ZENO'S MOTEL** 1621
Martin Spring Dr. (Route
66)

BRUNO'S A local favorite,
2001 Forum Dr.

**JOHNNY'S SMOKE
STEAK** For good barbecue!
201 Highway 72W.

WHERE TO STAY

ZENO'S MOTEL On Route
66 since 1955.

Waynesville

population 3200

WHAT TO SEE:

**FORT LEONARD WOOD
AND U.S. ARMY
ENGINEER MUSEUM** For
information call (573) 596-
4249.

OLD STAGECOACH STOP
On National Register of
Historic Places. An 1850
structure that has housed a
great deal of history! On the
square at 105 Linn St.

OLD COURT HOUSE Built
in 1903, housing the Pulaski
County Historical Society
Museum.

Tear greens into a large bowl. Pour hot
dressing over greens. Toss to wilt slightly.
Sprinkle with salt and pepper to taste and
serve immediately with crusty French bread. 8
to 10 servings.

GOOD FOOD IN WAYNESVILLE:

*At The Home Place Bed and Breakfast,
innkeeper Jean Hiatt offers her guests a memorable
opportunity to step back in time. The "giraffe-style"
stone house was built in 1940 on the site of
former Fort Waynesville, a camp for Union troops.*

*Home Place is filled with a large collection of
military memorabilia from the Civil War to the
present and Jean has added other unusual bits of
history including a victrola, pump organ, and
working antique phone booth.*

*Jean and her husband also own the Home
Place Mercantile, just down the street at 100 S.
Benton. She has remodeled the upstairs with a
great Route 66 theme to provide an additional
bed and breakfast suite that includes 2 bedrooms,
a kitchenette and bath, all for $66 per night!*

*Jean is a home economist who delights in
serving a full gourmet breakfast in the dining
room or upper porch that overlooks Roubidoux
Creek. Enjoy the peace and quiet of a small town
filled with memories to be rediscovered.*

THE HOME PLACE BED AND BREAKFAST
Blueberry Sour Cream Muffins

TOPPING:

  1/3 CUP BUTTER
  1/3 CUP BROWN SUGAR
  1/3 CUP FLOUR
  1/2 TEASPOON CINNAMON

MUFFINS:

1/3 CUP SOFT BUTTER OR MARGARINE

1 CUP SUGAR

1 EGG

1 TEASPOON VANILLA EXTRACT

2 CUPS FLOUR

2 TEASPOONS BAKING POWDER

1/4 TEASPOON SALT

3/4 CUP MILK

1/2 CUP SOUR CREAM

1 CUP FRESH BLUEBERRIES

Stir topping ingredients together and set aside.

Cream first 4 muffin ingredients. In a separate bowl, sift flour, baking powder, and salt. Add to creamed mixture alternately with milk and sour cream. Fold in blueberries. Spoon batter into greased muffin tins and sprinkle with topping.

Bake in a preheated 375° oven for 20 to 25 minutes. 16 to 18 muffins.

THE HOME PLACE BED AND BREAKFAST

Breakfast Strata

6 SLICES OF BREAD

SOFTENED BUTTER

2-1/4 CUPS CHEDDAR CHEESE

1 CUP CHOPPED COOKED HAM

5 EGGS, BEATEN

2 TABLESPOONS MINCED GREEN ONION

3/4 TEASPOON DRY MUSTARD

3/4 TEASPOON WORCESTERSHIRE SAUCE

1/4 TEASPOON GARLIC POWDER

DASH OF CAYENNE

SALT AND PEPPER TO TASTE

1-3/4 CUPS MILK

ANTIQUE SHOPS Several antique shops are around the square including The Dusty Attic.

HOME PLACE MERCANTILE On the corner of the town square. 100 S. Benton.

ROUBIDOUX SPRINGS AND PARK A 30-million-gallon-per-day spring and two streamside parks available for picnics.

WHERE TO EAT:

BENTON STREET CAFE AND TEA ROOM 100 N. Benton

IN NEARBY ST. ROBERT:

THE HUB

BAVARIAN HOUSE

WHERE TO STAY:

THE HOME PLACE BED AND BREAKFAST 302 S. Benton. (573) 774-6637

WHERE TO EAT:

BUCKHORN EXIT FROM I-44

WITMOR FARMS I-44 at Buckhorn Exit. Owner Roy Moorman helped build this first of the old Nickerson Farm chain. He and his wife, Norma, bought the cafe in 1963.

CAVEMAN BAR-BQ AND STEAK HOUSE Exit 150 from I-44, north, immediately make a right turn on State Road W. Drive 4 miles until pavement ends. Turn left for 1 mile on gravel road to parking lot. Shuttles take guests to the restaurant entrance, 100 feet above the Gasconade River. A must see experience! (573) 765-4554

Trim crusts from bread and butter lightly. Spray a 7 x 11 baking pan and place bread in pan to form a single layer. Sprinkle with half the cheese. Cover with ham. Combine remaining ingredients and carefully pour over the ham and cheese. Cover and refrigerate overnight. Bake uncovered in a preheated 350° oven for 30 minutes. Top with remaining cheese and return to oven for an additional 10 minutes or until cheese has melted. Let stand 5 minutes before cutting. 8 servings.

GOOD FOOD FROM RICHLAND:

In all likelihood, Caveman Bar-BQ and Steak House is the most unusual eatery along the length of Route 66 today. Missouri boasts over 5,000 caves, but none can compare to this unique bit of real estate located 100 feet above the Gasconade River. For those who want exceptionally good food as well as a setting like no other, this is the spot.

David and Connie Hughes bought the fishing resort along the river in 1984. David heard about the cave on his new property from old timers who remembered climbing up a ladder during the 1920s and 30s to the Saturday night speakeasy where dancing and home brew drew regular crowds.

When David finally borrowed a ladder to investigate the cave that is located high above the river, he found the perfect setting for a restaurant. The Hughes moved some 3500 tons of rock from the cave, cleaned every surface, and opened the Caveman Bar-BQ and Steak House in August of 1994. The fine food and unusual ambiance draw between five and six hundred customers a day on weekends.

Caveman Bar-BQ and Steak House
Grasshopper Pie

2 CUPS PREPARED WHIPPED TOPPING

1 JAR (7-1/2 OUNCES) MARSHMALLOW
CREAM

1 TEASPOON MINT EXTRACT

4 TO 6 DROPS GREEN FOOD COLORING

1 9-INCH PIE CRUST MADE FROM CRUSHED
OREO COOKIES

15 THIN CHOCOLATE MINT WAFERS,
CHOPPED

In a large bowl, gradually stir topping into marshmallow cream. Stir in mint extract and food coloring until evenly blended. Spoon mixture into crust. Sprinkle with chopped mint wafers. Freeze until firm. 6 slices.

GOOD FOOD FROM LEBANON:

The name Munger Moss has a long history along Route 66. In 1947 Jesse and Pete Hudson bought the Chicken Shanty Cafe and some adjoining land in Lebanon. They changed the name to Munger Moss Cafe and built a motel next door. Jim Sponseller bought the cafe in 1952 and operated it until 1979. The cafe is now gone but Bob and Ramona Lehman continue to operate the motel that has been home to thousands of Route 66 travelers.

Ramona shares this salad dressing that Mrs. Sponseller served to her many customers and has added one of her own favorite salads. Both recipes are excellent.

Lebanon:
population 10,000

WHERE TO EAT:

STONEGATE STATION
1475 S. Jefferson

WHERE TO STAY:

MUNGER-MOSS MOTEL
236 Seminole. A classic Route 66 location. Owners Bob and Ramona Lehman have many stories from Route 66 days!

Conway
population 650

WHERE TO EAT:

MCSHANES Home of the Little Round Pie. On the I-44 north access road. There's a great story about the pies here!

Munger Moss's
Thousand Island Dressing

1 CUP SALAD DRESSING
1/2 CUP CATSUP
2 HARD-COOKED EGGS, MINCED
1 TABLESPOON GRATED CHEDDAR CHEESE
1 SMALL GREEN PEPPER, CHOPPED
1 TEASPOON GRATED ONION OR CHIVES

Combine all ingredients and serve over salads. 1-1/2 cups dressing.

Ramona Lehman's
Vegetable Salad

1 SMALL HEAD CAULIFLOWER, CHOPPED
EQUAL AMOUNT OF BROCCOLI, CHOPPED
1 BUNCH GREEN ONIONS, CHOPPED
1 CUP LIGHT SALAD DRESSING
1/3 CUP SUGAR
2 TABLESPOONS VINEGAR

Combine vegetables. Mix dressing ingredients and pour over vegetables. Toss, chill, and serve. 8 to 10 servings.

Ada Moore of Lebanon, active in the Missouri Route 66 Association since its inception, shared this recipe for cinnamon rolls. Her mother, Emma Martley, prepared them often. Most of the guests who left their home also took away a bag of rolls. Ada remembers making bus trips from her home in Kansas City several times to see her grandparents in Springfield, Missouri. Before Ada left, her mother always handed her a bag of cinnamon rolls to eat on the way. The comfortable tradition has been carried on by the Martley's children and grandchildren.

Emma Martley's Cinnamon Rolls

2 PACKAGES DRY YEAST

1 CUP WARM WATER

1 CUP SHORTENING

1 TEASPOON SALT

2 CUPS WARM MILK

1 CUP SUGAR

2 EGGS

8 CUPS SIFTED FLOUR

FOR FILLING:

BUTTER

CINNAMON

SUGAR

NUTMEG

(ADD RAISINS AND NUTS, IF DESIRED).

Develop yeast in warm water. Add shortening, sugar, salt, warm milk, and eggs to the yeast mixture. Beat well then add 2 cups of the flour. Continue beating until smooth. Let mixture rest for 10 minutes.

Stir mixture, then gradually add remaining flour to make a soft dough. Place in well-greased bowl and turn to grease all surfaces. Cover and allow to double in bulk. Punch down and roll out on a lightly floured work surface to form a rectangle. Spread with butter, sugar, cinnamon, and a pinch of nutmeg. Add raisins or walnuts if desired.

Roll dough from lengthwise side and seal edges. Cut into 1-1/2 inch slices and place with cut side down in greased pan. Let rise again then bake in a preheated 375° oven for 20 to 25 minutes. 20 large rolls.

Marshfield

population 4500

WHAT TO SEE:

TELESCOPE A 1400-pound replica of the Hubble Space Telescope. Edwin Hubble was born in Marshfield in 1889.

SHOPS Antique and collectible shops.

WHERE TO EAT:

MOM'S CAFE 210 W. Jackson

TINY'S SMOKEHOUSE I-44 and Hwy 38

WHERE TO STAY:

THE DICKEY HOUSE 331 S. Clay St. **(417) 468-3000**

GOOD FOOD IN MARSHFIELD:

The Dickey House is a gracious Colonial Revival mansion, built at the turn of the century by Samuel Dickey, a prominent Marshfield attorney. It remained in his family until 1970. Bill and Dorothy Buesgen fell in love with the home when they found it for sale during a trip through Marshfield from their native California. They bought Dickey House in 1990, did extensive repair work to maintain the authentic character of the home, and opened it to guests in 1991. The home features three-foot diameter columns, intricate woodwork on the widow's walk, and a beveled glass front entrance. Dorothy serves a full breakfast each morning in Victorian splendor. While you are eating, share Bill's enthusiasm for the Hubble model he built to honor the city's most famous citizen.

THE DICKEY HOUSE
Caramel French Toast

1/2 CUP BUTTER

1 CUP BROWN SUGAR, PACKED

5 EGGS

1-1/2 CUPS MILK

1 TEASPOON VANILLA

2 TABLESPOONS SUGAR

1/4 TEASPOON SALT

1 LOAF FRENCH BREAD, SLICED 3/4 INCH THICK

In a small saucepan combine butter and brown sugar. Simmer until syrupy. Pour over bottom of a 9 x 13 inch glass dish. Remove crusts from sliced French bread and place slices over syrup mixture in dish. Beat eggs, milk, vanilla, sugar, and salt. Pour over bread, cover, and refrigerate overnight. Preheat oven to 350° and bake uncovered for 35 minutes. 10 to 12 servings.

Metropolitan population 450,000

I STICK BUTTER
I/2 CUP SUGAR
I CUP FLOUR
I-I/2 TEASPOONS BAKING POWDER
PINCH OF SALT
3/4 CUP MILK
I2 PRUNE PLUMS, PITTED AND HALVED OR 2
  CUPS SLICED PEACHES
I/4 TEASPOON CINNAMON
I/2 CUP SUGAR
GRATED ORANGE OR LEMON RIND

THE DICKEY HOUSE

Pumpkin Pancakes with Apple Cider Syrup

1-1/2 CUPS FLOUR

1 TEASPOON BAKING POWDER

1/4 TEASPOON BAKING SODA

1-1/2 TEASPOONS PUMPKIN PIE SPICE

1/4 TEASPOON SALT

1 EGG

1/4 CUP CANNED PUMPKIN

1-1/2 CUPS MILK

3 TABLESPOONS COOKING OIL

In a medium bowl, stir together the flour, baking powder, soda, salt, and pumpkin spice. In another bowl beat the egg, pumpkin, milk, and oil. Add milk mixture to the flour mixture and stir until just blended, but still lumpy. Pour about 1/4 cup of batter for each pancake onto a hot griddle or heavy skillet. Cook over medium heat until browned, turning to cook second side of pancakes. About 10 pancakes.

Apple Cider Syrup

1/2 CUP SUGAR

4 TEASPOONS CORNSTARCH

1/2 TEASPOON CINNAMON

1 CUP APPLE CIDER OR APPLE JUICE

1 TABLESPOON LEMON JUICE

2 TABLESPOONS BUTTER OR MARGARINE

In a small saucepan stir together the sugar, cornstarch, and cinnamon. Add the apple cider and lemon juice. Cook for 2 minutes over medium heat until mixture is thickened and bubbly. Cook an additional 2 minutes. Remove from heat and stir in the butter or margarine. Serve while warm over pancakes. 1 1/3 cups.

Springfield

population 150,000

ORIGINAL STRETCH OF OLD 66 Begin here to drive along a segment of original Route 66, without interstate interruptions, all the way to the edge of Oklahoma City. The few breaks that occur are minimized by the beautiful rolling hills, lush vegetation, and mom-and-pop stores. Includes that great original nine-foot-wide Route 66 ribbon in two segments between Miami and Afton.

Route 66 was Kearney, Glenstone, St. Louis, College, and Chestnut streets, then Highway 266 to Halltown.

HISTORIC DISTRICTS The Commercial Street Historic District, including Frisco Railroad Museum and several good restaurants, on Museum at 543 E. Commercial. The Walnut Street Historic District has several antique shops and restaurants.

OUTDOOR WORLD Bass Pro Shop containing Outdoor World and Hemingway's Blue Water Cafe. Make time to stop here. 1935 S. Campbell Ave.

GOOD FOOD IN SPRINGFIELD:

The Walnut Street Inn, an 1894 Queen Anne Victorian home, is a Springfield Designer Showcase restoration. COUNTRY INNS MAGAZINE has rated Karol and Nancy Brown's bed and breakfast as "one of the top twelve inns in the country." The inn has received numerous other awards for quality service and the tasteful design.

Located next door to Southwest Missouri State University, fourteen beautifully appointed guest rooms blend yesterday's charm with today's comfort. Sumptuous Ozark breakfasts add a final touch to this luxury getaway.

WALNUT STREET INN
Strawberry Soup

4 CUPS FROZEN STRAWBERRIES, THAWED

8 OUNCES CREAM CHEESE, SOFTENED

1/2 CUP SOUR CREAM

1/4 CUP POWDERED SUGAR

2 TABLESPOONS VANILLA

Place all items in a food processor. Blend until smooth but still thick. Serve chilled in small bowls. Garnish with a dollop of whipped cream and fresh mint or berries. 1 quart.

WALNUT STREET INN
Glory Morning Muffins

2 CUPS FLOUR

2 TEASPOONS BAKING SODA

2 TEASPOONS CINNAMON

1 TEASPOON NUTMEG

1/2 TEASPOON SALT

3 EGGS, BEATEN

3/4 CUP VEGETABLE OIL

3/4 CUP BUTTERMILK

2 CUPS SUGAR

2 TEASPOONS VANILLA

1 CAN (18 OUNCES) CRUSHED PINEAPPLE, DRAINED

1 CUP RAISINS

1 CUP COARSELY CHOPPED NUTS

2 CUPS GRATED CARROTS

1 CUP APPLES, PEELED AND CHOPPED

1/2 CUP GRATED COCONUT

Line 48 muffin tins with paper or foil liners. Sift flour, soda, cinnamon, nutmeg, and salt together; set aside. Mix eggs, oil, buttermilk, sugar, and vanilla. Add flour mixture, pineapple, raisins, nuts, carrots, apples, and coconut. Stir well. Spoon mixture into muffin tins. Bake in preheated 375° oven for 40 minutes or until a toothpick inserted in a muffin comes out clean. Muffins can be kept frozen for up to 3 months. 4 dozen muffins.

Lambert's Cafe, Home of the Throwed Rolls, was first opened in Sikeston, Missouri in 1942 by Agnes and Earl Lambert. Their Springfield location has been open since March of 1994. Famous for good food and plenty of it, the owners began throwing rolls to their guests in 1976 and the tradition has continued. You'll never leave hungry here or go out without a few laughs. A real Ozark welcome awaits.

Agnes Lambert raised her children on this recipe during World War II.

Agnes Lambert's Chicken and Dumplings

In a 2-gallon pot, cook a stewing chicken until meat can be pulled from the bone. Retain 1-1/2 gallons stock and chicken. In a large mixing bowl combine 2 eggs, 1 cup milk, and 1 teaspoon yellow food coloring.

CHRISTMAS Christmas City of Lights Spectacular. The city goes all out for the holidays.

FANTASTIC CAVERNS Three and a half miles northwest on Caverns Road. Tram tours through one of the states largest caves.

EXOTIC ANIMAL PARADISE In Strafford, 12 miles east. Phone **(417) 859-2159** for information.

DICKERSON PARK ZOO Exit 77 from I-44. 3043 N. Fort St.

WILSON'S CREEK NATIONAL BATTLEFIELD 1861 Civil War Battle where 2300 were slaughtered or wounded. Highway 182 and ZZ.

SPRINGFIELD CONVENTION AND VISITORS BUREAU 3315 East Battlefield . **(800) 678-8767**

WHERE TO EAT:

IN THE HEART OF DOWNTOWN:

RED ONION 305 S. Avenue A great Sunday brunch.

NONNA'S CAFE 306 S Avenue.Good Italian and American food.

LAMBERT'S CAFE "Home of the Throwed Rolls" 7 miles south on Hwy. 65.

Mix well. Add 2 cups flour, 1 teaspoon salt. Cut flour into liquid mixture until dough is smooth. On a well-floured board, roll dough to 1/4 inch thick. Cut into strips. Add to boiling stock. Reduce heat and simmer until dumplings are tender. About 20 servings.

SASSAFRAS! The Ozarks Cookbook is a treasured collection from the Junior League of Springfield. The cookbook contains 726 tested recipes from Ozark Mountain Country with 80,000 copies in print.

There are several outstanding Chinese restaurants in Springfield. This delicious Cashew Chicken recipe has become a community tradition!

SASSAFRAS!
Cashew Chicken

1/2 CUP MILK

2 TABLESPOONS WATER

2 EGGS, WELL BEATEN

SALT

4 LARGE CHICKEN BREAST HALVES, CUT INTO BITE-SIZED PIECES

2 TABLESPOONS CORNSTARCH

1-1/2 CUPS CHICKEN BROTH

2 TABLESPOONS OYSTER SAUCE

1 TEASPOON SUGAR

PEPPER TO TASTE

1 CUP FLOUR

VEGETABLE OIL FOR FRYING

1 CUP CASHEW NUTS

1/2 CUP CHOPPED GREEN ONIONS

SOY SAUCE

HOT FRIED RICE

Marinate chicken in milk, water, eggs and salt for 20 minutes. In a saucepan, dissolve cornstarch in a small amount of broth; add remaining broth gradually to make a paste.

Blend in oyster sauce, sugar, and pepper. Stir over medium-high heat until sauce boils and begins to thicken. Set aside.

Dredge chicken in flour. Fry in oil in a heavy skillet until crisp and golden. To prevent chicken pieces from sticking together, drop into hot oil one piece at a time. Drain on paper towels. Arrange chicken on a serving platter; sprinkle with cashews and green onions. Reheat sauce and pour over chicken. Serve immediately with soy sauce and rice. 4 servings.

GOOD FOOD IN HALLTOWN:

Thelma and Jerry White own Whitehall Mercantile, the oldest building still standing in Halltown. Built in 1900, the stark wooden structure housed a general store and post office on the first floor and the I.O.O.F. Lodge on the second floor. Today it is filled with antiques and collectables. The Whites are staunch Route 66 supporters who enjoy sharing stories of the road. Thelma says this good pie came with her to Missouri from her childhood home in Indiana. It was prepared originally by her Scottish grandmother.

Thelma White's
Sour Cream Raisin Pie

1 1/3 CUPS SUGAR
1-1/2 TABLESPOONS FLOUR
2/3 TEASPOON NUTMEG
2/3 TEASPOON CINNAMON
PINCH OF SALT
3 EGGS, LIGHTLY BEATEN
2 CUPS SOUR CREAM
2 CUPS SEEDLESS RAISINS

WHERE TO STAY:

WALNUT STREET INN 900 East Walnut St. (800) 593-6346

THE MANSION AT ELFINDALE 1701 S. Fort. (417) 831-5400

BIG CEDAR LODGE Affiliated with Bass Pro Shop, about 45 miles south of Springfield. An elegant Ozark experience! (417) 335-2777

Halltown
population 160

WHAT TO SEE:

At one time, Halltown had more antique shops per capita than any other community along Route 66. Whitehall Mercantile is one of the few survivors. Open daily except Wednesdays in the summer, and weekends only from November through March.

Carthage

WHAT TO SEE:

RED OAK II Stop by Red Oak II, Lowell Davis's whimsical reincarnation of his childhood home. Stroll the streets, visit artists, stop in at Belle Starr's home, the Salem country church, blacksmith shop, feed store, general store, old filling station, and restored motor courts now open as a "Bed and Baskets." Meet Lowell, internationally known artist of Little Critter collectable miniatures, and enjoy his unique art. **(417) 358-9018**

PRECIOUS MOMENTS CHAPEL AND VISITORS CENTER Artist Samuel Butcher's designs and creations are on display on the grounds. Nearby motels and restaurants. 480 Chapel Rd. **(800) 543-7975**

JASPER COUNTY COURTHOUSE Marvel at the Jasper County Courthouse, a magnificent Romanesque Revival structure completed in 1895 and built of Carthage marble, and browse the downtown square.

Combine dry ingredients and add eggs. Stir in sour cream and raisins. Pour mixture into two unbaked pie shells. Bake in preheated 425° oven for 20 minutes, then reduce heat to 375° and continue baking for another 30 minutes. Two 9-inch pies.

GOOD FOOD IN CARTHAGE:

Brewer's Maple Lane Farm makes a fascinating addition to the National Register of Historic Places. The 20-room mansion was built in 1900 by Cal Phelps, a miner and legislator. It was truly one of the great homes of the era. Arch and Renee Brewer bought the farm over forty years ago when the old house was "just a pile of rocks," according to Arch. After the Brewers reared their seven children in the 10,000 square foot expanse, they turned the Missouri marble estate into a bed and breakfast. Renee shared this favorite recipe with me on an unforgettable afternoon in the fall of 1994. Viewing this home is a Route 66 experience to be cherished.

BREWER'S MAPLE LANE FARM

Peanut Butter Cookies

1 CUP BUTTER OR MARGARINE

1-1/4 CUPS SUGAR

3/4 CUP FIRMLY PACKED BROWN SUGAR

2 EGGS

1 TEASPOON VANILLA

1 CUP PEANUT BUTTER

2-1/2 CUPS FLOUR

2 TEASPOONS BAKING SODA

1/2 TEASPOON SALT

Cream the butter or margarine and gradually add the sugar and brown sugar. Beat until light and fluffy. Add eggs and vanilla and blend well. Stir in the peanut butter.

Sift together the flour, baking soda, and salt. Add to the creamed mixture and blend. Drop by rounded teaspoonful on an ungreased baking sheet. Press with tines of a floured fork to make criss-cross pattern.

Bake for 10 to 12 minutes in a preheated 350° oven. Cool on wire racks. About 4 dozen cookies, depending on size.

Lowell and Charlotte Davis operate Red Oak II just east of Carthage. The Davis's wonderful re-creation of Lowell's childhood home offers visitors hours of pleasure reminiscing about the "good ol' days." Those who appreciate nostalgia at its best will want to stay a while to enjoy a recaptured era at the Frank Yant House, School Marm's House, or the Dalton Gang Homestead. This recipe for caramel corn was passed down from Lowell's mom, Nell Davis.

Red Oak II
Grandma Nell's Caramel Corn

8 CUPS POPPED CORN

2 CUPS BROWN SUGAR

2 STICKS MARGARINE

1/2 CUP WHITE CORN SYRUP

1 TEASPOON SALT

1/2 TEASPOON SODA

1 TEASPOON BUTTER FLAVORING

1 TEASPOON BURNT SUGAR FLAVORING

Sort out kernels that haven't popped and place the remaining in a large ovenproof pan.

Combine brown sugar, margarine, syrup, and salt in saucepan. Boil five minutes. Stir in flavorings and soda. Pour immediately over the popped corn. Stir and place in a 250° oven for one hour, stirring every 15 minutes. Cool and enjoy. 8 cups.

CIVIL WAR BATTLE OF CARTHAGE Learn about the city that was virtually destroyed during the Civil War. See the Civil War Battle of Carthage Historical Site and Civil War Museum. (417) 358-2373

VICTORIAN HOMES Take the Victorian Homes Driving Tour. Learn about the area during the late 19th and early 20th centuries at the Powers Museum or the Phelps House.

WHERE TO EAT:

TEA AND TRUFFLES 133 East Third (north side of town square).

CARTHAGE DELI AND ICE CREAM 301 S. Main (northwest corner of town square).

C.D.'S PANCAKE HUT 301 S. Garrison

TIFFANY'S, PRECIOUS MOMENTS COMPLEX

WHERE TO STAY:

THE LEGGETT HOUSE 1106 Grand Ave. (417) 358-0683

RED OAK II BED AND BASKET Rt. 1, Carthage. (417) 358-9018

Webb City

population 9,000

WHAT TO SEE:

HISTORIC HOMES Take a
driving tour to see many
turn-of-the-century homes.

WHERE TO EAT:

**BRADBURY BISHOP DELI
AND ROUTE 66 DINER**
Located in an 1887 building,
this Route 66 classic should
not be missed. 201 N. Main.

RED OAK II
Miss Charlotte's Corn Chowder

4 MEDIUM POTATOES, PEELED AND DICED
1 MEDIUM ONION, DICED
3 LARGE STALKS CELERY, CHOPPED
3 LARGE CARROTS, GRATED
2-1/2 CUPS WATER
2 CANS (15 OUNCES EACH) CREAM-STYLE
   CORN
2 CUPS SOUR CREAM
1 POUND BACON, FRIED CRISP AND CRUM-
   BLED
GRATED CHEDDAR CHEESE

Put potatoes, onion, celery and carrots in
cooking pot with water. Bring to boil then
simmer for 30 minutes. Add corn, sour cream
and bacon. Stir and simmer 2 minutes.
Provide a bowl of grated cheese so guests may
top their bowls if desired. 8 to 10 servings.

*Charlotte Davis says that she and Lowell
have eaten lots of good meals cooked by longtime
friend, Sharon Plate Griffith, now of Nashville.*

RED OAK II
Sharon's Spinach Cornbread

2 BOXES (8-1/2 OUNCES EACH) JIFFY CORN-
   BREAD MIX
8 EGGS, SLIGHTLY BEATEN
1-1/2 STICKS MARGARINE, MELTED
1 BOX (10 OUNCES) FROZEN CHOPPED
   SPINACH, THAWED AND DRAINED
1 CARTON (12 OUNCES) SMALL CURD COT-
   TAGE CHEESE

Combine cornbread mix with remaining
ingredients in a large mixing bowl. Transfer to
a greased 9 x 13 baking pan or large iron
skillet. Bake in preheated 425° oven for 25 to
30 minutes.

Note: Add 1/2 cup cooked, drained, crumbled sausage to the cornbread mixture if desired, or 1 tablespoon chopped hot peppers or 1/2 cup grated cheddar cheese. 15 squares.

The most elegant bed-and-breakfast in Carthage is The Leggett House at 1106 Grand. Nolan and Nancy Henry operate the 22-room Victorian stone home, built at the turn of the century by industrial pioneer J.P. Leggett.

LEGGETT HOUSE BED AND BREAKFAST
Coffee Cake

1/2 POUND BUTTER

1 CUP SUGAR

3 EGGS

2-1/2 CUPS FLOUR

2 TEASPOONS BAKING POWDER

1 TEASPOON SODA

1 TEASPOON SALT

1 CUP SOUR CREAM

1/2 TEASPOON VANILLA

Grease and flour a 10-inch tube pan. Cream butter until light and fluffy. Add sugar and eggs, one at a time, beating at least two minutes. Sift dry ingredients together and add to butter mixture, stirring until batter is smooth. Blend in sour cream, then spoon into cake pan. Bake for 50 minutes in a 350° oven. Cool slightly before slicing. 10 to 12 servings.

GOOD FOOD FROM JOPLIN:

FROM SEED TO SERVE by Leanna K. Potts of Joplin is based on her years of experience with herbs. Leanna has also collaborated with her young daughter to produce THYME FOR KIDS. This creative booklet introduces children to herb

Joplin
population 41,500

WHAT TO SEE:

HISTORICAL MUSEUM Dorothea Hoover Historical Museum in Schifferdecker Park includes a miniature animated circus and artifacts from Joplin's history. 4th and Schifferdecker Ave.

TRI-STATE MINERAL MUSEUM Also in Schifferdecker Park, includes displays of local mining.

MUNICIPAL BUILDING A Thomas Hart Benton mural can be seen in the lobby of the Municipal Building at 303 E. 3rd.

RICHARDSON'S CANDY STORE Great candy and a good antique store next door. S. 86 Highway. (800) 624-1615

WHERE TO EAT:

CLIFF SIDE A lovely spot 7 miles south of Joplin.

HIDDEN ACRES 2800 Range Line Rd.

HUNT'S BAR-B-Q RESTAURANT 1/4 mile south of Joplin Regional Airport. (417) 624-3858

BENITO'S Good Mexican food served by Claude Cupp. 2525 Range Line Rd.

gardening, suggests easy-to-follow recipes, and includes a variety of seeds along with planting directions.

FROM SEED TO SERVE

Baked Tarragon-Honey Onions

4 MEDIUM YELLOW ONIONS, PEELED

2 PATS BUTTER

2 TABLESPOONS HONEY

6 TABLESPOONS FRESH TARRAGON, FINELY CHOPPED

Place onions on sheet of foil large enough so that the onions may be wrapped completely in the foil. In the center of each onion, place a pat of butter, 1/2 tablespoon honey, and 1-1/2 tablespoons diced tarragon. Wrap in foil and bake in a 350° oven for about 1 hour or until onions are transparent. 4 servings.

THYME FOR KIDS

Green Bean Salad

2 TABLESPOONS PARMESAN CHEESE

1/3 CUP OLIVE OIL

1/3 CUP VINEGAR

1 TEASPOON SUGAR

2 TABLESPOONS FRESH BASIL, MINCED

1 LARGE CLOVE GARLIC, MINCED

1 TEASPOON FRESH CHIVES, MINCED

1 TEASPOON FRESH THYME, MINCED

1 CAN (15-1/2 OUNCES) FRENCH-STYLE GREEN BEANS, DRAINED

1 SMALL HEAD ICEBERG OR RED LEAF LETTUCE

In a jar or bottle combine cheese, olive oil, vinegar, sugar, and herbs. Shake well. Mix green beans with part of the dressing. Arrange lettuce on 4 to 6 salad plates and top with equal portions of green beans. Pour leftover dressing over greens and serve. 4 to 6 servings.

K A N S A S

K ansas: hearty, healthy, hospitable food from our heartland. Kansas cuisine is a composite of traditional dishes from European immigrants, Native American fare, and prairie kitchen nourishment from our no-nonsense grandmothers.

Pioneer cooks served fried chicken every Sunday, and prepared mashed potatoes, homegrown vegetables, biscuits, bread, and pies made from garden fruit to supplement the cowboys' diet of beans and coffee.

Kansas boasts only 13.2 miles of Route 66, yet it was the first state to completely pave the historic highway. The three Kansas Route 66 communities are diverse and rewarding. Galena is a mining community, Riverton was settled by Quakers, and Baxter Springs traces its roots to cowtown days. The heritage of Route 66 is strong here. The route's March Arch "Rainbow Bridge" has been preserved and is listed on the National Registry of Historic Places. And each October a half-marathon race spans Kansas 66 from the Oklahoma to Missouri line.

At Eisler Brothers Old Riverton Store customers can order one of the best sandwiches made along the highway and they can still raise the bright red lid of an old pop cooler, plunge an arm into the icy depths of the chest, and pull out a 6-ounce bottle of root beer or Coca Cola.

Kansas is Main Street at its best!

Galena

population 3400

GALENA MINING AND HISTORICAL MUSEUM
Howard Litch was the driving force behind this town treasure where more area history is shared than in many more prestigious stops. This is a very special museum. Located in the old Katy Depot on 7th St.

GOLDEN RULE STORE
Dorotha Senter is the extraordinary lady who operates the store founded by her father in 1912. Get your purchases wrapped in brown paper and tied with a string! Meet Dorotha Senter at 403 Main.

SCHERMERHORN HOME
The most elaborate of the early-day Victorian homes. Open only on special occasions for tours. 5th and Wood.

WHERE TO EAT:

LUCKY LADIES DINER
Cafe at 518 Main. Leased often to new tenants, but worth a stop to see the walk-in vault left in place when the turn-of-the-century Miner's State Bank was raised.

GOOD FOOD IN GALENA:

Gena and Scott Shockley live south of Galena where Scott grew up. Gena shared this recipe that her mother and grandmother have used for years to make pickles from their bounteous gardens.

Gena Shockley's Bread and Butter Pickles

5 POUNDS CUCUMBERS, SLICED THIN

2 OR 3 ONIONS, SLICED

1/2 CUP SALT

3 CUPS SUGAR

2 CUPS VINEGAR

2 TEASPOONS CELERY SEED

2 TEASPOONS MUSTARD SEED

1-1/2 TEASPOONS TUMERIC

1 TEASPOON GINGER

1 TEASPOON CLOVES

1/2 TEASPOON PEPPER

Place cucumbers and onions in a large pan. Add salt and cover with ice cubes. Let stand for 3 hours. Drain and rinse well in cold water. Combine remaining ingredients and pour over the cucumbers and onions. Bring to a boil. Reduce heat and simmer 3 to 4 minutes. Pack pickles in hot sterilized jars, and quickly seal. 4 pints.

GOOD FOOD IN BAXTER SPRINGS:

When I visited Mary Ellen Lee at her charming old home in Baxter Springs, I could feel the love and warmth she had poured into Lottie Keenan House. All of her beloved pieces fit perfectly into the renovated home that once belonged to early Baxter Springs resident, Lottie Keenan.

The home makes a nostalgic stop and Mary Ellen is an excellent cook. Mary Ellen shared these favorites. She says this orange juice special is a delicious eye-opener.

LOTTIE KEENAN HOUSE
Orange Juice Special

1 CAN (6 OUNCES) FROZEN ORANGE JUICE
2 CANS WATER
1 CAN (6-1/2 OUNCES) CRUSHED PINEAPPLE
1 LARGE BANANA

Combine all ingredients in a blender and fill to the top with ice. Pulse until ice is crushed. Serve immediately. Six 5-ounce servings.

LOTTIE KEENAN HOUSE
Cinnamon Roll Muffins

2 PACKAGES DRY YEAST
1/4 CUP WARM WATER
1 CUP LUKEWARM MILK
1 CUP MARGARINE, MELTED
2 EGGS, BEATEN
1/4 CUP SUGAR
1 TEASPOON SALT
4-1/2 CUPS FLOUR

FILLING:

2 STICKS SOFTENED MARGARINE
SUGAR AND CINNAMON AS DESIRED

Dissolve yeast in warm water. Combine yeast mixture with remaining ingredients in order given in a large mixing bowl. Beat until smooth, about one minute. Dough will be very soft. Cover with a damp cloth and place in refrigerator overnight.

Riverton
population 900

WHAT TO SEE:

EISLER BROTHERS OLD RIVERTON STORE Built in 1925, and still a real working general store. Operated today by Scott Nelson, president of the Kansas Historic Route 66 Association.

SPRING RIVER A beautiful stop for a picnic.

BIG BRUTUS Drive north on Highway 69 to West Mineral to see the second largest electrical shovel in the world, 16 stories high, 5,500 tons.

WHERE TO EAT:

EISLER BROTHERS OLD RIVERTON STORE Great sandwiches are concocted here!

SPRING RIVER INN This classic stop may be closed.

BAXTER SPRINGS MUSEUM An exceptionally good community museum. 8th and East Ave.

NATIONAL CEMETERY Take a driving tour of 16 Civil War sites. Included is the third national cemetery in the country featuring a monument that honors those killed in the Quantrill Massacre, October 6, 1886, who are buried here. The monument cost $4,000 in 1886.

RESTAURANT AT 1101 MILITARY "The restaurant in the bank that was robbed by Jesse James." Formerly was Bill Murphey's Restaurant, famous for pies since 1941.

MURPHEY'S RESTAURANT Now located in the old Baxter National Bank building diagonally across the street from 1101 Military.

VAN'S STEAKHOUSE 2447 S. Military

BLUE MOON CAFE A local favorite for good Vietnamese food. Located in Baxter Shopping Center.

The next morning, roll out half the dough into a rectangle and spread with one stick of softened margarine. Sprinkle dough with desired amount of sugar and cinnamon. Roll dough from long side in jelly roll fashion. Cut dough into 1-1/2 inch slices and place cut side down into greased muffin tins. Repeat process for remaining half of dough. Bake cinnamon rolls in preheated 350° oven for about 25 minutes. Cool and glaze with a powdered sugar icing if desired. About 2 dozen muffins.

LOTTIE KEENAN HOUSE

Baked Ham with Almond Flavoring

1 15 TO 20 POUND BONE-IN HAM, UNCOOKED

3 TABLESPOONS ALMOND EXTRACT

1 JAR (18 OUNCES) ORANGE MARMALADE

2 CANS (11 OUNCES EACH) MANDARIN ORANGES, DRAINED

1 JAR (6 OUNCES) MARASCHINO CHERRIES, UNDRAINED

1/2 TEASPOON TABASCO SAUCE

Place whole ham, fat side up, in an open roasting pan. Bake in 325° oven for 5 to 6 hours. Remove from oven, cool, and cut away the rind and fat from the ham. Score the ham and brush on the glaze made from almond extract, marmalade, and Tabasco sauce which has been heated in saucepan. Place the mandarin oranges and cherries with the juice on top of the ham and return to oven for 30 minutes. Let ham cool slightly before removing from roasting pan to platter. Slice, saving the oranges and cherries for garnish. 12 to 15 servings.

"Burnt Offerings" is a popular weekly food column that has appeared in the BAXTER SPRINGS CITIZEN since the late 1970s. Carolyn Nichols, who compiles the article, is a longtime Baxter Springs resident whose father started the paper. Carolyn's late husband followed as publisher and the paper is now in the capable hands of her son.

Carolyn has published one cookbook collection and supplement that sold out quickly and another is underway. She is also busy in a variety of community activities and is an enthusiastic Route 66 supporter who has served on the Kansas Historic Route 66 Association board of directors.

She says this delicious ice cream recipe came from Earsie Riddle, who handed it down to her daughter Dorothy Marsh. Granddaughter Andrea Tunnel now prepares the treat for special summer events.

WHERE TO STAY:

LOTTIE KEENAN HOUSE BED-AND-BREAKFAST
535 East 10th. (316) 856-4155

Old-Fashioned Vanilla Ice Cream

In a saucepan scald 4 cups milk. In a double boiler, mix 1-1/2 cups sugar with 2 tablespoons flour and a pinch of salt. Add 6 lightly beaten eggs and the milk to the flour/sugar mixture.

Cook over hot water for 10 minutes, stirring constantly. When thickened, add 1/2 gallon whole milk and 2 tablespoons vanilla. Stir and pour into ice cream freezer. Follow manufacturer's directions to freeze. 1 gallon.

Shirley Ellsworth shared this recipe for candy that was first made at Anthony's Candy Store in Galena. Called Mine Run Candy, many thought Mr. Anthony named it because the crisp porus texture reminded him of the minerals that were mined in the area. But he always said that it came about as an accident when he allowed some candy to caramelize while he wasn't paying attention and "let his mind run wild." Whatever the name, Mine Run Candy has become a local favorite.

Mine Run Candy

1 CUP SUGAR

1 CUP DARK CORN SYRUP

1 TABLESPOON WHITE VINEGAR

1 TABLESPOON SODA

Combine sugar, corn syrup, and vinegar in large pan and cook while stirring constantly until sugar dissolves. Cover pan for one minute to wash down crystals.

Uncover pan and insert candy thermometer and cook candy without stirring to 300° (hard crack stage). Remove from heat and stir in soda. Candy will foam, so be sure to use a large pan and a big spoon with a long handle.

Pour mixture into a buttered 9 x 13 dish. Do not spread. After it cools, break into bite-sized pieces and coat with chocolate.

CHOCOLATE COATING:

Melt a block of almond bark or dark chocolate for about 90 seconds in a microwave. Watch carefully and don't overcook. Dip the candy pieces into the melted chocolate and set on waxed paper to cool.

Carolyn Nichols shared her own favorite recipe for Watermelon Pickles that has been a family favorite for years. She says this is one of the most popular sale items at fall bazaars in the area.

Watermelon pickles are best when made with thick white rind. Large, oval, dark green Black Diamond melons make a perfect choice.

Carolyn Nichols's Watermelon Pickles

6 POUNDS WATERMELON RIND (ABOUT HALF A LARGE MELON)

Cut pink meat and green rind from white. Cut white rind into 1-inch squares or whatever shape you prefer.

Cover rind with cold salt water. (Do not use iodized salt.) Soak overnight. The next morning drain and rinse melon pieces thoroughly. Cook in clear water until rind is fork tender but don't overcook. Drain well.

MAKE A SYRUP OF:

8 CUPS SUGAR
I 2/3 CUPS CIDER VINEGAR
4 DROPS OIL OF CLOVES
6 DROPS OIL OF CINNAMON
A FEW DROPS OF GREEN COLORING (OPTIONAL)

Boil syrup for 5 minutes. Add rind and let stand overnight. The next morning add 1 cup sugar and bring to boil. Can in hot sterilized jars. If syrup is left, save for another batch. It will keep for 2 weeks in refrigerator. 4 pints per 6 pounds of melon rind.

In nearby Joplin, Fred and Red's on South Main serves up chile and spaghetti to a host of regulars who say their sauce is the best ever. Lea Ona Essley of Baxter Springs shares this spaghetti topping that is very close to the original recipe. She says the secret ingredient is the addition of tamales to the sauce, adding both body and flavor.

Fred and Red's Chile

1 LARGE CAN (28 OUNCES) TAMALES, MASHED
1 POUND COOKED HAMBURGER
1/2 CUP CHOPPED ONION
WATER TO MAKE A THICK SAUCE
1 CAN (8 OUNCE) TOMATO SAUCE
1 PACKAGE (1 OUNCE) WILLIAMS CHILE SEASONING MIX
1 POUND BRICK CHILE

Mash the tamales. Cook the hamburger and drain; add onion and mashed tamales, then enough water to make a sauce. Add tomato sauce, chile seasoning and brick chile and heat to boiling. Reduce heat and simmer for 10 minutes. Note: Serve this great chile plain or as a sauce over pasta. Approximately 9 cups.

Bordens Restaurant, 2615 East 11th St., Tulsa, Oklahoma

O klahoma is barbecue country. Barbecue, to the purist, is slow cooked meat served with one of the many rubs, marinades, mops, or sauces that make for culinary magic. True connoisseurs of smoked meat often pass on the extras, preferring their meat with only the smoke flavor created by this time-honored cooking method.

The contraptions that often look like locomotives are considered the best and often most expensive smokers. Steve Kennon, who designs and builds his own dry smokers, says the cookers vary in design. Most have a water pan, allowing skilled cooks to add tenderizing moisture around the meat as it slowly cooks with controlled heat from wood smoke. Dry smokers rely on perfectly designed equipment and the skill of the fire builders to provide flavor with a dry air process. Temperature in smokers should be maintained between 175° and 250°. Hardwoods like hickory, pecan, oak, Osage orange (bois d'arc), maple, or mesquite form the all-important bed of coals and provide flavor. "Smokewood" such as apple, cherry, peach, pear, and sassafras is added for distinctive flavor. A good smoker can never be rushed. It may take 10 to 24 hours to turn out mouth-watering hams, briskets, beef tenderloins, or ribs. Chicken, sausage links, and bologna rolls may be ready in 3 to 6 hours. A perfectly smoked ham will be blackened and crispy on the outside yet maintain a juicy, pink interior that is incredibly tender and flavorful.

Mike and his brother Steve, both Northeastern Oklahoma natives, say their favorite smoker has a separate chambers so they can prepare vegetables while the meat is smoking. Beans, corn-on-the-cob, potatoes, and squash are among their favorites. Vegetables cook in about two hours as natural smoke imparts a tangy outdoor flavor.

Steve says Oklahoma cooks seem to enjoy smoked pork and beef equally while Texans prefer beef, and folks in the Deep South smoke pork more often. Chicken is popular with health conscious cooks.

There are good barbecue sites all along Route 66. Here are a few of the best in Oklahoma: The Texas Toothpick in Commerce, The Pits and Cotton Eyed Joe's in Claremore, Wilson's and Billy Ray's in Tulsa, P.J.'s in Chandler, Dan's in Davenport, Billee's in Arcadia, and Jiggs Smoke House in Clinton. This all-American food is meant to be enjoyed. Just be sure there are plenty of napkins and dig in!

GOOD FOOD IN QUAPAW:

Amanda Greenback, a Seneca Indian who has lived in Northeastern Oklahoma all her life, is recognized as an outstanding cook who often prepares her native food for for large groups. Just after our visit, she began preparation of a full meal for a class on Indian culture taught by her daughter at Northeastern Oklahoma A&M College in Miami.

Amanda cooks by the look and feel of her food, so she emphasized that these directions may need slight adjustment.

Amanda Greenback's Fry Bread

4 TEASPOONS BAKING POWDER

I TEASPOON SODA

2 TABLESPOONS SUGAR

5 POUNDS FLOUR

2 TABLESPOONS MARGARINE, MELTED

I QUART BUTTERMILK

SHORTENING FOR FRYING

Stir baking powder, soda, and sugar into flour. Add margarine and buttermilk and stir until mixture is well blended. Heat shortening in large kettle to about 350°. Work dough in hands and pull off biscuit-size pieces. Flatten and drop into hot fat. Allow to brown on both sides then remove and drain. Serve hot.

Variation: After flattening the fry bread, place a small amount of cheese, cooked and seasoned ground meat, or a fruit such as drained canned apples in the center of the dough. Pull sides together to seal dough at the top. Fry as usual. Amanda says her grandchildren call these treats "turtles" because of the shape.

Amanda Greenback's Grape Dumplings

2 CANS (46 OUNCES EACH) GRAPE JUICE

I/2 CUP SUGAR

5 POUNDS FLOUR

4 TEASPOONS BAKING POWDER

I TEASPOON SODA

I QUART GRAPE JUICE

2 EGGS

2 TABLESPOONS MARGARINE, MELTED

I/4 CUP SUGAR

Quapaw

population 985

WHAT TO SEE:

SPOOKLIGHT ON DEVIL'S PROMENADE ROAD East of town, near the state line.

MURALS Murals on several old buildings.

ANNUAL QUAPAW POW-WOW One of the oldest gatherings in the country, 1997 marked the 125th year.

BEAVER SPRINGS PARK 4th of July weekend

WHERE TO EAT:

DALLAS' DAIRYETTE

Commerce

WHAT TO SEE:

MICKEY MANTLE'S HOME Plans are underway to restore the home as a museum. 319 S. Quincy.

HOWARD'S GARDEN CENTER Spectacular family-operated business on Mickey Mantle Blvd.

THE ROCK SHOP For everyone who loves to collect or just enjoys rocks, an extensive collection!

WHERE TO EAT:

THE LIL' CAFE 307 N. Mickey Mantle Blvd.

TEXAS TOOTHPICK BAR-B-QUE 610 N. Mickey Mantle Blvd.

Pour two cans of grape juice into large kettle. Add sugar and bring juice to a boil. Meanwhile, combine flour, baking powder and soda in a large bowl. Make a hole in center of dry ingredients and pour 1 quart of grape juice, eggs, margarine, and sugar into mixture. Blend by working flour from the sides.

Dumplings may be dropped into boiling grape juice by tablespoons or the dough can be rolled out and cut into approximately 2-inch pieces before cooking. Dumplings will be juicy. Ladle into serving dishes and eat while warm.

GOOD FOOD IN COMMERCE:

Dennis Gray spent 20 years in Texas law enforcement before he and his family moved to Commerce in 1992. Gray has enjoyed barbecuing all his adult life and has won many competitions. His skill was evident at the 1996 Miami Open Chile and BBQ Cookoff where he was proclaimed Grand Champion by winning in every BBQ division.

Friends who enjoy the results of his talent encouraged him to go into business, so the Texas Toothpick opened in the spring of 1996 in an unadorned location on the north edge of town.

Gray built his own smoker from a 150-gallon propane tank and designed it with a grill on one end and a smoker on the other. He depends on hickory to impart flavor.

The name for his business just happened. Friends in Texas always told Dennis his barbecue was not only finger lickin' good, it was toothpicking good. Texas Toothpick Bar-B-Que was a natural.

TEXAS TOOTHPICK

Bar-B-Que Pork Ribs

1 SLAB LEAN PORK RIBS
LEMON PEPPER
ZESTY ITALIAN DRESSING
ALUMINUM FOIL

Wash ribs in cold water. Trim all excess fat from both front and back of ribs. Shake lemon pepper on both sides and rub into meat. Pour zesty Italian dressing over top side of ribs and refrigerate at least a couple of hours. Wrap ribs in heavy duty aluminum foil and place over hot coals on grill for 1 to 1-1/2 hours. Remove foil and place ribs in smoker for another two hours. Slice ribs and serve from a big platter to folks who find the ribs so tender they'll say they're "toothpicking good!"

TEXAS TOOTHPICK

Texas Grilled Onion Blossom

1 LARGE ONION
LEMON PEPPER
PAPRIKA
MARGARINE
ALUMINUM FOIL

Cut around bottom of onion one layer deep and peel off outer layer; wash. Cut onion from the top into eighths so that the onion will open like a flower. Sprinkle with a healthy amount of lemon pepper and a touch of paprika. Top with about 4 tablespoons margarine. Wrap onion in heavy duty foil and place on grill, to the side of the fire and cook for 30 to 45 minutes.

To serve, cut foil open and place onion in a bowl. Spread open like a flower and serve with any dip of your choice.

Students at Alexander Elementary School in Commerce participated in a fund raiser during the 1994-1995 school year and brought favorite recipes from home to share with the community as a cookbook. Derek Bomen, a 3rd grader, did the art work on the cover and when the collection was assembled, the best of Commerce hometown cookery emerged. Here are two favorites.

Rachel Walker's Stuffed Green Peppers

4 LARGE GREEN BELL PEPPERS
I CAN (15-1/2 OUNCES) HUNT'S PRIMA SALSA
3/4 CUP WATER
I POUND VERY LEAN GROUND BEEF
2 CUPS COOKED RICE
1/4 CUP CHOPPED ONION
1-1/2 TEASPOONS SALT
1/8 TEASPOON PEPPER
I CUP SHREDDED CHEDDAR CHEESE

Wash and halve peppers lengthwise. Remove seeds. Parboil for 3 to 5 minutes and cool. Combine salsa with water. Lightly mix beef, rice, onion, salt, pepper and half the salsa. Pile into green pepper halves. Top with cheese. Arrange in 9 x 12 baking dish. Pour remaining salsa over. Cover and bake in preheated 350° oven for 1 hour. 4 to 6 servings.

Greg Cossairt's Zucchini Bake

I LARGE CARROT, CHOPPED OR SHREDDED
I OR 2 STALKS CELERY, CHOPPED
I CUP CHOPPED ZUCCHINI
I BELL PEPPER, CHOPPED

2 TABLESPOONS MARGARINE
2 EGGS
1-1/2 CUPS WATER
DASH OF THYME
1 CUP PREPARED STUFFING MIX
PEPPER, ONION SALT, AND SAGE TO TASTE

Combine vegetables and sauté in margarine. Combine remaining ingredients. Place vegetables in a greased 8 x 8 casserole dish and pour egg mixture over vegetables. Bake in a preheated 425° oven for 30 minutes. 6 servings.

Note: Using red pepper in place of green makes a more colorful dish. Browned ground beef, hot sausage, or corn may also be added.

GOOD FOOD IN MIAMI:

The First National Bank of Miami has a meeting room for community activities. This often includes luncheons, receptions, and other community functions. Several years ago, bank employees Peggy Angle and Anne Pendergraft began collecting recipes for some of the good food that passed through the doors. Soon THE BANKER'S BEST HOME COOKIN' was published, with the proceeds going to charitable Miami causes including the bank's adopted school and renovation at the Coleman Theater. Here are two delicious examples from the collection.

THE BANKER'S BEST HOME COOKIN'

Ann Pendergraft's Ozark Apple Pudding

1/2 CUP BUTTER OR MARGARINE
1 CUP SUGAR
1 EGG
1 CUP FLOUR
1 TEASPOON SODA

Miami

population 14,000

WHAT TO SEE:

COLEMAN THEATER Built in 1929 in the Spanish Mission style, now home to a Route 66 satellite exhibit. 103 N. Main.

DOBSON MUSEUM 110 A Street S.W.

NEOSHO RIVER BRIDGE Historic steel-truss Neosho River Bridge, built in 1937 and on Route 66.

RIBBON ROAD 2 stretches of original 9 foot wide road between Miami and Afton.

WHERE TO EAT:

PIZZA HUT EXPRESS Owners Renick and Jackie Kreger, Oklahoma Route 66 Association officers, have creatively decorated their business with a Route 66 theme. 101 A Street, N.W.; behind the Coleman Theater.

WAYLAN'S KU-KU BURGER A great place for a hamburger! 915 N. Main.

BE-BOP DINER Well done 1950s decor. 2019 N. Main.

MILAGROS MEXICAN RESTAURANT Outstanding Mexican food in the historic St. James Hotel. 103 E. Central.

1 TEASPOON CINNAMON

1 TEASPOON NUTMEG

1/2 TEASPOON SALT

2-1/4 CUPS CHOPPED APPLES (ABOUT 4 SMALL)

1 CUP CHOPPED NUTS (OPTIONAL)

Cream together the butter, sugar, and egg. Add flour, soda, cinnamon, nutmeg, and salt. Stir together with the apples and nuts. Pour mixture into a buttered 9 x 9 baking dish and bake in preheated 325° oven for 1 hour. Serve with a whipped cream topping if desired. 8 servings.

THE BANKER'S BEST HOME COOKIN'

Peggy Angle's Chocolate Mousse

1 ENVELOPE UNFLAVORED GELATIN

2 TABLESPOONS COLD WATER

4 TABLESPOONS BOILING WATER

1 CUP SUGAR

1/2 CUP COCOA

2 TEASPOONS VANILLA

2 CUPS VERY COLD HEAVY CREAM

Sprinkle gelatin over cold water; stir and let stand for 1 minute. Add boiling water and stir until gelatin is dissolved. Set aside. Combine sugar and cocoa in a cold mixing bowl. Add the vanilla and cream. Beat at medium speed until stiff peaks form. Pour in gelatin mixture; continue beating until blended. Spoon into serving dishes and chill until ready to serve. 6 to 8 servings.

In the historic St. James Hotel, beneath the imposing murals painted by Bronson Edwards, and part of the National Historic Registry, Milagros Mexican Restaurant offers delicious mainstream Mexican flavor.

Russ and Rebecca Sano opened their dream restaurant in May of 1996 after making a conscious decision to leave California to be nearer family. Rebecca's father and four brothers have all been in the restaurant business, so other family members naturally have followed. When the Sanos found this Miami location, they knew it was right. Other opportunities soon fell into place and Milagros (meaning "miracles" in Spanish) became reality.

MILAGROS MEXICAN RESTAURANT
Sopaipillas

12 CUPS FLOUR

1/3 CUP SUGAR

3 TEASPOONS BAKING POWDER

2-1/3 CUP WATER

2 CUPS MILK

3 TABLESPOONS DRY YEAST

HONEY, SUGAR, AND CINNAMON

Combine flour, sugar, and baking powder. Warm the water and milk and sprinkle in the dry yeast. Allow liquid to stand a few minutes before adding to the flour mixture. Stir to combine, then lightly knead the dough. Place dough in a greased bowl and allow to rise for an hour. Punch down and store in refrigerator until ready to use.

When ready to cook sopaipillas, pull off small balls of dough, flatten slightly and drop into shortening that has been heated to 350°. Fry until lightly browned. Serve with honey and a sprinkling of sugar and cinnamon.

Chile Verde

10 POUNDS PORK ROAST, TRIMMED AND
BONED
1/2 CUP CHILE POWDER
3 BELL PEPPERS
1 ONION
1/4 CUP GARLIC POWDER
1/4 CUP SALT
1/2 TABLESPOON BLACK PEPPER
3 TABLESPOONS CUMIN
1 CUP CRUSHED TOMATOES
1/2 CUP FLOUR, OR MORE AS NEEDED TO
THICKEN

Cube the pork roast and brown slowly in oil for 20 minutes. Add remaining ingredients except flour and cook an additional 10 minutes. Cover the meat with water to a level of about 4 inches. Bring to boil and cook 15 minutes longer. Combine flour with some of the liquid and stir until smooth. Return to cooking pot to thicken slightly. Adjust seasoning if desired. Serve stew while hot. 30 servings.

At Waylan's Ku-Ku-Burger, owner Gene Waylan says, "Don't just ask for a burger, ask for a Waylan's." One of the best hamburger stops in Green Country, and the sole survivor of a chain that once numbered over two hundred, Waylan's Ku-Ku Burger has been a part of Miami since 1973. The giant neon sign out front adds a nostalgic touch but the real quality here comes hot off the grill.

For those who enjoy an occasional break from hamburgers, try the chile dogs. Here is the giant recipe used to top the dogs.

WAYLAN'S KU-KU BURGER
Chile Dog Chile

7-1/2 POUNDS CHILE MEAT, BROKEN INTO
  SMALL PIECES
3 CANS (46 OUNCES EACH) TOMATO JUICE,
  WITH JUST ENOUGH WATER TO RINSE
  CANS
3 HEAPING TABLESPOONS COARSELY
  GROUND PEPPER
3 HEAPING TABLESPOONS SALT
3 GOOD HANDFULS OF CHOPPED ONIONS
1 CUP WILLIAMS CHILE SEASONING
1 CAN (#10 SIZE) PINTO BEANS, UNDRAINED

Combine all ingredients except chile seasoning and beans.

Heat, stirring to prevent burning. Bring chile to a good boil then add the chile seasoning and cook mixture for 30 minutes. Puree beans in a blender or food processor and add to chile dog mixture. Stir well to blend. Freeze and store in several containers until needed.

J-M Farms and J-M Foods, Inc. in Miami grow mushrooms and other fresh salad produce delivered daily in an eight-state area. This family-operated business began in 1979 and now has a payroll of over 400.

J-M FARMS
Mexicali Jumping Mushrooms

1 CUP SHREDDED SHARP CHEDDAR CHEESE
1/4 CUP SOUR CREAM
3 TABLESPOONS SLICED GREEN ONIONS
3-1/2 TABLESPOONS FINELY CHOPPED
  CILANTRO OR PARSLEY
3 TABLESPOONS CANNED DICED GREEN
  CHILES

Afton

WHAT TO SEE:

BUFFALO RANCH On Route 66 since 1953. See buffalo and other exotic animals. Includes a restaurant and trading post. Intersection of Highway 60 and 69.

COLLECTIBLES Ada Martin's Matchbook collections. Stop to see her antique shop, Hidden Treasures, and Ada will be glad to take you next door to see her lifelong hobby, the world's largest matchbook collection. 101 S.E. 1st Street, 3 doors east of the old Palmer Hotel.

HAR-BER VILLAGE 3-1/2 miles west of Grove. Take Highway 59, 14 miles from Afton to see an outstanding display of antiques housed in over 100 well-designed buildings. A must-see! (918) 786-6446

CHEROKEE QUEEN RIVERBOAT CRUISE Take U.S. 59 north to Grove. (918) 786-4272

WHERE TO EAT:

LINDA'S ROUTE 66 CAFE 5 N.E. 1st St.

BUFFALO RANCH RESTAURANT Intersection of Highways 60 and 69

1/4 CUP BUTTER
1 CLOVE GARLIC, PRESSED
16 FRESH MUSHROOM CAPS, 2 INCHES IN DIAMETER
GRATED PARMESAN CHEESE

In mixing bowl toss cheddar cheese, sour cream, onions, cilantro, and chiles to mix evenly; set aside. In small saucepan combine butter and garlic; warm over low heat to melt butter. Brush mushroom caps with garlic butter. Fill each cap with about 1 tablespoon cheese mixture. Sprinkle generously with Parmesan cheese. Broil until bubbly and golden, about 3 minutes. 8 servings.

J-M FARMS

Shrimp and Mushroom Creole

1 GREEN PEPPER, SLICED IN THIN STRIPS
2 MEDIUM ONIONS, SLICED IN THIN STRIPS
1/2 CUP DICED CELERY
1 CUP SLICED MUSHROOMS
2 TABLESPOONS COOKING OIL
1 CAN (14-1/2 OUNCES) TOMATOES
1/4 CUP CHILE SAUCE
1/4 CUP SEEDLESS RAISINS
1 BAY LEAF
1 TEASPOON PARSLEY FLAKES
1/4 TEASPOON EACH OF THE FOLLOWING: THYME, CURRY POWDER, CAYENNE PEPPER, SALT, AND PEPPER
1 POUND DEVEINED COOKED SHRIMP
1/2 CUP SLIVERED ALMONDS
3 CUPS HOT COOKED RICE

In a large skillet heat the cooking oil and sauté the vegetables. Add all other ingredients except the shrimp, almonds, and rice. Cover and simmer for 50 minutes. Add shrimp and cook over medium heat for another 10 minutes. Stir in the almonds. Serve over hot rice. 8 servings.

GOOD FOOD IN VINITA

Vinita is the uncontested "Calf Fry Capitol of the World."

Over 12,000 attend the annual September festivities. In addition to the cook-off, the festival features cowboy games, family entertainment, arts, and crafts. Guests cay buy an all-you-can-eat calf fry tasting kit. For the less venturesome, a variety of other good food is on hand.

Here is an authentic recipe courtesy of Mr. George Schumacher.

Oklahoma Calf Fries

10 POUNDS FRESH CALF FRIES
2 POUNDS CORNMEAL
1 CUP FLOUR
1 BOX (12 OUNCES) CORNFLAKE CRUMBS
SALT, PEPPER, SPICES TO TASTE
OIL FOR FRYING

Cut calf fries into thin pieces. Mix with other ingredients. Deep fry until they float to the top. Remove and drain well. Eat while warm. 35 to 40 servings.

Phyllis DeWitt is a former Vinita resident who now practices law in Tulsa. She and her husband, Tom, love barbecue and often spend weekends on their motorcycle, searching for good barbecue stops or revisiting favorite eateries across the state. They use a smoker to prepare good meat at home and love to compare notes with other enthusiasts about their latest success stories. Phyllis has perfected this excellent recipe for refried beans that incorporates great flavor but is not as high in fat as many recipes.

Vinita

population 6,000

"The Calf Fry Capitol of the World"

WHAT TO SEE:

The oldest Oklahoma town on Route 66, founded in 1871.

LITTLE CABIN CREEK PECAN COMPANY Don and Michel Gray are enthusiastic members of the Oklahoma Route 66 Association. 1.5 miles east of Vinita on Route 66.

EASTERN TRAILS MUSEUM 215 W. Illinois

AMERICA'S LARGEST MCDONALDS Built as the Glass House in 1958, spans I-44 today.

CALF FRIES The World's Largest Calf Fry Festival and Cook-Off, each September.

WHERE TO EAT:

CLANTON'S CAFE A three-generation Route 66 eatery. 319 E. Illinois

DJ'S GOLDEN SPIKE 414 E. Illinois

DEWARD AND PAULINE'S RESTAURANT 611 S. Wilson

Chelsea

population 1600

WHAT TO SEE:

A fiercely loyal, close-knit community of residents who are proud of their bountiful history.

OIL WELL The state's first oil well was drilled here in 1889, 1 mile south and 4 miles west of Route 66.

FIRST BANK The Bank of Chelsea, established in 1896, was the first state bank chartered in Indian Territory.

GENE AUTRY Notable Chelsea citizens include Will Rogers's two sisters and singing cowboy Gene Autry.

MAIL ORDER HOUSE The J.S. Hogue Home, placed on the National Register of Historic Places in 1983, is a Sears Roebuck and Co. mail-order house.

Foyil

population 90

WHAT TO SEE:

TEAM-PENNING The fastest growing rodeo sport in the country can be watched every Friday night and Sunday afternoon at Lucky Barbee's Ranch, between Chelsea and Foyil. "A cowboy thing for the whole family."

Phyllis DeWitt's Refried Beans

1 POUND DRIED PINTO BEANS

1 BONELESS PORK ROAST (1-1/2 TO 2 POUNDS)

1 TABLESPOON CHILE POWDER

2 TEASPOONS HOT SAUCE

2 TEASPOONS CUMIN

3 CLOVES GARLIC, MINCED

1 TABLESPOON SUGAR

1-1/2 TO 2 TEASPOONS GARLIC SALT

1/2 TEASPOON SALT

Wash beans thoroughly; cover with water and soak overnight.

Drain beans and place in a large, heavy Dutch oven. Add pork roast and enough water to cover. Add remaining ingredients except garlic salt and salt.

Bring beans to boil and reduce heat to simmer, cooking 3-1/2 to 4 hours. Remove the pork and shred. Mash the beans, add garlic salt and salt to taste. Return 1/3 to 1/2 of the shredded pork to the beans, as desired. Serve beans with sour cream, guacamole, and/or cheese. 8 servings.

GOOD FOOD IN CHELSEA:

Erskine Stanberry lives in her family's Sears Roebuck home that came to Chelsea on the Frisco Railroad, precut and ready to assemble in 1913 at a price of $1600. The home is located at 1001 Olive Street. A community leader and teacher for 43 years, Mrs. Stanberry remembers well the time Will Rogers patted her on the shoulder and said, "Erskine, are you going to be a schoolteacher all your life?"

Erskine Stanberry's Mama's White Cake with Caramel Filling

1 CUP BUTTER

2 CUPS SUGAR

3 CUPS CAKE FLOUR

2 TEASPOONS BAKING POWDER

1 CUP ICE WATER

1 TEASPOON VANILLA EXTRACT

8 EGG WHITES, BEATEN UNTIL STIFF

Cream the butter and sugar thoroughly. Stir in flour, baking powder, ice water, and vanilla to make a smooth batter. Fold in the beaten egg whites. Place in two 8-inch baking pans that have been greased and floured. Bake in preheated 375° oven for about 30 minutes. Test for doneness with toothpick.

CARAMEL FILLING:

10 TABLESPOONS BROWN SUGAR

5 TABLESPOONS MELTED BUTTER

6 TABLESPOONS EVAPORATED MILK

POWDERED SUGAR

Combine brown sugar, butter, and milk in saucepan. Cook over medium heat until sugar dissolves. Allow to cool then beat in enough powdered sugar to spread nicely.

GOOD FOOD IN CLAREMORE:

Leland and Kay Jenkins offer the peace and quiet of a rural country setting south of Route 66 between Foyil and Claremore. The Country Inn Bed and Breakfast includes a five-acre yard covered with big shade trees. Comfortable chairs offer the perfect place to relax near a peaceful stream. Try a game of horseshoes, take a swim, or ride bicycles along country roads.

ED GALLOWAY'S TOTEM POLES East on State Highway 28A. One of the best examples of folk art in the country. Don't miss this opportunity.

ANDY PAYNE MONUMENT Monument to favorite son Andy Payne, winner of the 1928 Bunyon Run that earned him $25,000 to help pay off his family farm.

WHERE TO EAT:

TOP HAT DAIRY BAR Crossroads of Highway 66 and 28A. Owner Wanda DeRosia has assembled some fine road memorabilia and serves up good food.

Claremore

population 13,500

WHAT TO SEE:

WILL ROGERS MEMORIAL AND TOMB 1720 W. Will Rogers Blvd.

DOGIRON RANCH Will Rogers's birthplace, the Dogiron Ranch, off Hwy. 88 between Claremore and Oologah.

WILL ROGERS HOTEL Corner of Old Highway 66 and Highway 88

J.M. DAVIS GUN MUSEUM The largest one-man collection in the world. 333 N. Lynn Riggs

129

COUNTRY INN BED AND BREAKFAST
Paper Bag Apple Pie

6 BAKING APPLES

1/2 CUP BROWN SUGAR

2 TABLESPOONS REGULAR OATMEAL

1/2 TEASPOON NUTMEG

1/2 TEASPOON CINNAMON

9-INCH UNBAKED PIE SHELL

TOPPING:

1/2 CUP SUGAR

1/2 CUP REGULAR OATMEAL

1 TABLESPOON FLOUR

1/2 CUP BUTTER

9-INCH UNBAKED PIE SHELL

Sprinkle brown sugar, oatmeal, nutmeg,
and cinnamon over sliced apples. Place in pie
shell. Prepare topping by combining sugar,
oats and flour. Cut in the butter and mix until
crumbly. Sprinkle on top of apple mixture.

Slide pie into heavy brown paper bag and
fasten with paper clips. Place on baking sheet
in preheated 425° oven for one hour. Split bag
open and remove pie to cool. 8 servings.

*Claremore is home to the Hammett House,
one of the best known eating places in northeastern
Oklahoma. The landmark restaurant first opened
in 1969 and soon gained a reputation for
excellence. Jim and LaNelle Hammett took pride
in quality and served her favorite recipes until they
retired and closed the Hammett House doors in the
mid-1980s. Today's owners, Bill and Linda Biard,
keep the tradition alive with "pamper" fried
chicken, potato rolls, and fourteen varieties of
humongous pies. Many recipes come from Mrs.
Hammett, who enthusiastically helped them
recreate the restaurant to cater to the 90s taste.*

Baker Patsy Van Deventer turns out as many as 40 pies a day for her appreciative customers. The Biards are also owners of Venice Gardens.

HAMMETT HOUSE
German Chocolate Pie

4 CUPS MILK

1-1/2 CUPS SUGAR

PINCH OF SALT

3/4 CUP CORNSTARCH

5 EGG YOLKS

3/4 STICK BUTTER

1 TEASPOON VANILLA

1/2 CUP CHOCOLATE CHIPS

1 CUP COCONUT

1 CUP PECANS

9-INCH BAKED PIE SHELL

TOPPING:

2 CUPS HEAVY CREAM, STIFFLY WHIPPED
(WHIPS TO 4 CUPS)

1/4 CUP CHOCOLATE SYRUP

1/3 CUP COCONUT

1/3 CUP PECANS

Heat milk to scald. Mix sugar, salt, and cornstarch in a bowl. Add dry ingredients to milk while stirring constantly. Add 1 cup hot mixture to egg yolks and blend. Add back to remaining milk and bring back to boiling for 1 minute, stirring constantly. Cook until thick. Add unmelted butter, vanilla, chocolate chips, coconut, and pecans. Stir until well blended. Cool briefly then pour into a 9-inch baked pie shell.

To prepare topping, combine whipped cream with chocolate syrup to color. Add coconut and pecans and pile high on pie. Decorate with chocolate syrup. 6 slices.

Lemon Pecan Pie

6 WHOLE EGGS
1/3 STICK MARGARINE, MELTED
2-1/4 CUPS SUGAR
3/4 CUP PECAN PIECES
1 TEASPOON LEMON EXTRACT
JUICE OF 1/2 LEMON
8-INCH UNBAKED PIE SHELL

Mix ingredients in order given, but do not use a mixer or beat until frothy. Pour into pie shell. Place in preheated 350° oven and bake 10 minutes. Reduce oven temperature to 300° and bake until crust is browned and pie is set. 6 slices.

Claremore's Carriage House Bed and Breakfast Inn was opened in October of 1995 by Dean and Sara Selvy. The circa 1910 home belonged to community leader Ocie Mayberry for over 50 years. Many local residents still refer to the lovely home with the large wrap-around front porch as the Mayberry House. Guests may choose from the Paris Room or Charlotte's Suite on the second floor of the main house or take advantage of the beautifully redecorated carriage house that offers comfort and privacy for a getaway weekend. Sara serves a gourmet breakfast each morning.

CARRIAGE HOUSE BED AND BREAKFAST
INN

Refrigerator Angel Biscuits

1 PACKAGE ACTIVE DRY YEAST

1/2 CUP WARM WATER

5 CUPS FLOUR

1 TEASPOON BAKING SODA

3 TEASPOONS BAKING POWDER

1 TEASPOON SALT

3 TABLESPOONS SUGAR

3/4 CUP SHORTENING

2 CUPS BUTTERMILK

Dissolve yeast in warm water (115° F). Combine dry ingredients and work in shortening with a biscuit cutter or fork. Add yeast mixture and buttermilk. Blend well. Place biscuit mix in a greased bowl. Cover and chill if not using immediately. (If dough is covered and refrigerated, it will keep for 3 to 4 days.) When ready to use, roll out dough on a lightly floured board and cut 3/4-inch thick biscuits. Let rise for 20 minutes; allow an hour if dough is cold. Bake in a preheated 425° oven for 20 minutes. Approximately 30 biscuits.

Lora Montgomery and Faye Hyde collaborated on A TREASURE CHEST OF OKLAHOMA'S WILDLIFE RECIPES. The book was released in 1995 and includes oldtime favorite recipes, remedies from the past, and memories from elderly family and friends. Lora and Faye explain how they prepare and cook wildlife that their hunting families bring home. With fish, they often serve these hush puppies.

Catoosa

population 3,000

WHAT TO SEE:

BLUE WHALE THEME PARK Favorite landmark that is coming to life again as a Route 66 rest stop.

ARKANSAS RIVER NAVIGATION SYSTEM Turn basin for the Kerr-McClellan Arkansas River Navigation System (the farthest inland port in the world).

HISTORICAL MUSEUM Arkansas River Historical Society Museum , 5350 Cimarron Road.

LIBERTYFEST CELEBRATION July 4th each year.

WHERE TO EAT:

LIL' ABNER'S DAIRYETTE Dine-In or Carry Out. Lil' Abner's Sweet Shoppe on Route 66 since 1959. 501 S. Cherokee St.

MOLLY'S LANDING On the Verdigris River next to the twin bridges and surrounded by old Route 66.

Hillbilly Hush Puppies

2 CUPS CORNMEAL

1 CUP FLOUR

2 TEASPOONS BAKING POWDER

1 TEASPOON SALT

3/4 CUP MILK

1 EGG

1/2 MEDIUM ONION, CHOPPED

1/2 CUP WHOLE KERNEL CORN

1/2 CUP CREAM-STYLE CORN

CANOLA OR OTHER LIGHT OIL FOR FRYING

Combine all the ingredients except oil. Heat the oil and drop mixture one spoonful at a time, into deep fat. Brown nicely then drain on paper towels before serving while hot. About 4 dozen.

GOOD FOOD IN CATOOSA:

At Catoosa's annual Libertyfest Celebration, three days of outdoor fun surround the 4th of July holiday, the most popular activity is the Chile Cookoff. The winner in 1995 was Joe Giles, principal of the Prairie Grove, Arkansas, Elementary School. Joe is an avid chile cook whose mentor was R.T. Miles, one of Joe's teachers and "a grand old chile man of Texas."

With his recipes, Joe has won first place in the Arkansas, Oklahoma, Missouri, and Kansas Mens' State Championships, has produced a winning bowl of fire at the annual Terlingua Cookoff, and has won numerous other awards and recognitions.

Joe promises that diced raw apple alongside every steaming bowl of his chile makes a perfect accompaniment. I followed his advice and agree!

LIBERTYFEST JULY 4TH CELEBRATION
1995 FIRST PRIZE WINNING RECIPE
PERPETRATED BY JOE GILES

Loose Stool Chile

2 POUNDS OF CUBED LEAN STEW MEAT
ENOUGH WATER TO COVER
1 CAN (8 OUNCES) TOMATO SAUCE
1 TABLESPOON LE GOUT BEEF BASE
2 TEASPOONS ONION POWDER
1-1/2 TEASPOONS GARLIC POWDER
1/2 TEASPOON GARLIC SALT
1 TEASPOON WHITE PEPPER
1 TEASPOON MONOSODIUM GLUTAMATE
  (MSG)
5 1/2 TEASPOONS CHILE POWDER
1 TABLESPOON CUMIN
1/8 TEASPOON CAYENNE
SALT AND PEPPER TO TASTE

Cover the stew meat with water and boil for 45 minutes.

Add tomato sauce, beef base, and the "white spices" of onion powder, garlic powder, garlic salt, white pepper and MSG.

Boil for 25 minutes, stirring occasionally. Add "red spices" of chile powder, cumin, and cayenne. Simmer for 35 minutes, stirring frequently. Add salt and pepper to taste just before serving. 6 to 8 servings.

GOOD FOOD FROM TULSA:

Ruth Sigler Avery is the daughter-in-law of Tulsan Cyrus Avery, the "Father of Route 66." Ruth says this soup has been a family favorite for years.

Tulsa

*Metropolitan population
750,000*

WHAT TO SEE:

GILCREASE MUSEUM
One of the best western art and history collections in the nation. 1400 Gilcrease Museum Rd. (918) 596-2700

PHILBROOK MUSEUM OF ART Italian Renaissance revival villa on 23 acres, once home to Waite Phillips, now houses extensive permanent art collections. 2727 S. Rockford Rd. (800) 324-7941

OXLEY NATURE CENTER
800 acres of natural vegetation and walking trails. 6700 E. Mohawk Blvd. (918) 669-6644

ART DECO WALKING TOUR Central downtown area. Tulsa has the largest collection of Art Deco buildings on Route 66; includes Boston Avenue Methodist Church (1301 S. Boston) and the Philtower Building (527 S. Boston) among many others. Call the Chamber of Commerce at (918) 585-1201 for information.

ORAL ROBERTS UNIVERSITY 7777 S. Lewis. Call (918) 495-6807 for campus tour information.

SHOPPING AND GOOD
RESTAURANTS IN UTICA
SQUARE 21st St. and Utica
Ave.

CAIN'S BALLROOM Bob
Wills and the Texas Playboys
performed on KVOO radio
from here for 9 years. Filled
with memorabilia. 423 N.
Main. (918) 584-2309

DISCOVERYLAND
Summertime outdoor live
performances of *Oklahoma!*
A not to be missed production! (918) 245-6552

WHERE TO EAT:

MUSEUM RESTAURANTS
Gilcrease Rendezvous Room
and La Villa at Philbrook.

THE SPUDDER Top steaks
in a nostalgic oil field atmosphere. 6536 E. 50th St.

THE GREEN ONION
Handsome restaurant with
consistently good food.
4532 E. 51st St.

POLO GRILL Choice
American and world cuisine.
2038 Utica Square.

JODY'S RESTAURANT
2300 Riverside. Superb food
in an elegant setting.

NELSON'S BUFFETERIA
Chicken fried steak at its
best. 514 S. Boston.

METRO DINER 1950s
decor, neon, 66 roadhouse
atmosphere, 3001 E. 11th.

Ruth Avery's
Potato and Noodle Soup

NOODLES:

2 EGGS BEATEN
2 CUPS FLOUR
1 TEASPOON BAKING POWDER

SOUP:

1 CAN (10- 3/4 OUNCES) CHICKEN BROTH
2 MEDIUM POTATOES, PEELED AND DICED
    INTO 1/2 INCH CUBES
2 LARGE BERMUDA ONIONS, SLICED INTO
    1/4 INCH PIECES
6 STALKS CELERY WITH LEAVES, CHOPPED
    INTO 1/4 INCH PIECES
2 CUPS WATER
1/2 TEASPOON SALT, OR TO TASTE
1 PINCH ROSEMARY
1 PINCH THYME
2 CUPS MILK

Combine eggs, flour, and baking powder.
Knead to make firm noodles. Set mixture
aside. Combine all soup ingredients except the
milk. Bring to boil and cook until vegetables
are done. Meanwhile, mold noodles by hand
into round balls about a teaspoon in size. Drop
noodles into hot soup. Allow noodles to cook
thoroughly. Add the milk and again heat but
do not boil. Serve with crackers, a green salad,
and fruit for a complete meal. 2 quarts.

*Michael Wallis, Tulsa author of ROUTE 66,
THE MOTHER ROAD, has done more to chronicle
Route 66 than any other one person. This popular
Oklahoman is also the author of PRETTY BOY:
THE LIFE AND TIMES OF CHARLES ARTHUR
FLOYD. The books earned Wallis two of his trio of
Pulitzer Prize nominations.*

Wallis points out that when Pretty Boy was not on the outlaw trail making "withdrawals" from banks, he loved to get into the kitchen and bake apple pie. In 1933 one of his pies won top honors at a country pie supper where the respected sheriff, unaware of who had done the baking, tasted the slice and declared it the best pie he'd ever put in his mouth.

Wallis says the 30-year-old bandit left an apple pie behind in his Buffalo, New York hideaway when, in 1934, he decided to head toward home in Sallisaw. A final shootout ended his life on that trip and he never saw Oklahoma again. This pie recipe is considered Pretty Boy's best version.

Michael Wallis's Pretty Boy's Apple Pie

PIE CRUST:

2 CUPS FLOUR
3/4 CUP LARD
1 TEASPOON SALT
6 TO 7 TABLESPOONS COLD WATER

Prepare crust by working the flour, lard, and salt together until crumbly. Mix in cold water until dough holds together in big pieces. Divide into two equal balls.

On a floured surface roll out one ball thin enough to line a 9-inch pie tin. Roll out second ball for the top crust.

Preheat oven to 450°.

WEBER'S GRILL Credited with inventing the hamburger by owners Harold and Rick Bilby who say their great-grandfather was serving burgers in Indian Territory by 1891. Weber's root beer is also a classic. 3817 S. Peoria.

WILSON'S BAR-B-Q Most often rated the best in Tulsa. 1522 E. Apache.

RICARDO'S MEXICAN RESTAURANT 5629 E. 41st

RON'S HAMBURGERS AND CHILI Six local locations including 6548 E. 51st, 5239 S. Peoria, and 3239 E. 15th.

ROUTE 66 DOWNTOWN DINER On early 66 alignment 402 E. 2nd.

OLLIE'S RESTAURANT On Route 66, near Tulsa's 1st oil well. Train buffs love this place, great hometown atmosphere. W. 41st St. and Southwest Blvd.

WHERE TO STAY:

MCBIRNEY MANSION BED & BREAKFAST 1414 S. Galveston

APPLE FILLING:

1 POUND FRESH APPLES, PEELED AND SLICED OR 1 CAN (16 OUNCES) SLICED APPLES
2 TABLESPOONS FRESH LEMON JUICE
1/2 TEASPOON GROUND NUTMEG
1/2 TEASPOON GROUND CINNAMON
1/2 CUP WHITE SUGAR
1/4 CUP SEEDLESS RAISINS
1 CUP BROWN SUGAR
2 TABLESPOONS FLOUR
2 TABLESPOONS BUTTER
1/2 CUP SHELLED OKLAHOMA PECANS
1/4 CUP MILK

HARD SAUCE:

1/2 CUP BUTTER
1-1/2 CUPS POWDERED SUGAR
1 TABLESPOON BOILING WATER
1 TABLESPOON BRANDY OR RUM ("MOONSHINE" IS PREFERABLE)

Place the apples in the lined pan. Sprinkle with lemon juice, nutmeg and cinnamon. Spread the white sugar and raisins evenly over the apples.

Mix the brown sugar, flour, and butter in a bowl. When well blended, spread over the apples and sprinkle with pecans. Add most of the milk and cover with the top crust. Seal the edges and prick top with a fork. Brush the remaining milk on the crust.

Bake for 10 minutes at 450°, then reduce heat to 350° and bake another 30 minutes until crust is golden.

To make hard sauce, cream the butter until light. Beat in the sugar and add water. Then beat in the liquor and serve sauce on each slice of pie. If you dare, add a scoop of homemade vanilla ice cream. 6 slices.

Jody Walls is a well-known caterer and Tulsa's first noted female chef. She has been associated with several of the city's best restaurants. Ms. Walls now owns and operates Jody's Restaurant at 2300 Riverside. This excellent Italian Cream Cake goes back almost 20 years when the idea for the cake came from a customer. Ms. Walls elaborated on the original recipe, adjusted flavorings, made the icing richer and the cake lighter. The outstanding result has appeared at many prestigious functions and is as delicious as it is beautiful.

Jody Walls's Italian Cream Cake

1 CUP BUTTERMILK

1 TEASPOON SODA

1/2 CUP BUTTER

1/2 CUP SHORTENING

2 CUPS SUGAR

5 EGGS, SEPARATED

2 CUPS FLOUR, SIFTED

1 TEASPOON VANILLA EXTRACT

3-1/2 OUNCES COCONUT

1 CUP PECANS, CHOPPED

ICING:

1 PACKAGE (8 OUNCES) CREAM CHEESE, SOFTENED

8 CUPS POWDERED SUGAR, SIFTED

1-1/2 CUPS PECANS, CHOPPED

1 CUP BUTTER, SOFTENED

1 TEASPOONS VANILLA EXTRACT

Preheat oven to 350°. Grease and flour three 9-inch cake pans. Combine buttermilk and soda; set aside. Cream butter, shortening, and sugar. Add egg yolks one at a time, beating after each addition. Alternately add buttermilk and flour, small amounts at a time. Add vanilla extract.

Beat egg whites to stiff peak; fold into batter and flour mixture. Stir in coconut and pecans. Pour equally into pans and bake for 25 minutes. Cool on racks.

To make icing, cream together the cream cheese and butter. Add sugar slowly to spreading consistency. Stir in pecans and vanilla. Frost cake. 12 to 15 servings.

The Spudder Restaurant has served quality steaks to Tulsans and their guests since 1979. The rustic building is decorated with an extensive collection of oil field memorabilia. Signs from old gas stations, hundreds of early drilling photographs, gas pumps from the 1930s and 1940s, and a sizeable collection of tools remind diners that Tulsa was once the "Oil Capital of the World." Food here is plentiful and good. Most meals begin with a small bowl of hearty potato soup followed by a steak, baked potato, green salad, and delicious hot rolls brought to the table in old fashioned tin lunch pails to keep them warm. Owners Duane and Shirley Croxdale share this recipe for the potato soup, scaled to family-size portions.

THE SPUDDER RESTAURANT
Potato Soup

3 CUPS DICED, PEELED POTATOES

1/3 CUP DICED CELERY

1/2 CUP DICED ONION

1/2 CUP DICED HAM

3 CUPS WATER

2 TABLESPOONS CHICKEN BOUILLON
   GRANULES

SALT AND WHITE PEPPER TO TASTE

3 TABLESPOONS BUTTER

3 TABLESPOONS FLOUR

2 CUPS MILK

Cook potatoes, celery, onion, and ham in a large stockpot with water until potatoes are tender but not mushy. Add bouillon, salt, and white pepper to taste. (The Spudder soup is very peppery. Combine butter and flour to make a roux, add milk, and thicken. Stir into potato mixture, heat, and serve. 8 to 10 first course servings.

Blackberries grow wild throughout Oklahoma Green Country. Each year, Patsy Rowland and her family arm themselves with long-sleeved shirts and gloves to pick gallons of the luscious fruit on their rich farmland property some 25 miles southeast of Tulsa in what is often referred to as Kadashan Bottom country.

Patsy entered this blackberry ice cream recipe that she perfected in 1995 for the first annual Freeze Out Benefit for the Tulsa County 4-H Foundation. She has successfully defended her winning title every succeeding year. This scrumptious recipe is a tribute to her skill.

Wild Kadashan Bottom Blackberry Ice Cream

4 EGGS

2-1/2 CUPS SUGAR

4 CUPS WHIPPING CREAM

1 TABLESPOON VANILLA

1/2 TEASPOON SALT

1 QUART BLACKBERRIES, PROCESSED IN A
   BLENDER AND STRAINED

2 CUPS MILK (OR ENOUGH TO FILL A
   1-GALLON FREEZER)

Beat eggs until frothy. Add sugar gradually, beating until mixture thickens. Add vanilla, salt, and strained blackberries; blend thoroughly. Pour mixture into a 1-gallon ice cream maker and add milk to fill. Freeze ice cream according to freezer manufacturer's instructions. 1 gallon.

Dr. Steve Gerkin is a busy Tulsa dentist who shares his love of good food with friends in a gourmet cooking club. He is also an enthusiastic runner who has participated in the Boston Marathon and several other prestigious running events. Here is a mouthwatering recipe that he recently included in his quarterly newsletter to patients. He says it is the perfect dessert to prepare for a favorite valentine.

GERKIN'S GOURMET
Raspberry Soufflé

1 PACKAGE (10 OUNCES) FROZEN
   RASPBERRIES
4 EGG WHITES AT ROOM TEMPERATURE
1/2 CUP SUGAR
1 CUP COLD WHIPPING CREAM
2 TABLESPOONS GRAND MARNIER

Preheat oven to 375°. Butter up to six individual souffle dishes and coat with sugar.

Whirl the raspberries with their syrup in food processor until smooth. Beat the egg whites to soft peak stage. Beat in the sugar, one tablespoon at a time and continue beating until the peaks are stiff and glossy. Gently fold in the raspberry puree.

Pour the batter into the prepared dishes. Bake until puffed and lightly golden, about 12 to 15 minutes.

While the souffles are baking, whip the cream with the liqueur to soft peaks. Serve the souffles hot from the oven topped with whipped cream. 6 servings.

GOOD FOOD IN SAPULPA:

Each November, the SAPULPA DAILY HERALD publishes a recipe contest under the direction of Laurie Quinnelly, Lifestyle Editor. Eight judges made the 1995 selections. Here are two of the best.

FIRST PLACE WINNER

Debbie Pruitt's Barbecued Meatballs

3 POUNDS LEAN GROUND BEEF

I CAN (I2 OUNCES) EVAPORATED MILK

I CUP OATMEAL

I CUP CRACKER CRUMBS

2 EGGS

I/2 CUP FINELY CHOPPED ONION

I/2 TEASPOON GARLIC POWDER

2 TEASPOONS SALT

I/2 TEASPOON PEPPER

2 TEASPOONS CHILE POWDER

Combine all ingredients. Mixture will be soft. Shape into walnut-sized balls. Place meatballs in a single layer on a waxed-paper lined cookie sheet. Freeze until firm. Store meatballs in freezer bag until ready to use.

SAUCE FOR MEATBALLS:

2 CUPS CATSUP

I CUP BROWN SUGAR

I/2 TEASPOON LIQUID SMOKE

I/2 TEASPOON GARLIC POWDER

I/4 CUP FINELY CHOPPED ONION

Combine all ingredients and stir until brown sugar is dissolved. Place frozen meatballs in 9 x 13 baking pan. Pour sauce over meat. Bake in preheated 350° oven for one hour. Serve while warm, preferably in chafing dish. 60 to 70 walnut-sized meatballs.

Sapulpa

population 18,500

WHAT TO SEE:

FRANKOMA POTTERY Popular pottery made from local clay. A large showroom with tours available. 2400 Frankoma Rd.

SAPULPA HISTORICAL MUSEUM A superior community museum, located in the 3-story, 1910 Lee Hotel. Includes an Oklahoma Route 66 satellite museum. Open 10:00-3:00, Monday–Thursday, 100 E. Lee.

COLLINS BUILDING Originally a 1925 Masonic Temple, restored interior is original and ornate. 317 E. Lea.

MR. INDIAN COWBOY STORE Native American owned and operated. 1000 S. Main .

WHERE TO EAT:

NORMA'S DIAMOND CAFE Great Route 66 classic stop that opened in 1950. Stop in for good road food and an opportunity to meet "Mr. Norma." 408 N. Mission.

FREDDIE'S BBQ AND STEAKHOUSE 1425 New Sapulpa Rd.

ROUTE 66 CAFE Open 6:00-2:00 daily. 219 S. Dewey.

Jeanie Thoos Spradlin's Holiday Bread Pudding with Whiskey Sauce

1 LOAF (10 OUNCES) FRENCH BREAD, 2 TO 3
   DAYS OLD (OR 6 TO 8 CUPS DRY,
   CRUMBLED BREAD)

4 CUPS MILK

2 CUPS SUGAR

1/2 CUP BUTTER, MELTED

3 EGGS

2 TABLESPOONS VANILLA

1 CUP RAISINS

1 CUP COCONUT

1 CUP CHOPPED PECANS

1 TEASPOON CINNAMON

1 TEASPOON NUTMEG

WHISKEY SAUCE:

   1/2 CUP BUTTER

   1-1/2 CUPS POWDERED SUGAR

   2 EGG YOLKS

   1/2 CUP BOURBON, SCOTCH, RUM, OR FRUIT
      JUICE

Combine all ingredients to form a moist mixture. Pour into a buttered 9 x 12 baking dish. Place in a non-preheated oven and bake for 1 hour, 15 minutes at 350° or until pudding is golden brown.

To make whiskey sauce, cream butter and sugar over medium heat until butter melts and sugar is dissolved. Remove from heat and add egg yolks. Pour liquor into mixture gradually, stirring constantly. Sauce will thicken as it cools.

Serve pudding warm with whiskey sauce. 10 to 12 servings.

GOOD FOOD IN KELLYVILLE:

Helen Krause began experimenting with a wide variety of chiles in her garden soon after moving to the tiny Route 66 community of Kellyville in 1970. Helen calls the taste of chiles "sensational," and has discovered many favorites from the Hispanic and native American cultures. Her book, HELEN'S SOUTHWEST SPECIALTIES reflects her love for the tongue tingling dishes.

Helen makes chile powder at home to create the best and freshest flavor. She suggests experimenting by using mild Anaheims, popular jalapeños, or any other favorite variety. Here are her directions:

Roast the chiles, leaving seed and stems intact, by spreading them, a few at a time, on a cookie sheet in a 250° oven for about 10 minutes. Watch chiles to keep from burning. Turn off the oven and allow chiles to cool completely. Break open and discard the seeds and ribs. Use a coffee grinder, blender, or food processor to grind chile to powder consistency. To make a hotter chile powder, discard only the stems, leaving the chile whole, then grind as directed above.

HELEN'S SOUTHWEST SPECIALTIES
Terrific Tortilla Torte

2 CUPS PINTO BEANS, COOKED
1/2 CUP CHOPPED ONION
1 CLOVE GARLIC, MINCED
1/4 TEASPOON GROUND CUMIN
1/4 TEASPOON CHILE POWDER
1/4 CUP PICANTE SAUCE
1 CUP CANNED GREEN CHILES, CHOPPED
4 FLOUR TORTILLAS (8-INCH SIZE)
3/4 CUP JACK CHEESE, SHREDDED
2 TABLESPOONS SLICED RIPE OLIVES

Kellyville
population 985

Bristow
population 4,300

WHAT TO SEE:

BRISTOW MUSEUM, RAILROAD DEPOT E. 7th at the tracks.

DOWNTOWN DISTRICT Many old brick buildings in good condition and several antique shops. More brick-paved streets than any other Oklahoma town, most paved in the late 1800s.

WHERE TO EAT:

ANCHOR DRIVE IN 630 S. Roland. A family-run hamburger and barbecue stop on Route 66 since the late 1940s.

OSCAR'S SANDWICH HOUSE 104 W. 9th

MID AMERICA SALE BARN Where local residents enjoy home cookin' on Fridays and Saturdays.

2 CUPS SHREDDED LETTUCE
1 MEDIUM TOMATO, CHOPPED
2 JALAPEÑO PEPPERS, THINLY SLICED
VEGETABLE COOKING SPRAY

Place beans in a strainer and drain. Coat a large skillet with nonstick spray and place on medium heat. Add onion and garlic. Sauté until tender. Turn heat to low and add beans, cumin, and chile powder. Cook uncovered over low heat for 25 minutes, stirring occasionally. Mash bean mixture with masher and set aside, keeping warm.

Combine picante sauce and green chiles and set aside.

Wrap tortillas in foil to keep them from drying out. Heat in oven until warm, about 8 minutes. Lightly coat a baking sheet with cooking spray. Place a tortilla on the baking sheet and top with 1/3 of the bean mixture, 1/4 cup cheese, and 2 teaspoons sliced olives. Repeat layer twice. Top with remaining tortilla. Cover with foil and bake at 350° for 15 minutes.

Transfer to serving platter, arrange lettuce around torte, top with tomatoes and garnish with jalapeño slices. 4 servings.

GOOD FOOD IN BRISTOW:

Bristow was originally settled by Lebanese immigrants whose ancestors continue to share the foods they have grown to love.

Lebanese cooks impart their own special touch to tabouleh, even though the dish appears in the cuisine of other Middle Eastern cultures. Here is a good recipe that is a composite from several excellent Bristow cooks.

Tabouleh

8 OUNCES BULGUR (FINE CRACKED WHEAT)

5 BUNCHES PARSLEY, STEMS REMOVED AND FINELY CHOPPED

1 POUND RIPE TOMATOES, FINELY CHOPPED

5 GREEN ONIONS, FINELY CHOPPED

2 TABLESPOONS FRESH MINT LEAVES, MINCED

1/8 TEASPOON ALLSPICE (SOMETIMES OMITTED)

1/2 CUP LEMON JUICE (ADJUST TO TASTE)

1/2 CUP OLIVE OIL

SALT AND PEPPER TO TASTE

Cover the bulgur in cold water and soak for 1 hour. Squeeze dry. Pick the parsley leaves from the large stems. Discard stems. Wash and dry parsley leaves. Chop all vegetables. Mix parsley, tomatoes, onions, and mint together. Combine allspice, lemon juice, and olive oil. Pour over bulgur and toss lightly. Salt and pepper to taste. 20 small servings.

I met Jackie Hutson at a lovely Bristow Garden Club Luncheon while sharing the Route 66 story. Jackie's mother's banana pie is a nostalgic dish very special to Jackie, who agreed to share it.

Jackie Hutson's Mother's Banana Cream Pie

2 HEAPING TABLESPOONS FLOUR

2/3 CUP SUGAR

1/2 CUP MILK

2 EGG YOLKS

2 CUPS MILK

PINCH OF SALT

1 TEASPOON VANILLA

2 LARGE OR 3 SMALL BANANAS

1 BAKED 9-INCH PIE SHELL

Stroud

population 3,000

WHAT TO SEE:

TANGER FACTORY OUTLET CENTER Revitalized Main St. with antique stores and an old ghosted Coca-Cola sign.

THE ROUTE 66 SHOE TREE LaVonne Plute's farm, a small tree is waiting. Stop and see shoes that others have left and add your own pair to a new highway memorial.

WHERE TO EAT:

ROCK CAFE Opened August 4, 1939, a Route 66 classic. 114 W. Main.

SPECIALTY HOUSE FAMILY RESTAURANT A local favorite for good home cooking. 721 W. 7th.

Davenport

population 980

WHERE TO EAT:

DAN'S BAR-B-QUE PIT Rated as one of the 10 best barbecue outposts in the country by Rich Davis, creator of K.C. Masterpiece barbecue sauce. On Route 66.

MERINGUE:

2 TO 3 EGG WHITES

4 TABLESPOONS SUGAR

Combine flour with sugar, in a medium saucepan. Add milk and stir vigorously. Add egg yolks, one at a time, stirring thoroughly after each addition then pour in remaining milk and salt. Cook over medium heat, stirring constantly until filling thickens. Add vanilla and cool mixture. Slice bananas into pie shell. Add cooled filling. Top with meringue made by beating egg whites with sugar until stiff. Brown pie in preheated 350° oven for 10 minutes. 6 to 8 slices.

GOOD FOOD IN STROUD:

Diana Stobaugh and her mother, Vi Mason started their first restaurant in Stroud in 1987 as Specialty House Family Restaurant. Vi's pies and soups were an immediate hit. Loyal customers return regularly. The restaurant is known for outstanding catfish and barbecue as well as the scrumptious pies. Diana credits good employees, a dedicated family, and plenty of hard work for their success. This apple pie is spectacular, covered with a cinnamon sauce that Vi developed after trying a great pie in another location.

SPECIALTY HOUSE FAMILY RESTAURANT
Vi's Blue Ribbon Apple Pie

2 UNBAKED 9-INCH DEEP DISH PIE CRUSTS

7 MEDIUM-SIZED COOKING APPLES

2 TABLESPOONS CORNSTARCH

3/4 CUP SUGAR

1 TEASPOON CINNAMON

4 TABLESPOONS MARGARINE

SAUCE:

> 1/2 CUP SUGAR
> 1/2 CUP APPLE JUICE FROM PEELINGS
> 4 TABLESPOONS MARGARINE
> 1-1/4 TABLESPOONS CORNSTARCH
> 1/2 TEASPOON CINNAMON
> 1/2 TEASPOON NUTMEG

Peel and slice apples, saving the peelings. Place peelings in a cup of boiling water, simmer a few minutes and save the juice.

Combine cornstarch, sugar and cinnamon. Sprinkle a small amount of the sugar mixture in the bottom of pie shell. Layer apples and sprinkle more sugar. Continue until apples are used and shell is filled. Slice the margarine on top of apples. Put top crust in place. Bake pie in preheated 450° oven for 15 minutes. Reduce heat to 350° and continue baking for 45 minutes.

For sauce, combine all ingredients in a small saucepan. Bring to boil and cook until mixture is thickened. Pour on top of pie. 6 to 8 scrumptious slices!

The Rock Cafe has experienced a renaissance under the capable guidance of Christian and Dawn Herr. This 1939 vintage eatery has been a second home to thousands of cross-country truckers and a favorite hangout for local high school students. Today Christian serves up delicious dishes from his Swiss background and offers buffalo burgers for those who want to experience something new. The giraffe stone exterior came from the roadbed as Route 66 was built through the area. This Rock Cafe recipe is for a national dish from Zurich, Switzerland.

Zueri Gschnaetzlets

2 TEASPOONS BUTTER

I LARGE ONION, DICED

I POUND VEAL OR CHICKEN BREAST, CUT IN
2-INCH STRIPS

5 OUNCES MUSHROOMS

I CUP WHITE WINE

2 CUPS WHIPPING CREAM

I PACKAGE (I2 OUNCES) KNORR BROWN
GRAVY MIX

I OUNCE PAPRIKA

RED AND BLACK PEPPER TO TASTE

MINCED PARSLEY, OPTIONAL

Melt butter in skillet, add onions. After about a minute, add meat and the paprika and pepper. Cook until meat is almost done, stirring so it will brown evenly. Add mushrooms and wine and cook for about 2 more minutes. Stir brown gravy mix with the cream and pour over meat. Cook and stir constantly. Serve with parsley as a garnish. 4 servings.

Note: For a side dish, cook several potatoes until half done, let them cool then grate them. Fry with butter until golden brown.

Agnes Brewer and Donna Baker were next-door neighbors for years. Donna has now moved to a country home near Stroud, but first she found time to collaborate with Agnes on an unusual recipe collection, POTATOES AND MORE!. The self-published booklet was released in 1995. The "potato sack" cover features rough brown textured paper tied carefully with cord. Their research led to over 80 potato recipes along with more bits of information about potatoes than they ever expected to find! Sweet Potato Pie is a modern adaptation of an old Southern favorite.

POTATOES AND MORE!

Creamy Sweet Potato Pie

1 UNBAKED 9-INCH PASTRY SHELL

1 CUP MASHED, COOKED SWEET POTATOES

1 CAN (14 OUNCES) SWEETENED CON-
DENSED MILK

2 EGGS

1 TEASPOON CINNAMON

1/2 TEASPOON GINGER

1/2 TEASPOON NUTMEG

1/2 TEASPOON SALT

In a large bowl combine sweet potatoes, condensed milk, eggs, spices, and salt. Blend well and pour into pie shell. Bake in a preheated 400° oven for 35 to 40 minutes, or until a knife inserted in the center comes out clean. Cool thoroughly before cutting. Garnish with whipped cream and nuts if desired. Refrigerate any leftovers. 6 servings.

When Stroud native Keith Easton decided to leave the oil business and return home in 1992, he and his wife Shelly began looking for a special home. When they heard that the home of J.W. Stroud, the town founder, was for sale they knew it would fit their needs perfectly. The 1900 Victorian house is on the National Register of Historic Buildings and Easton remembered visiting friends there many times as a child.

The Eastons opened their home as a bed and breakfast for several years but have now retired. Shelly is a wonderful cook who is known for the famous Stroud House cookies she bakes. She shared this breakfast favorite that was often served to their bed-and-breakfast friends.

Chandler

population 2,600

WHAT TO SEE:

MUSEUM OF PIONEER HISTORY Lincoln County Historical Society/Route 66 Satellite exhibit. An excellent museum! 717 Manvel.

WHERE TO EAT:

PJ'S BARBECUE Located on a corner where a filling station once served Route 66 travelers. Many good stories, a great bottle collection, plus quality food. 1423 S. Manvel.

GRANNY'S COUNTRY KITCHEN Old-fashioned country breakfasts and blue plate specials. 917 Manvel.

WHERE TO STAY:

LINCOLN MOTEL Clean but simple, a return to 1939 when this Route 66 motor court was built. 740 E. 1st St.

Luther

population 1,100

WHAT TO SEE:

ORCHARDS Native pecan orchards can be found from here eastward to Miami. "Old-time" pecan grower Gordon Couch raises his pecans along this stretch of Route 66.

THE STROUD HOUSE

Santa Fe Eggs

1 PACKAGE (3 OUNCES) CREAM CHEESE, SOFTENED
1 CUP MILK
6 LARGE EGGS
2 CUPS COTTAGE CHEESE
1 POUND MONTEREY JACK CHEESE, SHREDDED
1 TEASPOON BAKING POWDER
1 TEASPOON SALT,
1 TEASPOON SUGAR
1/2 CUP MARGARINE
1/2 CUP FLOUR
SALSA

Beat softened cream cheese into milk until mixture is smooth; set aside. In another bowl, beat the eggs and add cottage cheese, Monterey Jack cheese, baking powder, salt, and sugar. Melt the margarine in a small saucepan and add flour. Blend well then pour into egg mixture. Stir in milk and cream cheese. Grease a 9 x 13 baking pan and pour egg mixture into pan. Refrigerate overnight. The next morning bake the eggs uncovered in a preheated 350° oven for 45 minutes or until lightly browned. Let stand five minutes before cutting into squares. Serve with salsa. 12 servings.

GOOD FOOD IN ARCADIA:

HILLBILLEE'S CAFE
City Slicker Chicken

Grill an unbreaded unskinned chicken breast in 1 tablespoon olive oil for about 4 to 5 minutes. Season with a touch of basil, salt, and freshly ground black pepper. Finely chop 2 green onions, 1 slice of bell pepper and a small piece of fresh ginger root. Sprinkle on grill to gently sear. Place on top of grilled chicken breast. Serve with slices of tomato and potato salad. 1 serving.

GOOD FOOD IN EDMOND:

The 1908 home of Dr. A.M. Ruhl is unique in many ways. In 1928, Dr. Ruhl had the house raised 12 feet in order to build another story beneath, giving him a full three stories. Other features include a basement, some 80 windows, and a grand wraparound porch.

In 1989 Hershel and Edith Hall with their son and daughter-in-law, Gary and Martha Hall, bought the landmark home and began renovating it as a bed and breakfast. Today they offer guests two suites and four rooms, all with private baths. Breakfast at The Arcadian Inn is served privately in the suites, or in the large dining room on the ground floor. Martha serves gourmet food and has put together her own cookbook of favorite dishes.

Arcadia
population 350

WHAT TO SEE:

ROUND BARN Built in 1898 from native burr oak. Open 10:00-5:00 Tuesdays—Sundays. **(918) 396-2398**

WHERE TO EAT:

HILLBILLEE'S CAFE Features pecan-smoked barbecue done next door at Lil' Billee's, chicken-fried steak, and classic hamburgers with fries. Live music several nights each week. 206 E. Highway 66.

WHERE TO STAY:

HILLBILLEE'S BED AND BREAKFAST Rebuilt from a Route 66 log motor court by Wade and Norma Braxton. Several rooms have been carefully restored .This is a comfortable getaway. 206 E. Highway 66.

Edmond
population 53,000

WHAT TO SEE:

EDMOND HISTORICAL SOCIETY MUSEUM Includes a Route 66 satellite exhibit. 431 S. Blvd.

"A TASTE OF EDMOND"
Kicks off the annual 4th of
July Libertyfest Celebration
each year. Participants can
sample food from over 50
local restaurants.

ENTERPRISE SQUARE
Enterprise Square, USA, an
Epcot Center-style hands-on
attraction explaining the
free enterprise system. 2501
E. Memorial. **(405) 425-
5030**

W H E R E   T O   E A T :

AROUND THE CORNER
11 S. Broadway

CAFE 501 501 S. Boulevard

FANNIES ON BROADWAY
706 S. Broadway

MCLAREN'S PANTRY 3210
S. Boulevard

**TWELVE OAKS
RESTAURANT** 6100 N.
Midwest Blvd.

W H E R E   T O
S T A Y :

**THE ARCADIAN INN BED
AND BREAKFAST** 328 E.
1st. (405) 348-6347

ARCADIAN INN
Piña Colada Muffins

1 BOX DUNCAN HINES BUTTER RECIPE
   GOLDEN CAKE MIX
1 CUP BISCUIT MIX
1/2 CUP BUTTER, MELTED
3 EGGS
1 CAN (20 OUNCES) CRUSHED PINEAPPLE
1 TEASPOON COCONUT EXTRACT
1 TEASPOON RUM EXTRACT
1 CUP SHREDDED COCONUT
1 CUP SLICED ALMONDS
MARASCHINO CHERRIES

Mix all of the above ingredients except
maraschino cherries until moistened. Do not
over mix. Grease muffin tins and fill cups 1/3
full. Bake in preheated 400° oven for 10
minutes. Take muffins from oven and quickly
place 1/2 of a cherry on top of half-baked
muffins. Return to oven, turn heat down to
350° and bake 5 to 8 minutes longer or until
muffins are done. 36 muffins.

*Grace Deason says she moved to Edmond by
way of Arkansas and Texas. She comes from a
family of good cooks who have always had large
gardens and preserved their own food. At well past
eighty, Grace still enjoys canning. The day we
visited there were several jars of squash relish
cooling on the kitchen counter and she had fresh
greens cooking on the stove for lunch. We talked
about many of her favorite recipes. She said this
peanut brittle recipe is one that is used by all the
family. No one seems to remember where it came
from, but it never fails.*

Grace Deason's Peanut Brittle

2 CUPS SUGAR

1 CUP WATER

1 CUP WHITE CORN SYRUP

1/4 TEASPOON SALT

2-1/2 CUPS RAW PEANUTS

2 TEASPOONS SODA

Combine sugar, water, and corn syrup in a saucepan and cook to the hard-crack stage (310° F.). Quickly add salt and peanuts and continue cooking until syrup takes on a golden color and peanuts no longer pop. Remove from heat, add soda, and pour into two greased jelly roll pans or on other greased surface. Pull with tongs to stretch and flatten. Break into pieces when cool. 3 pounds.

GOOD FOOD IN OKLAHOMA CITY:

Cathy Keating, wife of Frank Keating, Governor of Oklahoma, is a native Tulsan who led the way in restoring the 1928 Governor's Mansion. The home is open for tours each Wednesday afternoon. Call 521-2342 for information.

FROM CATHY KEATING

Kay Bird's Chicken Breasts with Mushrooms

2 SKINLESS AND BONELESS BREASTS OF CHICKEN

4 WELL BEATEN EGGS, SALTED TO TASTE

1 CUP FINE BREAD CRUMBS (CORN FLAKE CRUMBS MAY BE SUBSTITUTED)

1/2 CUP BUTTER

6 LARGE MUSHROOMS, SLICED (SLICED CANNED MUSHROOMS MAY BE USED)

Oklahoma City

population 445,000

WHAT TO SEE:

STATE CAPITOL Oklahoma State Capitol Complex. The only state capitol with working oil wells located on the grounds. N.E. 23rd and Lincoln. **(405) 521-3356**

NATIONAL COWBOY HALL OF FAME 1700 N.E. 63rd. **(405) 478-2250**

REMINGTON PARK RACE TRACK World class pari-mutuel horse racing. 1 Remington Place. **(405) 424-9000**

CULTURE Kirkpatrick Center Museum Complex: Omniplex, planetarium, Indian Center, Air Space Museum, Photography Hall of Fame, gardens. 2100 N.E. 52nd. **(405) 427-5461**

OKLAHOMA CITY ZOOLOGICAL PARK One of the 10 best in the country. 2101 N.E. 50th . **(405) 424-3344**

HARN HOMESTEAD AND 1889ER MUSEUM Oklahoma heritage at its best! 313 N.E. 16th. Call **(405) 235-4058** for tour information.

6 THIN STRIPS PARMESAN, GRUYERE OR
    MUENSTER CHEESE (GRATED PARMESAN
    MAY BE SUBSTITUTED)
1/2 CUP RICH BROTH
1 LEMON
PARSLEY

Cut chicken breasts in thin slices. Immerse them in well beaten eggs for at least 1 hour. Roll gently in crumbs. Heat half the butter in a skillet and brown chicken until golden, turn and brown on other side. Heat remaining butter in small casserole and add chicken. Cover with sliced mushrooms. Baste with chicken stock. Place casserole in preheated 350° oven and bake for 30 minutes, basting occasionally with the chicken stock. Add cheese the last ten minutes before serving. When done, squeeze lemon juice to taste over chicken. Garnish with parsley and lemon slices and serve with rice pilaf.

Note: When preparing for a crowd, allow 2 breasts per person. This can be made ahead of time and baked just before serving. 3 to 4 servings.

Kamp's Grocery at 1310 N.W. 25th is a hidden treasure amidst the bustle of the state capital. Locals flock to Kamp's for the deli menu and great box lunches as well as family dinners to go, all in conjunction with the Yippee-Yi-Yo Cafe inside the 1910 store with its tin ceilings, wood floors, old fixtures, and vintage photographs. Mary Ellen Flanagan, an owner and manager of the store today, says their coconut cake has been carefully resurrected to copy original owner Alfred Kamp's popular recipe. The croissant sandwich is typical of the good food served at the deli today.

KAMP'S GROCERY

Alfred Kamp's Coconut Cake

2-1/2 CUPS ALL PURPOSE FLOUR

2 CUPS SUGAR

1 TEASPOON BAKING POWDER

1/2 TEASPOON BAKING SODA

1/2 CUP BUTTERMILK

1/2 CUP BUTTER, SOFTENED

1 TEASPOON VANILLA

4 EGG WHITES

FROSTING:

1 PINT HEAVY CREAM

SUGAR

COCONUT

MARASCHINO CHERRY

In a large bowl, combine all dry ingredients. Using an electric mixer, slowly add buttermilk and butter. Add vanilla and beat for 2 minutes. Add egg whites and beat for 2 minutes more or until batter is very smooth and fluffy. Pour batter into two greased and floured 9-inch round baking pans. Bake in a preheated 375° oven for 25 to 30 minutes or until toothpick inserted in center comes out clean. Cool before frosting.

To frost, whip cream until fluffy. Sweeten to taste. Fill and frost cake with cream. Sprinkle with coconut until top and sides are completely covered. Top with a single maraschino cherry. 8 servings.

YIPPE YI YO CAFE Inside Kamp's Grocery, a great 1910 establishment with old-fashioned charm and quality food. 25th and Classen Blvd., 1310 N.W. 25th.

CATTLEMEN'S STEAKHOUSE Established in 1910 next to the stockyards. A must-see for western history and locals say the best steaks in town. 1309 S. Agnew.

TERRALUNA Creative combinations with Mediterranean, Italian, Asian, and California touches. 7403 N. Western Ave.

TEAROOMS Two tearooms with special appeal: Rose Garden Tea Room 4413 N. Meridian and Cathy's Cupboard, Nichols Hills Plaza, 63rd and Western.

ANN'S CHICKEN FRY Great Route 66 decor inside and out. 4106 N.W. 39th.

SLEEPY HOLLOW A longtime local favorite. 1101 N.E. 50th.

HAUNTED HOUSE 7101 Miramar

BEVERLY'S PANCAKE CORNER The final resting place for the famous "Chicken in the Rough" chain, an OKC legend. 2115 N.W. Expressway (at Pennsylvania).

MEIKI'S ROUTE 66
RESTAURANT Route 66
decor, Italian food 4533
N.W. 39th.

**WHERE TO
STAY:**

GRANDISON INN 1200 N.
Shartel. (405) 521-0011 or
800-240-INNF

WILLOW WAY At 27
Oakwood Dr. (405) 427-
2133

FLORA'S BED AND
BREAKFAST 2312 N.W.
46th. (405) 840-3157

KAMP'S GROCERY
Smoked Turkey Croissant

1 FRESH CROISSANT
4 OUNCES THINLY SLICED SMOKED TURKEY
  BREAST
1 TEASPOON TARRAGON MAYONNAISE
LETTUCE
TOMATO SLICES
1 TABLESPOON GORGONZOLA VINAIGRETTE

Toast the croissant. Heat the turkey. Place
turkey, mayonnaise, lettuce and tomato on half
the croissant. Top with Gorgonzola vinaigrette.
1 sandwich.

Gorgonzola Vinaigrette:

4 OUNCES GORGONZOLA CHEESE
4 OUNCES OLIVE OIL
2 OUNCES BALSAMIC VINEGAR

Combine and stir until well blended. Keeps
in refrigerator for 2 weeks when well sealed.
Use as needed for salads and sandwiches.

*The Grandison at Maney Park meets all the
criteria for Victorian accommodations at their best!
The lovely old home features three floors of rich
mahogany woodwork, leaded glass windows,
antique furnishings in the nine bedrooms, in a
historical setting. Hosts Bob and Claudia Wright,
their family and staff, have added other special
amenities: mystery weekends, ice cream socials,
unique classes, tasting parties, and much more add
to the pleasures found in this award winning inn.
The Grandison is a stop for those who love to be
pampered.Claudia shares her mother's easy recipe
for ice cream that is creamy, sherbet-like, and a
delightful color. The salsa egg recipe is very popular
with breakfast guests.*

GRANDISON BED AND BREAKFAST INN

Grape Ice Cream

1 CUP SUGAR (OR MORE IF YOU LIKE ICE
  CREAM VERY SWEET)
1 PINT GRAPE JUICE
MILK TO FILL A 1-1/2 GALLON FREEZER

Dissolve sugar in grape juice. Pour into
1-1/2 gallon freezer. Add milk to fill. Follow
manufacturer's instructions for freezing. 1-1/2
gallons.

GRANDISON BED AND BREAKFAST INN

Salsa Eggs

FOR EACH SERVING:

1/4 CUP DANISH HAM, COARSELY CHOPPED
1 TABLESPOON SALSA
1 LARGE EGG
1 TABLESPOON SHREDDED CHEDDAR
  CHEESE

Coat an individual baking dish with
nonstick cooking spray. Sprinkle ham in the
bottom of the dish. Top with salsa. Break the
egg gently into dish and bake in a preheated
350° oven until whites of the egg are just set,
about 15 minutes. Sprinkle with cheese and
return to oven until cheese melts. Serve
immediately in the baking dish.

Note: At the Grandison, salsa eggs are
served with fresh fruit and hot flour tortillas
or jalapeño corn muffins.

Flora's Bed and Breakfast was opened in 1985 by JoAnn and Newt Flora who were among the very first bed-and-breakfast operators in Oklahoma City. Their two story contemporary home makes a comfortable stop for those who have business in the nearby Penn Square area or just want a relaxing quiet time away from the everyday routine. Two beautifully appointed rooms await guests.

JoAnn shares this popular breakfast strata that is both easy and delicious.

FLORA'S BED AND BREAKFAST
Breakfast Strata

6 SLICES BREAD, ANY KIND

4 TABLESPOONS MARGARINE

2 CUPS CHEDDAR CHEESE, GRATED

2 CUPS JACK CHEESE, GRATED

1 CAN (4 OUNCES) DICED GREEN CHILES

6 EGGS

2 CUPS MILK

2 TEASPOONS PAPRIKA

1 TEASPOON OREGANO

1/2 TEASPOON PEPPER

1/4 TEASPOON GARLIC

1/4 TEASPOON MUSTARD

Spread bread slices with margarine. Arrange in single layer in a 9 x 13 baking dish. Sprinkle cheese and chiles over bread.

Beat eggs and add remaining ingredients to eggs. Pour over bread and allow mixture to stand overnight. Bake in a preheated 350° oven for 1 hour. Let set 10 minutes before cutting and serving. 6 to 8 generous servings.

Note: Ham pieces, diced bacon, or onion may be added if desired.

Willow Way Bed and Breakfast is a lovely two-story English Tudor home hidden away in a elegant eastside area that features native trees, large lots, winding streets, and the quiet associated with country living.

Johnita and Lionel Turner offer friendly hospitality and are quick to share the warmth of a fireplace, luxurious appointments, a landscape filled with squirrels and birds, and American horse country gentility. Remington Park, a world-class pari-mutuel race track, is nearby.

Guests may choose one of the upstairs bedrooms and suites or the restored and gracefully decorated greenhouse. Willow Way offers an experience to remember.

WILLOW WAY BED AND BREAKFAST
Scones

2 CUPS FLOUR

1 TEASPOON BAKING POWDER

1/2 TEASPOON SALT

2 TABLESPOONS SUGAR

1/2 CUP BLACK WALNUTS, CHOPPED

1 TABLESPOONS LEMON PEEL, STIRRED INTO
  2 TABLESPOONS SUGAR

1/4 CUP BUTTER

ENOUGH MILK TO MIX

FRUIT FOR FILLING (OPTIONAL)

Combine and blend all ingredients except milk and butter. Cut butter into mixture. The blend may be stored in refrigerator at this stage. When ready to use, add enough milk to make a sticky dough. Turn onto a floured breadboard. One cup of scone mix will make 8 to 10 small scones. Pat dough into rectangle about 3 x 10 inches. Cut into triangles and fold in half. Brush with milk and sprinkle with sugar. Bake in a preheated 400° oven for 12 to 15 minutes.

Bethany

population 21,000

WHAT TO SEE:

BETHANY HISTORICAL SOCIETY MUSEUM 6700 N.W. 36th

DOWNTOWN A refurbished downtown area that hosts antique shops, a bakery, and specialty stores.

BRIDGES Lake Overholser steel-truss bridge on west edge of town may be closed to traffic.

YEARLY EVENTS Special crowd-pleasing events each year include: Spring Fest, 1st Saturday in May; Harvest Jamboree, 1st Saturday in October; Christmas in Bethany, near Thanksgiving; Farmers Market, Tuesdays and Fridays from June through October.

Bethany is home to astronaut Shannon Lucid

WHERE TO EAT:

CYNTHIA'S PANTRY AND TEA ROOM 6730 N.W. 39th Expressway.

WHERE TO STAY:

ROSEWOOD BED AND BREAKFAST 7000 N.W. 39th St. (405) 787-7641

If stuffed scones are desired, microwave any sliced favorite fresh fruit for 30 seconds and place in scone before folding in half. Bake as usual. 16 to 20 small scones.

WILLOW WAY BED AND BREAKFAST
Aunt Kay's Brisket

5 TO 7 POUND TRIMMED BRISKET (10 TO 12 POUNDS UNTRIMMED)
GARLIC SALT
ONION SALT
LOWERY'S SEASONED SALT
MEAT TENDERIZER
4 TABLESPOONS LIQUID SMOKE
4 TABLESPOONS WORCESTERSHIRE
3 TABLESPOONS SOY SAUCE
3 TABLESPOONS ITALIAN DRESSING
2 TABLESPOONS CATSUP
1 TEASPOON PREPARED MUSTARD
1 TEASPOON CELERY SEED

Sprinkle brisket generously with the garlic, onion, and Lowery's seasoned salts and meat tenderizer. Place meat in a large cooking bag and add remaining ingredients. Marinate overnight. Bake in cooking bag in a preheated 275° oven for 4 to 5 hours or until tender. Begin testing at about 3-1/2 hours in order not to overcook meat. Slice after meat has cooled and serve with basting juice. 12 or more servings.

GOOD FOOD IN BETHANY:

Rosewood Bed and Breakfast is a very different "old home" because it is actually a collection of several old homes. Val and Dana Owens tore down several small older places in order to recycle lumber, doors, cabinets, bath tubs, and stained glass windows. As a result Rosewood now includes the best of both worlds. New appliances, electrical wiring, heating and air conditioning provide for comforts we have grown to expect, yet the solid oak doors and claw foot bath tubs contribute to the classic atmosphere.

The design at Rosewood is patterned after Victorian homes and work was completed so that the bed and breakfast could open in July of 1995. Located at 7000 N.W. 39th Street, it is hidden only a block off 39th Expressway, Old Route 66. Two rooms are available and a full country breakfast awaits.

ROSEWOOD BED AND BREAKFAST
Quiche

PIE CRUST:

- 1 CUP FLOUR
- 1/2 CUP SHORTENING
- 1/2 TEASPOON SALT
- 2 TABLESPOONS SUGAR
- 4 TO 6 TABLESPOONS WATER

Mix dry ingredients. Cut shortening into mixture with pastry cutter. Add water to make a soft dough. Knead into ball and roll out to fit a 9-inch deep pie pan or a 10-inch pie pan. Prick crust and bake in a preheated 450° oven for 5 minutes.

FILLING:

- 4 EGGS, SLIGHTLY BEATEN
- 2 CUPS MILK OR HALF-AND-HALF
- 2 CUPS CHEDDAR AND MOZZARELLA CHEESE, MIXED AND SHREDDED
- 6 SLICES COOKED BACON
- 1/2 CUP CHOPPED ONIONS
- 1/4 CUP SLICED BLACK OLIVES

Yukon

The Czech Capitol of
Oklahoma.

WHAT TO SEE:

CZECH FESTIVAL 1st
weekend, each October.

**CHISHOLM TRAIL
FESTIVAL** 1st weekend
each June. Cattle coming
from Texas and headed to
railheads in Kansas passed
through Yukon on this
famous trail from 1867 until
just before the land run in
1889.

MURAL Wall mural at 4th
and Main.

YUKON FLOUR MILL Sign
atop Yukon Flour Mill can
be seen for miles at night.
The mill operated from
1900 until 1970.

**YUKON'S BEST
RAILROAD MUSEUM**
Housed in several cars and
cabooses, contains a Route
66 Satellite exhibit. 3rd and
Main (Route 66).

GARTH BROOKS Yukon is
home to Dale Robertson
and Garth Brooks. Highway
92 through town has been
named Garth Brooks Blvd.

WHERE TO EAT:

YAKITY YAK CAFE 1233
Garth Brooks Blvd.

JERRY MACK'S BBQ
126 W. Main

Combine all ingredients and pour into pie
crust. Add or substitute other ingredients if
desired. Example: a small bit of broccoli,
spinach, tomato, or chopped cooked chicken.

Bake in preheated 450° oven for 15
minutes. Turn temperature to 350° and
continue baking for 40 to 45 minutes.
Remove from oven and allow to set for 15
minutes before slicing. 6 slices.

GOOD FOOD FROM YUKON:

*Prior to the annual Czech Festival, Yukon
Czech women bake some 36,000 kolaches to be
sold during the festivities. Kolaches are unique
pastries made of sweet yeast dough baked until
golden and topped with a spoonful of sweetened
poppyseed, pureed prunes, cottage cheese, glazed
apricots, or other sugary tidbits. Here is a typical
recipe as shared at the 1995 Czech Festival.*

Yukon Czech Festival Kolaches

1 CUP BUTTER
2/3 CUP SUGAR
1-1/2 TEASPOONS SALT
2 EGGS, WELL BEATEN
1/8 TEASPOON NUTMEG
GRATED RIND AND JUICE OF 1/2 A LEMON
2 PACKAGES DRY YEAST
1 CUP WATER
1 CUP MILK, SCALDED AND COOLED TO
  LUKEWARM
7 CUPS (OR MORE) SIFTED FLOUR

PRUNE FILLING:

1 POUND UNPITTED PRUNES
SUGAR
1/4 TEASPOON VANILLA
1/8 TEASPOON GROUND CLOVES
GRATED RIND OF 1/2 LEMON (OPTIONAL)

Poppy Seed Filling:

I CUP GROUND POPPY SEED
I/2 CUP BUTTER
I/4 CUP MILK
I-I/2 TEASPOONS LEMON JUICE
I/4 TEASPOON CINNAMON
I/4 CUP SUGAR

Cream together the butter, sugar, and salt. Add eggs, nutmeg, lemon juice, and rind. Mix yeast with water. Add milk and blend the liquid with 3 cups of the flour. Beat until smooth, then add butter mixture and remaining flour to make a medium soft dough, (as stiff as can be mixed with a wooden spoon.) Knead with the wooden spoon.

Let dough rise in a warm place until doubled then turn dough out on a board and knead down. Let stand for a few minutes.

Make rolls by pinching off a piece of dough the size of a large walnut, smooth it round and place rolls two inches apart on buttered cookie sheet.

Prepare fillings while dough is rising. For prune filling, cook prunes until tender, remove pits and sweeten to taste. Add vanilla and cloves. Add lemon rind if desired. Cook mixture until thick. For poppy seed filling, combine all ingredients and simmer 5 minutes.

Let kolaches rise until doubled, then with finger tips, stretch but do not mash rolls into shape of tiny pie shells.

Fill each pastry with a teaspoon of desired filling. Brush edges with butter and let rise again for about 15 minutes. Bake in preheated 375° oven for 20 minutes. About 7 dozen.

The Chisholm Trail Festival is held each year on the historic Kirkpatrick homestead property, located at Vandament and Garth Brooks Boulevard. Several thousand participants share a piece of authentic history and pioneer spirit during the two-day event. Drovers, Indians, mountainmen, pioneer school children, chuckwagon cooks, and other enthusiastic participants bring history back to life. Yukon resident J.W. "Jim" Parker is the knowledgeable and enthusiastic resource person for the highly successful event. Ninth Street in Yukon follows the Chisholm Trail. A marker is located at 2200 S. Holly.

Here is a favorite pioneer recipe that is just as good today as it was when cowboys ate at the chuckwagon. Cracklings are pork skins, crisply fried and flavorful. Many Oklahoma pioneers drank buttermilk with their cornbread or cracklin' bread for an evening meal.

UNCLE "RED" SMITH'S FAVORITE
Cracklin' Bread

1 CUP SWEET MILK

1 EGG

1 TEASPOON SALT

1 TEASPOON BAKING POWDER

2 TABLESPOONS FLOUR

1 CUP CORNMEAL

1/2 CUP CRISP-FRIED CRACKLINGS

Mix all together and pour into a hot cast iron skillet in which 1 tablespoon lard has been melted. Bake 30 minutes in 400° oven. When done, break chunks of bread into a big goblet of fresh sweet milk and eat. "It's mustache-lickin' good!" 4 to 5 servings.

The women at First United Methodist Church in Yukon recently compiled COOKING WITH LOVE. The popular book includes over 400 mouth-watering hometown recipes. Here are two fine examples.

This recipe for poppyseed dressing is wonderful on grapefruit and avocado salad and equally delicious on other fresh fruit.

COOKING WITH LOVE

Jane Shedeck's Poppyseed Dressing

2/3 CUP SUGAR

1 TEASPOON PAPRIKA

1 TEASPOON POPPY SEED

4 TABLESPOONS VINEGAR

1/3 CUP HONEY

1 TABLESPOON DRY MUSTARD

1/4 TEASPOON SALT

1 TEASPOON GRATED ONION

2 TABLESPOONS LEMON JUICE

1 CUP VEGETABLE OIL

Combine all ingredients using low speed on the mixer or blend in a food processor. Store in refrigerator until needed. About 1-1/2 cups.

COOKING WITH LOVE

Joyce Munyon's Oatmeal Buttermilk Pancakes

2 CUPS QUICK OATS, UNCOOKED

1/2 TEASPOON SODA

2-1/2 CUPS BUTTERMILK

1 CUP SIFTED ALL-PURPOSE FLOUR

2 TEASPOONS BAKING POWDER

1 TEASPOON SALT

2 TABLESPOONS SUGAR

1/3 CUP MELTED SHORTENING

2 EGGS, BEATEN

El Reno

Onion Fried Burger Capital of the World.

WHAT TO SEE:

CANADIAN COUNTY MUSEUM AND HERITAGE PARK 300 S. Grand

EL RENO HOTEL Built in 1892.

ONION BURGER DAY 1st Saturday in May each year. The burgers were first cooked here in 1926.

BPOE LODGE A part of the Oklahoma Territory exhibit at the St.Louis World's Fair in 1904, dismantled and saved. 415 S. Rockford .

BIG 8 MOTEL Where scenes from the movie *Rain Man* were filmed. "Amarillo's Finest" is still on the sign. 1705 E. Hwy. 66.

WHERE TO EAT:

HENSLEY'S RESTAURANT A family-run Route 66 original that now operates behind the oil derrick next to I-40 serving good home cooking. Country Club Exit, south from I-40.

Add oats and soda to buttermilk. Let stand 5 minutes. Sift together the flour, baking powder, salt, and sugar. Add sifted dry ingredients, shortening and eggs to oat mixture. Stir to combine.

For each pancake, pour about 1/4 cup batter onto hot, lightly greased griddle. Bake to golden brown, turning only once. Serve hot with butter and syrup. 14 to 16 small pancakes.

GOOD FOOD IN EL RENO:

Ed Elliott opened the Old Opera House Tea Room in the historic downtown section of El Reno in 1992. The two story brick building that also houses an Antique Mall has an exterior wall covered with murals depicting nine segments of local history beginning with Coronado in 1541.

The tea room itself is tastefully decorated in plum and forest green with art along the walls. It is open from 11 a.m. to 2 p.m. each weekday, which allows Ed to take care of a busy catering schedule. Local residents return regularly for his exceptional chicken salad and chocolate walnut pie. This rich apple pie is another favorite and is baked fresh daily along with all of the other items on the enticing menu.

OLD OPERA HOUSE
Sour Cream Apple Pie

1 UNBAKED 9-INCH PIE SHELL

3/4 CUP SUGAR

1/3 CUP FLOUR

1 EGG

1 TEASPOON VANILLA

1 CUP SOUR CREAM

3 OR 4 GRANNY SMITH OR OTHER TART GREEN APPLES

TOPPING:

1/2 STICK BUTTER
1/2 CUP FLOUR
1/2 CUP SUGAR

Combine the sugar and flour. Whisk in the egg, vanilla, and sour cream. Slice apples into pie shell and pour creamy mixture over the apples. Bake in a preheated 350° oven for 40 to 45 minutes or until lightly browned. Meanwhile cut the butter, flour, and sugar together until mixture is the consistency of small peas. Take pie from oven and sprinkle topping over pie. Return to oven and bake an additional 15 minutes. Serve warm. 6 slices.

OLD OPERA HOUSE TEA ROOM 110 N. Bickford

JOHNNIE'S GRILL 301 S. Rock Island

ROBERT'S GRILL 300 S. Bickford

SID'S DINER 300 S. Chocktaw

Calumet

population 540

GOOD FOOD IN CALUMET:

Pat Lafoe is a busy resident who has never slowed down after her 29-year career as an elementary teacher. Today she sells real estate, caters, makes wedding cakes, teaches swimming, raises a large garden, preserves most of her vegetables, and finds time to travel with her husband, both here and abroad. Cooking comes naturally to this mother of three grown children and busy community leader. Pat says that anyone who loves sauerkraut will enjoy this hearty main dish. The oatmeal cookie recipe was her mothers and remains her all-time favorite.

Pat Lafoe's
Pork, Kraut, and Dumplings

1 PORK ROAST (2 TO 3 POUNDS)
2 PACKAGES (1 POUND EACH) OF POLISH OR
  SMOKED SAUSAGE
2 CANS (14-1/2 OUNCES EACH) SAUERKRAUT
CARAWAY SEEDS TO TASTE
SALT AND PEPPER

Hydro

WHAT TO SEE:

LUCILLE HAMON'S GAS STATION North access road of I-40, old Route 66

JOHNSON PEANUT COMPANY North access road of I-40, old Route 66

HYDRO FREE FAIR Each August. A typical old-time country fair.

WHERE TO STAY:

CROSSWIND RANCH BED-AND-BREAKFAST Rt.1, Box 16A. (405) 663-4051

DUMPLINGS:

4 CUPS FLOUR
1/2 TEASPOON SALT
1/4 TEASPOON PEPPER
6 EGGS, BEATEN
MILK

Boil the pork roast until tender. Cool and remove all fat and bones. Cut pork into small pieces. Place broth in refrigerator until cold and remove solidified fat.

Cut sausage into bite-sized pieces. Add broth and pork. Combine with sauerkraut, caraway seeds, and salt and pepper to taste. Add enough water to broth so that dumplings can be added later. Bring liquid to a boil then simmer for 1 hour.

To make dumplings, combine flour, salt, pepper and eggs and add enough milk to make a stiff dough.

Bring pork mixture to a boil. Add dumplings by teaspoonsful. Boil until dumplings are thoroughly cooked, 10 to 15 minutes.

Serve while hot in bowls as soup or entree. 12 to 14 generous servings.

Pat Lafoe's Oatmeal Cookies

1 CUP MARGARINE
1 CUP BROWN SUGAR
1 CUP GRANULATED SUGAR
1 TEASPOON VANILLA
2 EGGS, WELL BEATEN
1-1/2 CUPS FLOUR
3 CUPS OATMEAL
1 TEASPOON SODA
1 TEASPOON SALT
1 TEASPOON CINNAMON
1/2 CUP RAISINS, OPTIONAL

Cream margarine and add brown sugar and eggs. Add dry ingredients and mix well. Drop by teaspoonsful on ungreased cookie sheet. Bake in preheated 350° oven for 10 minutes. 100 cookies.

GOOD FOOD IN HYDRO:

The country home of Charlie and Margie Moxley stands next to original Route 66 between Hinton and Hydro. The land is part of Mrs. Moxley's grandfather's original homestead claim dated 1901. A framed deed to L.H. Crosswhite hangs on the porch and is signed by Teddy Roosevelt. Their Crosswind Ranch Bed and Breakfast pastures are dotted with Texas Longhorn cattle. The red skin of western Oklahoma is evident along here. Winter wheat holds the land in place despite the continuous wind. This is a place to appreciate natural beauty and contemplate the hard work of our pioneer ancestors. The bed and breakfast is open only during the summer.

CROSSWIND RANCH

Margie Moxley's Homemade Yogurt

2 CUPS WARM MILK

1/3 CUP DRY MILK

2 TABLESPOONS PLAIN YOGURT WITH ACTIVE CULTURES

FRUIT AS DESIRED

Combine milk with dry milk. Scald and cool until lukewarm. Add plain yogurt and pour mixture into a quart jar. Use a yogurt maker if available, otherwise, set the jar in a small cooler and pour very warm water around the jar. Cover the jar with a lid and keep warm for several hours until yogurt is solid.

Add fresh or canned fruit to taste.

Weatherford

population 10,300

WHAT TO SEE:

ASTRONAUT THOMAS STAFFORD NASA MUSEUM Located at the airport, northeast of town.

FARMERS MARKET Every Saturday morning during the growing season. Corner of Main and Kansas.

COTTER BLACKSMITH AND MACHINE SHOP Family operated since 1913, an Oklahoma historic place and oldest business in town. 208 W. Rainey.

WHERE TO EAT:

THE CITY DINER A 1994 addition to Weatherford with diner decor guaranteed to remind customers of the 50s. 1231 E. Main

THE MARK Built in 1959, The Mark is the oldest restaurant in Weatherford still in business along Route 66. Good homestyle cooking. 601 E. Main

CASA SOTO Good Mexican food. 121 S.W. Main

Clinton

population 9,300

WHAT TO SEE:

ROUTE 66 MUSEUM 2229 W. Gray Blvd. (Exit 65 from I-40)

MOHAWK LODGE INDIAN STORE First Indian trading post in Oklahoma, relocated here. East of town on Route 66.

WHERE TO EAT:

POP HICK'S RESTAURANT 223 W. Gary

BIG PA'S 200 S. 4th Bill and Connie Cummins.

BUDDY BURGER 200 S. 4th

WHERE TO STAY:

"DOC" MASON'S BEST WESTERN TRADE WINDS INN Elvis Presley and his entourage stayed here on four occasions in the 1960s. 2128 W. Gray Blvd.

Lucille Hamons began selling gas on Route 66 in 1941. Motel rooms behind the station were often filled with folks who broke down while heading across the state. Lucille's is one of the few remaining establishments operated by an original owner along Route 66. She says she doesn't cook much any more, but has made many a burrito in her day. She prefers the old-fashioned kind made with plenty of ground meat rolled inside the tortillas.

Here is a more contemporary version, guaranteed to be popular with the hungriest traveler, yet low in fat.

Black Bean and Rice Burritos

1 REGULAR SIZE BOIL-IN-BAG CONVERTED RICE

1 TABLESPOON GARLIC POWDER

1/2 TEASPOON GROUND CUMIN

1 CAN (15 OUNCES) BLACK BEANS, UNDRAINED

6 FLOUR TORTILLAS (8-INCH SIZE), WARMED

3/4 CUP SHREDDED SHARP CHEDDAR CHEESE

1/4 CUP SLICED GREEN ONIONS

1/4 CUP SALSA

1/4 CUP PLAIN LOW-FAT YOGURT

Cook rice according to package directions. Combine garlic, cumin, and black beans in saucepan. Bring to a boil then reduce heat to simmer and continue cooking in uncovered pan for five minutes. Remove from heat and stir in rice. Spoon about 1/3 cup of the bean and rice mixture down the center of each tortilla. Top each with cheese, green onions, salsa and yogurt and roll up. 6 servings.

Elk City

population 11,000

Each year the ELK CITY DAILY NEWS publishes a treasury of favorite recipes that deals with only one subject. The 1995 anthology was entitled, ONLY ONIONS. Compiled and edited by Jo Ann Medders, Women's Editor, this annual supplement is a popular addition that is saved, enjoyed, and used frequently by local cooks.

WHAT TO SEE:

NATIONAL ROUTE 66 MUSEUM A part of Old Town Museum Complex. Route 66 and Pioneer Rd.

ANADARKO BASIN MUSEUM OF NATURAL HISTORY 107 E. 3rd

Barbara Passmore's Cheesy Green Onion Muffins

1-3/4 CUPS ALL-PURPOSE FLOUR

4 TEASPOONS BAKING POWDER

1 TABLESPOON SUGAR

1 TEASPOON SALT

3 CUPS RICE CHEX CEREAL, CRUSHED TO 1 CUP

2 EGGS, BEATEN

1-1/4 CUPS MILK

1/3 CUP VEGETABLE OIL

1/2 CUP FINELY CHOPPED GREEN ONIONS WITH TOPS

3 OUNCES GRATED CHEDDAR CHEESE

WHERE TO EAT:

COUNTRY DOVE GIFTS AND TEA ROOM For the best lunch in town. 610 W. 3rd.

FLAMINGO RESTAURANT A popular Route 66 restaurant in the same location since 1961. Where the locals have breakfast. 2010 W. 3rd.

SARAH'S FINE DINING 108 Blue Ridge Drive (2 blocks south of I-40 at Main Street exit).

BAR-B-QUE SHACK 221 N. Main

JIGGS SMOKE HOUSE Parkersberg Road exit from I-40

Preheat oven to 400°. Grease 18 2-1/2-inch muffin cups. In a large bowl, combine flour, baking powder, sugar, and salt. In a second bowl combine cereal, eggs, milk, oil, and green onions. Add cheese and blend thoroughly. Pour liquid mixture into flour mixture and stir only until moistened. Fill muffin cups and bake for 20-25 minutes or until muffins are browned. 18 muffins.

Note: One 3-ounce package of cream cheese may be substituted for cheddar cheese. Cut cream cheese into 1/4 inch cubes before adding to batter.

Sayre

WHAT TO SEE:

GRAPES OF WRATH
Courthouse that achieved
30 seconds of fame as backdrop for film version of *The
Grapes of Wrath.*

EXOTIC ANIMALS Largest
ostrich population in the
country plus other exotic
animals, privately owned but
visible from I-40.

OWL DRUG STORE Built
in the 1920s with the original oak shelves and marble-
topped back fountain still in
place. 101 W. Main.

**RS AND K RAILROAD
MUSEUM** 411 N. 6th

**SHORT GRASS COUNTRY
MUSEUM, ROCK ISLAND
DEPOT** Both museums
open by appointment. 106
E. Poplar.

BRIDGE Steel-truss bridge
Near Exit 26 from I-40 and
once a part of Route 66.

WHERE TO EAT:

66 DINER N.E. Highway
66, across from college.

**FAMILY HOUSE
RESTAURANT** Once oper-
ated by Gene Hill, a long-
time Route 66 cafe owner.
108 E. Main.

*The United Methodist Cookbook in Elk
City is a lovely collection that includes many
favorite recipes from church members and
community leaders. When I asked for suggestions,
this vegetable casserole was mentioned several times.*

UNITED METHODIST COOKBOOK

Lori Reed's
Mixed Vegetable Casserole

1 PACKAGE (20 OUNCES) FROZEN MIXED
   VEGETABLES
1 CUP CHOPPED ONIONS
1 CUP CHOPPED CELERY
1 CUP SHREDDED CHEDDAR CHEESE
1 CUP LOW-FAT MAYONNAISE
1-1/2 CUPS BUTTERY CRACKER CRUMBS
1/2 CUP BUTTER OR MARGARINE, MELTED

Cook frozen vegetables according to
package directions; drain well. Combine
cooked vegetables, onion, celery, cheese, and
mayonnaise in a large bowl, stirring well.
Spoon mixture into a greased 7 x 11 x 1-1/2
inch baking dish. Combine cracker crumbs and
butter; stir well. Sprinkle crumb mixture
evenly over casserole. Bake in preheated 350°
oven for 30 to 35 minutes or until thoroughly
heated. 8 to 10 servings.

The United Methodist Women of Sayre put their first cookbook together in 1993, Come Grow With Us. Their women's group has been a vital part of Sayre since 1902. Many of the recipes use garden-fresh produce and all are delicious.

Come grow with us

Vicki Ivester's Marinated Vegetables

1 POUND FRESH BABY CARROTS, CLEANED

8 OUNCES FRESH MUSHROOMS, TRIMMED
AND CLEANED

1 BUNDLE FRESH ASPARAGUS STALKS,
TRIMMED

FOR THE MARINADE:

8 OUNCES RANCH ITALIAN DRESSING

2 TABLESPOONS SNIPPED FRESH PARSLEY

2 TEASPOONS FINE HERBS

In a saucepan steam carrots for 8 minutes. Steam asparagus 3 to 4 minutes. Drain and cool. Layer carrots, mushrooms and asparagus (in order) in a flat dish. Shake marinade ingredients together and pour over vegetables. Cover and refrigerate at least 6 hours or overnight. Turn occasionally, taking care not to break asparagus spears. To serve, remove vegetables with a slotted spoon and arrange on a platter or plate. 12 servings.

Erick

population, 1,100

WHAT TO SEE:

HONEY FARM 2 miles west and a mile north

BECKHAM COUNTY HONEY FESTIVAL 2nd weekend in November.

100TH MERIDIAN MUSEUM Corner of Roger Miller and Sheb Wooley. Open by appointment. (405) 526-3221.

VINTAGE MOTELS Both the West Winds and Elm Motels are reminiscent of the old-fashioned stops that featured narrow garages between the rooms.

WHERE TO EAT:

CAL'S COUNTRY COOKING Cal Rogers has cooked good road food since 1949. A Route 66 classic stop! I-40 and Exit 7, north.

COME GROW WITH US

Sharon Ivester's Eggplant Pasta Sauce

1/2 CUP SALAD OIL

1 EGGPLANT (1 POUND), CUT INTO 1/2 INCH CUBES

1 CUP CHOPPED ONION

1 CUP SLICED MUSHROOMS

1 CLOVE GARLIC, MINCED

1 CAN (10 3/4 OUNCES) TOMATO SOUP

1 CAN (28 OUNCES) TOMATOES, CUT UP

1 TEASPOON OREGANO LEAVES

1/2 TEASPOON THYME

1 BAY LEAF

6 DROPS HOT PEPPER SAUCE

In a 4-quart Dutch oven over medium heat, cook the eggplant, onion, mushrooms and garlic in hot oil for 10 minutes, stirring frequently. Add remaining ingredients and bring to a boil. Reduce heat and simmer uncovered 45 minutes or until desired consistency. Discard bay leaf. Serve over hot pasta. 6 one-cup servings.

GOOD FOOD IN ERICK:

The annual Beckham County Honey Festival each November includes a parade, arts and crafts exhibit, tours of the OK Honey Farm, antique car show, and live entertainment. Local cooks vie for prizes for their favorite honey treats. Ben and Margie Snowden North own and operate the former Wilhelm Honey Farm, established in 1962. With the support of the Riverview Family and Community Education Group, they completed A HONEY OF A COOKBOOK in 1996. It is for sale at the Honey Farm just north of I-40 and in several nearby locations. Margie also enjoys writing poetry.

Her ode to Route 66 introduces the book.

Old 66

BY MARGIE SNOWDEN NORTH

Ghost road.
Crumpled, sometimes threadbare ribbon
That tied the nation together
Starting 1926;
Pitted and pock-marked now
By time and Oklahoma elements
And by tires of a half-century's
Worth of hurrying automobiles.

Road to freedom for dust-weary Okies;
Road back home when a way out
Was no longer needed,
Snaking over humps and gashes in the terrain,
Through patches of shinnery and sage and sunflowers,
Once host to tourists and Model T's,
To hobos and wagon loads of watermelons,
To new-fangled motor courts
And Burma Shave signs, and
Neon lights beckoning from big cities.

From west to east,
Texola to Quapaw,
A strip of concrete sections
That once made Oklahoma
The very heart of the Main Street of America.
Old 66,
Phantom from the past,
Cracked and fading,
Obliterated or by-passed...
But remembered still.

Many Honey Festival winning recipes are
included in the cookbook as well as many other
good dishes made with honey. Here are two of the
winners.

Joy Mayfield's Pumpkin Roll

3 EGGS

1 CUP SUGAR

2/3 CUP PUMPKIN

3/4 CUP FLOUR

1-1/2 TABLESPOONS HONEY

1 TEASPOON BAKING POWDER

2 TEASPOONS PUMPKIN PIE SPICE

1 TEASPOON CINNAMON

1/2 TEASPOON SALT

FILLING:

4 TABLESPOONS BUTTER OR MARGARINE

1 PACKAGE (8 OUNCES) CREAM CHEESE

1/2 TEASPOON VANILLA

1 CUP POWDERED SUGAR

Beat eggs at high speed for 5 minutes. Mix in remaining ingredients. Bake in a greased and floured jelly roll pan in a 375° oven for 15 minutes. Turn out on towel sprinkled with flour and powdered sugar. Immediately roll in towel and allow to cool.

Prepare filling by creaming butter, cream cheese, and vanilla together. Beat in powdered sugar. Unroll pumpkin cake; spread filling evenly and re-roll. Refrigerate at least 1 hour before slicing. About 12 servings.

Ann Mills's Caramel Apple Cake

1-1/2 CUPS VEGETABLE OIL

1 CUP SUGAR

1/2 CUP PACKED BROWN SUGAR

1/2 CUP HONEY

3 EGGS

3 CUPS FLOUR

2 TEASPOONS CINNAMON

1/2 TEASPOON NUTMEG

1 TEASPOON SODA

1/2 TEASPOON SALT

3 1/2 CUPS PEELED, DICED APPLES

1 CUP CHOPPED NUTS

2 TEASPOONS VANILLA

ICING:

1/2 CUP BROWN SUGAR

1/2 CUP LIGHT CREAM

1/4 CUP BUTTER OR MARGARINE

DASH OF SALT

1 CUP POWDERED SUGAR

1/2 CUP NUTS (OPTIONAL)

In a large mixing bowl, combine oil, sugars, and honey. Add eggs, 1 at a time, beating well. Combine dry ingredients and add to batter, stirring well. Fold in apples, nuts, and vanilla. Pour batter into greased and floured 10-inch tube pan. Bake in 325° oven for 1-1/2 hours or until cake tests done. Cool in pan for 10 minutes. Remove to wire rack. Cool completely before icing.

For icing, in top of a double boiler over simmering water, heat brown sugar, cream, butter, and salt until sugar dissolves. Cool to room temperature. Beat in powdered sugar until smooth. Drizzle over cake and sprinkle with nuts, if desired. 10 to 12 servings.

Texola

population 100

WHAT TO SEE:

OLD TERRITORIAL JAIL
Old Territorial Jail with no
windows or doors. One
block north of 66 on Main.

**SIGN ON THE LAST STOP
BAR**

*At Kay's Kountry Kreations across the street
from the Old Territorial Jail, Kay Atkins and her
mother, Rosalee Admire, stitch up a variety of
items including Route 66 orders. Rosalee was a
child of ten when the Bunyon Run took place. She
remembers being very scared of the strangers as
they came running by her home. The men were all
thirsty so she overcame her fear and was soon
providing water as they paused briefly on their run
down Route 66.*

*Most Texola residents are avid gardeners.
Okra and black-eyed peas are always included so
Rosalee shared her favorite okra salad. This salad
is good, even without the dressing.*

Rosalee Admire's Fried Okra Salad

6 SLICES BACON, FRIED CRISP AND DRAINED

2 TOMATOES, CHOPPED

1 SMALL ONION, CHOPPED

1/2 BELL PEPPER, CHOPPED

1 LARGE BAG (20 OUNCES) FROZEN OKRA,
FRIED, DRAINED, AND COOLED OR 4 CUPS
HOME-GROWN FRIED OKRA

DRESSING:

1/3 CUP VINEGAR

1/4 CUP SUGAR

1/4 CUP VEGETABLE OIL

Fry the bacon and set aside. Combine the
tomatoes, onion, pepper, and okra. Mix the
vinegar, sugar and vegetable oil in a jar and
shake until blended. Crumble the bacon over
the vegetables and pour the dressing over all
just before serving. 8 servings.

*T*he Texas Panhandle: cactus and Cadillacs, real cowboys, and plaster cows on the roofs of barbecue hang-outs. Panhandle residents take beef seriously in this rich flat country where the sky never ends.

Amarillo's Western Stockyard claims the largest cattle auctions in the world. On an average sale day 3,500 to 4,000 head of cattle change hands. Amarillo is the largest city on the Llano Estacado or "Staked Plains," the heart of the high plains region. Steaks around here are considered to be some of the best in the country. Prime rib, barbecue, and rich thick chile compete for popularity. Guides for the preparation of quality meat abound but several basics hold true. Prime beef comes first, and is most often served rare. Broiling is the preferred means of preparation and most steaks are served without accompanying sauces that hide the succulent flavor. In addition to beef, Panhandle cuisine reflects a spin-off from traditional southern, Hispanic, cowboy, Cajun, and no-nonsense prairie cooks. To best experience Texas, have a "cowboy morning" breakfast on the edge of Palo Duro Canyon. Then consider the challenge of a 72-ounce steak at The Big Texan. And finally, enjoy a piece of luscious coconut cream pie at The Adrian Cafe where a sign in the window says:

← 1139 Miles to Chicago and 1139 Miles to Los Angeles →.

Shamrock

population 2,300

WHAT TO SEE:

MUSEUM Visit the Pioneer West Museum in the former Reynold's Hotel.

BLARNEY STONE Discover a fragment of genuine Blarney Stone from County Cork, Ireland in Elmore Park.

TALL TOWER Gaze at the tallest water tower in Texas.

ST. PATRICK'S Join in the St. Patrick's Day Celebration each March.

WHERE TO EAT:

U DROP INN This vintage 1936 Route 66 classic offers a superb example of Art Deco architecture but may be closed.

WESTERN RESTAURANT Intersection of Route 66 and Highway 87, across the street from the U Drop Inn.

WHERE TO STAY:

YE OLDE HOME PLACE BED AND BREAKFAST 311 East 2nd St. (806) 256-2295

GOOD FOOD IN SHAMROCK:

Texans boast that more chile is prepared in Texas than any other state. After all, it is the official state dish and the jalapeno is the official state pepper. There are hundreds of variations of the fiery dish and most Texas chile cooks have strong opinions on whether the meat should be cut in cubes or coarsely ground. They also differ on the use of tomatoes, spices, and flavoring. At the granddaddy of all chile cook-offs in Terlingua, Texas, chile is prepared with meat and spices only.

In most Texas recipes, beans are added for family consumption but only after the master brew has cooked to perfection. Here is a typical recipe. It can be adjusted easily for those who have tender palates.

Route 66 Chile

2 POUNDS TRIMMED BEEF, CUT IN SMALL CUBES OR COARSELY GROUND

2 TEASPOONS VEGETABLE SHORTENING

1/2 TEASPOON HOT SAUCE

1 TEASPOON WORCESTERSHIRE SAUCE

8 OUNCES TOMATO SAUCE

3 BEEF BOUILLON CUBES

SPICE MIX:

3 TABLESPOONS CHILE POWDER

2 TEASPOONS CUMIN

2 TABLESPOONS DRIED ONION FLAKES

1 TABLESPOON GARLIC POWDER

1/2 TEASPOON SALT

1/2 TEASPOON PEPPER

1/2 TEASPOON OREGANO

1 BAY LEAF

Cook meat over medium heat in melted shortening until lightly browned. Add remaining hot sauce, Worcestershire sauce, tomato sauce, bouillon cubes and enough water to barely cover the meat mixture. Cover and simmer for about 45 minutes. Stir occasionally and add water if needed.

Combine spices. Add half of the combined spices including the bay leaf. Cook another hour, adding water as needed. Add remaining spices and continue cooking another 15 minutes. Adjust water to desired thickness. Remove bay leaf and taste to adjust salt and spices.

Note: Cooked pinto beans may be added for the last 15 minutes of cooking time, 4 to 6 cups, or according to personal preference.

Side dishes may include cornbread or tortillas, a green salad, guacamole, and fresh fruit. Beer is most often the Texas drink of choice. 6 to 8 servings without beans.

Ye Olde Home Place in Shamrock was built in 1904 of wood frame. In 1933, Amarillo architects Berry and Hatch remodeled and enlarged the home to reflect the art deco period. The exterior was redesigned and the home was enlarged to 5,000 square feet. The home was built as a showplace, and the interior cornices, arches, ceilings, lighting fixtures, and the walnut staircase have been carefully preserved. The Pendleton family has kept several fine examples of the original period furniture, including the dining room suite and a unique victrola still in working order. This is truly an unexpected jewel on the prairie—a reflection of what oil money brought to the Texas Panhandle.

Anaruth Pendleton and her staff offer a warm greeting, serve a full Texas-style breakfast, share the large terraced garden, and will direct you to area quarter horse ranches or other Panhandle points of interest. Anaruth says this chicken dish is popular at the luncheons she often serves for local groups.

McLean

Population 860

WHAT TO SEE:

DEVIL'S ROPE AND OLD ROUTE 66 MUSEUM This jewel of a museum is one of the best along Route 66, not to be missed! Corner of Kingsley and Old Route 66.

ALANREED-MCLEAN AREA HISTORICAL MUSEUM An excellent example of pioneer history. 117 N. Main.

PHILLIPS 66 Restored 1930s Phillips 66 station. On old westbound Route 66.

YE OLDE HOME PLACE
Hot Chicken Salad Casserole

2 CUPS COOKED DICED CHICKEN BREAST

1 CUP CHOPPED CELERY

1/2 CUP SLICED ALMONDS

1 CAN (2-1/4 OUNCES) SLICED RIPE OLIVES

2 TABLESPOONS FINELY CHOPPED ONION

1 CAN (10-3/4 OUNCES) CREAM OF CHICKEN SOUP

3/4 CUP LOW-FAT MAYONNAISE

1 TABLESPOON LEMON JUICE

1 CUP CRUSHED POTATO CHIPS

1/2 CUP GRATED CHEDDAR CHEESE

Combine chicken with celery, almonds, olives, onion, chicken soup, mayonnaise, and lemon juice. Stir well. Sprinkle half the chips on the bottom of a 9 x 9 inch casserole. Cover with chicken mixture. Top with remaining chips and cheese. Bake in a 400° oven for 15 to 20 minutes or until cheese melts. 8 to 9 servings.

GOOD FOOD IN MCLEAN:

CRUSINE DOWN OLD ROUTE 66, a community cookbook produced by the women at First United Methodist Church, has sold over 500 copies at the Devil's Rope and Old Route 66 Museum Store. Ruth Trew suggested the title that has proved to be a winner for the group. Not only are the hearty regional recipes good, but the ladies have a perfect market at the museum. The book was first published in 1990 and includes recipes from fellow UMW members in several other Route 66 communities.

CRUSINE DOWN OLD ROUTE 66

Vera Ann Johnson's Western Flapjacks

1-1/4 CUPS FLOUR

1 TEASPOON SUGAR

1 TEASPOON BAKING POWDER

1/2 TEASPOON SODA

1/2 TEASPOON SALT

1 EGG, LIGHTLY BEATEN

1-1/4 CUPS BUTTERMILK

1 TABLESPOON MELTED SHORTENING

Sift together the flour, sugar, baking powder, soda, and salt.

Stir in the egg, buttermilk, and shortening. Beat until smooth and cook on a hot griddle. Eight 5-inch flapjacks.

CRUSINE DOWN OLD ROUTE 66

Ruth Magee's Chicken Spaghetti

1 LARGE HEN, COOKED, BONED, AND CUT INTO BITE-SIZED PIECES

2 BOXES (7 OUNCES EACH) SPAGHETTI, COOKED IN CHICKEN BROTH

1 GREEN PEPPER, DICED

2 ONIONS, DICED

3 STALKS CELERY, SLICED

1 CLOVE GARLIC

1/4 POUND (1 STICK) MARGARINE

SALT AND PEPPER TO TASTE

1 CAN (28 OUNCES) TOMATOES

1 SMALL JAR PIMENTO, DICED

1 CAN (10-3/4 OUNCES) MUSHROOM SOUP

1 CAN (10-3/4 OUNCES) TOMATO SOUP

1 POUND VELVEETA CHEESE

Boil the hen, saving the broth. Sauté pepper, onions, celery, and garlic in margarine. Cook spaghetti in chicken broth and drain. In a large mixing bowl, combine chicken, vegetables, spaghetti, salt and pepper, tomatoes, pimento, and soup. Add a little milk if needed for moisture. Pour mixture in a 9 x 13 greased baking pan. Grate cheese over top. Bake in a 325° oven for 30 minutes. 10 to 12 servings.

Mabel Faulkner Wilson was born on the UV Ranch between McLean and Lefors soon after the turn of the century. As a small girl, she attended the First Methodist Church in McLean and grew up with strong family values and a love for good food. She became a home demonstration agent and home economics teacher. Mabel's love for the prairie, the sky, and the space in the Texas Panhandle made her typical of residents who think there is no better place to settle down than in this vast land of a thousand echoes.

Mabel Wilson's Frisky Lizzies

1/3 CUP MARGARINE

2/3 CUP BROWN SUGAR

3 EGGS

2 CUPS ALL-PURPOSE FLOUR

1-1/2 TEASPOONS SODA

1/2 TEASPOON SALT

1 TEASPOON PUMPKIN PIE SPICE

3 TABLESPOONS RUM OR RUM FLAVORING

1-1/2 TABLESPOONS MILK

1 POUND DATES

1 POUND CANDIED CHERRIES

1 POUND CANDIED PINEAPPLE

1 POUND NUTS

Cream margarine and sugar. Add eggs one at a time, beating well after each addition. Sift 1 cup of flour with the remaining dry ingredients and add to creamed mixture. Sift remaining cup of flour over chopped fruit and nuts and stir to coat. Add rum or rum flavoring, milk, and fruit to the creamed mixture and stir well to blend. Drop cookies by teaspoons on ungreased cookie sheets. Bake in 275° oven for 30 minutes. 5 dozen cookies.

Alanreed

Population 60

WHAT TO SEE:

VINTAGE SERVICE STATION A well-preserved service station from the 1930s. Also the dilapidated ruins of a reptile farm, and a forgotten cafe.

GOOD FOOD IN ALANREED:

Delbert and Ruth Trew remain the driving force behind the Old Route 66 Association of Texas. From their ranch near Alanreed, the Trews are also active in the Devil's Rope and Old Route 66 Museum and many church and civic endeavors in the McLean and Alanreed area.

CRUSINE DOWN OLD ROUTE 66
Ruth Trew's Chocolate Zucchini Cake

2 EGGS

1/2 CUP SOFT MARGARINE

1/2 CUP OIL

1-3/4 CUPS SUGAR

4 TABLESPOONS COCOA

I TEASPOON VANILLA

I TEASPOON SODA

I TEASPOON CINNAMON

1/2 TEASPOON GROUND CLOVES

1/2 CUP SOUR MILK

2-1/2 CUPS FLOUR

2 CUPS FINELY CHOPPED ZUCCHINI

1/4 CUP CHOCOLATE CHIPS

Groom

WHAT TO SEE:

CROSS OF JESUS
Experience the powerful 190-foot "Cross of the Lord Jesus Christ" and the 15 bronze stations of the cross currently being completed.

BRITTEN USA TOWER
Built intentionally with one short leg.

WHERE TO EAT:

GOLDEN SPREAD GRILL
Rubye Denton began serving customers in 1951 and bought the grill in 1957. This is the place where the locals gather for coffee then return for a hearty lunch.

Mix together all ingredients except zucchini and chocolate chips. Stir zucchini into batter last. Pour cake batter into greased and floured 9 x 13 cake pan. Sprinkle chocolate chips on top. Bake in 325° oven for 45 to 50 minutes. Needs no icing. 12 servings.

CRUSINE DOWN OLD ROUTE 66,
Paula Wilson's Sweet and Sour Chicken

1 CHICKEN, CLEANED AND CUT INTO PIECES
1 PACKAGE (1.15 OUNCES) DRY ONION SOUP MIX
1 JAR (12 OUNCES) APRICOT-PINEAPPLE JAM
1 JAR (8 OUNCES) CREAMY FRENCH DRESSING

Layer chicken pieces in roasting pan. Combine soup, jam, and dressing. Spread over chicken. Cover and bake in a 350° oven for 1-1/2 hours. (This sauce recipe is enough for two chickens.) 4 to 5 servings.

GOOD FOOD IN GROOM:

Both yellow crookneck and zucchini squash grow prolifically in the hot panhandle sun. Here is an exceptionally good squash casserole that Rubye Denton serves at the Golden Spread Grill. Enjoy!

GOLDEN SPREAD GRILL
Squash Casserole

3 1/2 POUNDS YELLOW SQUASH, TRIMMED AND SLICED
1/2 CUP GREEN PEPPER, CHOPPED FINE
1 LARGE ONION, DICED
2 RIPE TOMATOES, CHOPPED

8 TABLESPOONS MARGARINE OR BUTTER

4 EGGS

1/2 CUP SUGAR

1-1/2 TEASPOONS SALT

1/4 TEASPOON PEPPER

1/4 POUND HAM, DICED

3/4 CUP GRATED CHEDDAR CHEESE

3/4 CUP CRUSHED CHIPS FOR TOPPING

Combine squash, green pepper, onion and tomatoes in a large saucepan. Add a small amount of water, cover, and cook until tender, about 20 to 30 minutes, stirring occasionally to mash the squash. Drain thoroughly in a colander.

Add all remaining ingredients except chips. Pour mixture into a 9 x 12 lightly greased casserole and top with the crushed chips. Bake uncovered in a 350° oven for 30 to 45 minutes until top is golden brown. 10 to 12 servings.

GOOD FOOD IN AMARILLO:

Real ranchers and real cowhands greet guests at the Figure 3 Ranch each morning just in time for a ride across the plains to the rim of Palo Duro Canyon where sourdough biscuits, sausage, gravy, scrambled eggs, and cowboy coffee await.

The scenery itself is worth the trip. A breathtaking view awaits as early morning mist often rises from the northern edge of the canyon that drops some 700 to 800 feet below the level plain. Stories come naturally whether guests are interested in geology, prehistoric Indians, Coronado, Charles Goodnight, or other bits of Texas history significant to the area. Hosts Tom and Anne Christian and their cowhands can answer most questions.

Amarillo

Population 165,000

WHAT TO SEE:

PALO DURO CANYON

Take a 30-minute detour to Palo Duro Canyon State Park stretching 110 majestic miles, the second longest canyon in the United States. (806) 488-2227

TEXAS See "Texas," an outstanding summer musical drama with Palo Duro Canyon as the backdrop. A spectacular outdoor production! Drive 25 miles south of I-40 on I-27 to SR 217 or take FM 1541 south to the canyon. For "Texas" reservations call (806) 655-2181

COWBOY FIXINS AT PALO DURO CANYON

Indulge in Cowboy Morning Breakfasts or Cowboy Evening Dinners on the rim of Palo Duro Canyon. Cowboys on the Figure 3 Ranch provide all the authentic fixin's. April through October. One hour southeast of Amarillo. (800) 658-2613 or (806) 944-5562

CREEKWOOD RANCH OLD WEST SHOW AND CHUCKWAGON SUPPER

South of Amarillo on Washington (FM 1541). May through September, weather permitting. Call (800) 658-6673 for reservations

AMERICAN QUARTER HORSE HERITAGE CENTER AND MUSEUM The largest horse registry in the world. 2601 I-40 East. (806) 376-5181

SCIENCE CENTER Stop at Don Harrington Discovery Center. A hands-on science discovery center for families. Closed Mondays. (806) 355-9548

SHOPPING Shop at antique stores on 6th Street. Begin at the restored Nat Ballroom and continue 13 blocks to the west.

TRAFFIC SIGNS Find "Art for Art's Sake" traffic signs. Stanley Marsh 3 has the city talking. Over 750 signs have gone up (and come down) sporting a wide range of unusual statements.

CADILLAC RANCH Photograph the Cadillac Ranch. 10 vintage Cadillacs with tail fins pointing skyward at the same angle as the Cheops pyramids. Stanley Marsh's favorite art. West edge of Amarillo on I-40 and Route 66.

The spectacular 7,000-acre working ranch is only a small slice of Texas, but portrays real ranch life. The Christians began serving breakfast on the canyon rim back in 1981 and now offer Cowboy Evening Dinners that include steaks and burgers. This is an authentic Texas experience that shouldn't be missed.

FIGURE 3 RANCH

Cowboy Morning Sourdough Biscuits

5 CUPS FLOUR
2-1/2 CUPS SOURDOUGH STARTER
1 TEASPOON SUGAR
1 TEASPOON BAKING SODA
1/2 TEASPOON SALT
1/4 CUP COOKING OIL

Place flour in a large bowl and make a well in the flour. Pour starter into the well and add all the other ingredients. Stir until mixture no longer picks up flour. Cover and let rise three to four hours, or overnight. Place dough on floured board and roll to 1/2 inch thick. Cut out biscuits and place in greased cast-iron Dutch oven. Set by the campfire to rise for one to two hours.

Place hot lid on oven, set oven on coals, and place coals on lid. Cook until browned, 5 to 8 minutes. 15 large biscuits, 18 inch Dutch oven.

Sourdough Starter

4 MEDIUM BAKING POTATOES, PEELED AND
   QUARTERED
4-1/2 CUPS WATER
1 CUP ALL-PURPOSE FLOUR
2 TEASPOONS SUGAR
1/2 TEASPOON SALT

Place potatoes and water in medium saucepan. Cover and boil until potatoes are done, about 30 minutes. Drain liquid into measuring cup. (Do not use potatoes.) Measure 2-1/2 cups of the potato water into large mixing bowl. Add flour, sugar, and salt. Stir well. Cover with cheesecloth and let stand at room temperature until starter begins to bubble, about 4 days. Place in covered plastic container in refrigerator.

To use, take 2-1/2 cups of starter out for biscuit recipe. To remaining starter, add 1-1/2 cup flour and 1-1/2 cups warm water. Let starter stand at room temperature overnight then replace lid and return to refrigerator. Use regularly and enjoy! Note: Some cooks like to add 1 package of dry yeast to the original starter to give it an extra boost. If this is done, the starter will begin to bubble in 2 days.

One of the trendiest antique districts along Route 66 can be found on Sixth Street in Amarillo. This 13-block segment of the historic highway was inducted into the National Register of Historic Places in October of 1994. Bounded on the east by The Nat, a 1922 natatorium turned dinner-dance club that is now an antique mall, the street is undergoing a renaissance. Primarily known for antiques and collectibles, Sixth Street is also home to The Golden Light Cafe, the oldest restaurant in Amarillo continuously operating in the same location, and The Neon Grill and Fountain, a re-creation of the old Neon Cafe once located on the same site. At Puckett Antiques and Collectibles, customers always find freshly brewed coffee or tea along with home-baked goodies to enjoy while shopping. Owner Dorothy Puckett takes great pleasure in sharing her mother's good recipes by including several on her cards, ready for customers to take home and try for themselves.

WHERE TO EAT:

BIG TEXAN STEAK RANCH Home to the 72-ounce steak, Big Texan Opry Stage, Saturday Morning Cowboy Poetry, and Reptile Ranch housing the largest western diamondback rattlesnake in Texas. 7701 I-40 east.

THE GOLDEN LIGHT CAFE Marc Reed and his staff will make you feel welcome in this oldest cafe in the same location in Amarillo—great hamburgers! 2908 West 6th.

THE GOLDEN LIGHT BAR Stop next door to the cafe for beer, wine, peanuts, and music! The old signs on the walls were discovered under the shingles of a barn that was being demolished.

BLUE FRONT CAFE Comfortable and friendly with good food. 801 W. 6th.

NEON GRILL AND SODA FOUNTAIN Re-creation of the glory days along Route 66. 3209 W. 6th.

DYER'S BAR-B-QUE In Wellington Square. Good Texas-style barbecue.

MARTY'S For steaks and prime rib. 34th and Georgia (Westhaven Village).

SCOTT'S OYSTER BAR A local favorite. 4150 Paramount Blvd.

BEANS AND THINGS
Some of the finest barbecue
and chile you will find in
Texas. Look for the cow on
top! 1700 Amarillo
Boulevard East (Old 66).

**W H E R E   T O
S T A Y :**

**ADABERRY INN BED AND
BREAKFAST** 6818 Plum
Creek Dr. Kyle and Shannon
Adams. (806) 355-4118

**PARKVIEW HOUSE BED
AND BREAKFAST** 1311 S.
Jefferson. (806) 373-9464

AUNTIE'S HOUSE 1712 S.
Polk. (806) 371-8054

GALBRAITH HOUSE 1710
S. Polk. (806) 374-0237

Dorothy Puckett's
Mom's Chocolate Pie

1-1/2 CUPS SUGAR

4 TABLESPOONS CORNSTARCH

2 TABLESPOONS COCOA

PINCH OF SALT

2 CUPS MILK

3 EGGS, SEPARATED

1/2 TEASPOON VANILLA

2 TABLESPOONS BUTTER, MELTED

1 BAKED 9-INCH PIE SHELL

Mix sugar, cornstarch, cocoa, and salt. Add
milk and egg yolks. Blend thoroughly then
bring to a boil and cook until thick, stirring
constantly. Add vanilla and butter and
immediately pour into pie shell. Top with
beaten egg whites and brown for 5 minutes in
400° oven. 6 to 8 servings.

*In the canyonlands a few miles west of Sixth
Street and Route 66 is an unexpected treasure,
Adaberry Inn Bed and Breakfast. The 8,500-
square foot home of sand-colored brick towers three
stories above a Texas size panorama.*

*Northwest Amarillo has developed rapidly
because of its space, peace, and quiet with an
added bonus of rugged terrain formerly home to
only tumbleweeds, devil's claw, prairie chickens,
and a few rattlesnakes. Kyle and Shannon Adams
saw opportunity here and the need for a
comfortable, home-like stop for businessmen,
travelers, and those wanting a relaxing atmosphere
near Amarillo's large medical complex just south.
Adaberry Inn Bed and Breakfast opened in 1997
with 9 rooms or suites, each unique in flavor. The
Augusta Room comes complete with a putting
green, and the Santa Fe Room is decorated in
authentic southwestern style.*

Those traveling on business have comfortable work stations and modem lines. For relaxation, guests enjoy private patios, fireplaces, Jacuzzis, a complete workout room, a movie room, and a snack area for those who crave a peanut butter sandwich at midnight. A full breakfast awaits guests in the formal dining room or in the privacy of their suites.

Adaberry Inn
Overnight Pecan Waffles with Cran-Blueberry Topping

3 CUPS ALL-PURPOSE FLOUR

2 TABLESPOONS BROWN SUGAR

1 TEASPOON SALT

1 PACKAGE DRY YEAST

2 CUPS MILK

1/2 CUP WATER

1/3 CUP MARGARINE

3 EGGS

1/2 CUP CHOPPED PECANS

Lightly spoon flour into measuring cup; level off. In a large bowl, combine flour, brown sugar, salt, and yeast. In a small saucepan heat milk, water, and margarine until warm (120 to 130°). Add hot liquid to flour mixture; blend well. Stir in eggs. Cover bowl with plastic wrap. Refrigerate several hours or overnight.

Heat waffle iron. Stir down batter and add pecans. Bake in hot waffle iron until steaming stops and waffles are golden brown. Repeat with remaining batter. Serve immediately. Sixteen 4-inch waffles.

1/4 CUP COLD WATER

2 TABLESPOONS CORNSTARCH

1-1/2 CUPS SUGAR

1 CUP FRESH OR FROZEN BLUEBERRIES

3 CUPS FRESH OR FROZEN CRANBERRIES

1 TEASPOON CINNAMON

1/2 TEASPOON NUTMEG

3/4 CUP WATER

In a small bowl, combine 1/4 cup cold water and cornstarch; blend well and set aside. In medium saucepan, combine all remaining ingredients. Cook over medium high heat until mixture boils and berries are soft, stirring frequently. Stir in cornstarch mixture; continue to cook until mixture is thickened and bubbly, stirring often. Cool slightly and serve with waffles. About 4 cups.

COOKIN' WITH AMARILLO'S CORPORATE COWBOYS is a unique collection from Texans who love to eat! Several years ago, Art Force, the volunteers who promote and support the Fine Arts Division of Amarillo College, asked prominent Amarillo businessmen to share their favorite recipes as a scholarship fundraiser. The resulting cookbook has great food and a Texas-size sense of humor!

COOKIN' WITH AMARILLO'S CORPORATE COWBOYS

Ben Konis's Hot Damn Texas Panhandle Salami

2 POUNDS LEAN CHOPPED MEAT

2 TABLESPOONS MORTON'S TENDERQUICK

1-1/2 TEASPOONS LIQUID SMOKE

1/4 TEASPOON EACH GARLIC POWDER AND ONION POWDER

1 CUP COLD WATER

SCANT TEASPOON PEPPERCORNS

Mix all ingredients well. Shape into two tight rolls, wrap in waxed paper and refrigerate for 24 hours. Remove wrap and bake salami on cookie sheet in preheated 225° oven for 2 hours.

(My mother-in-law, Rosie, gave me this secret recipe. Great eating with rye bread, Dijon mustard, and a beer with ice and lime.) Two 1-pound rolls.

COOKIN' WITH AMARILLO'S CORPORATE COWBOYS

W. E. Juett's Horseradish Sauce for Cream Cheese

- 1 JAR (16 OUNCES) APPLE JELLY
- 1 JAR (18 OUNCES) APRICOT-PINEAPPLE PRE-SERVES
- 1 CAN (1-1/2 OUNCES) DRY MUSTARD
- 1 JAR (5 OUNCES) CREAMED HORSERADISH
- 1 BLOCK (8 OUNCES) CREAM CHEESE

Mix all ingredients except cream cheese. Spoon generously over cream cheese. Serve on a platter with a cheese knife and assorted crackers. Unused sauce can be stored in refrigerator, covered, for up to two months. About 4 cups.

COOKIN' WITH AMARILLO'S CORPORATE COWBOYS

Carlton Clemens's Chicken-Fried Steak and Gravy

Select 1 pound round steak or cutlet of desired thickness. Cut into four pieces. Pound with meat tenderizer (cleaver) or edge of small plate. Cover with flour and dust off excess. Dip slices in wash made of 1/2 milk and 1/2 buttermilk. Replace in flour and dust off excess. Deep fry at 350° until the steak floats.

Continue by pan frying at 300° until meat is browned on both sides. Serve hot with gravy.

To make the gravy, combine equal parts of flour and vegetable oil. In a heavy skillet, heat the oil until hot—about 300°. Add the flour, stirring carefully so the mixture doesn't stick to the pan. When the oil and flour mixture is hot, add milk and continue to cook until desired thickness is reached. Salt and pepper to taste. 4 servings.

COOKIN' WITH AMARILLO'S CORPORATE COWBOYS

Stanley Marsh 3's Wild Plum Jelly from the Frying Pan Ranch (Recipe for Husbands)

Approach house carefully. Do not disturb any workers, paid or volunteer, who are moving around strange contraptions, pans, and containers.

Expect to find all edible food out in small refrigerator near bedroom, in cans, or in the cupboards. Refrigerators are full of berries.

Be careful when you get up in the middle of the night not to jiggle any pans on the stove or island or countertops because they may be brimming full of plum juice in one stage of jell or another.

Do not be alarmed when your wife jumps up out of bed or out of the bathtub at various times and runs in the kitchen, moving about containers.

Do not ask the cowboys why they have coolers full of berries sunning in the front yard. They are ripening. It would just look foolish.

Smile and enjoy it. It's a beautiful harvest. The jelly tastes great and you will get a lot of compliments for just having stayed out of the way.

P.S. Bring your wife ice water or snacks; at

night take her for a ride or to the movie on the weekend. She is tired being on her feet. Let her choose the TV show. Encourage her to rest.

Parkview House is a two-story prairie home built around 1908 for Amarillo Mayor J.H. Patton and moved to its present location in the 1920s as the Waldorf Hotel. It has been a boarding house for railroad workers and a home to Amarillo college students. Present owners Carol and Nabil Dia have restored and updated the home and filled it with antiques from their travels. Five guest rooms await travelers who will enjoy Carol's lovely garden and continental breakfasts.

PARKVIEW HOUSE BED AND BREAKFAST
Fruity Bread Pudding

I POUND QUICK BREAD, PREFERABLY LEMON
  OR ORANGE
I CUP TOASTED COCONUT
I CAN (15-1/4 OUNCES) OF ONE OF THE
  FOLLOWING FRUITS, DRAINED: PITTED
  CHERRIES, PINEAPPLE CHUNKS, APRICOT
  HALVES, SLICED PEACHES, PEAR HALVES
I CAN (21 OUNCES) CHERRY PIE FILLING
1/2 CUP BRANDY OR RUM

Thinly slice the bread. Toast both the bread and coconut on a shallow pan in a 375° oven until crispy and firm. Crumble, mix, and layer half of the bread and coconut into a 2-1/2 quart ovenproof bowl. Add fruit, cover with pie filling and then with remaining bread and coconut. Cover and refrigerate 8 hours or overnight. Let stand for 30 minutes at room temperature. Preheat oven to 350° and bake pudding for 35 minutes. Serve warm for breakfast or as a dessert with whipped cream or ice cream. 10 servings.

Former Amarillo resident Donna Lea is a lifelong Texan who made several Route 66 excursions with me searching for good food. She has doubled as photographer, recordkeeper, and driver at various times. Country breakfasts aren't one of Donna's favorite meals, so she shared this substitute one day. Since then, I've developed a craving for these great "buffalo chips" and keep them in the freezer for mornings when I need a quick start.

Donna Lea's Buffalo Chips

2 CUPS MARGARINE

2 CUPS BROWN SUGAR

2 CUPS GRANULATED SUGAR

4 EGGS

4 CUPS FLOUR

2 TEASPOONS BAKING POWDER

2 TEASPOONS SODA

1/2 TEASPOON SALT

2 CUPS CORN FLAKES

2 CUPS OATMEAL

1 PACKAGE (6 OUNCES) CHOCOLATE OR BUT-
TERSCOTCH CHIPS

1 PACKAGE (7 OUNCES) COCONUT

1 CUP RAISINS

1 CUP PECANS, PEANUTS OR MIXED NUTS

Prepare these cookies in a very large mixing bowl or a roaster pan. Cream margarine with sugar and eggs. Stir in flour, baking powder, soda, and salt. Add remaining ingredients and blend well. Use an ice cream scoop to dip mixture. Place cookies on greased cookie sheet, flatten slightly allowing space for cookies to spread.

Cookies will be 3 to 4 inches in size. Bake in 350° oven for 15 to 18 minutes. Approximately 48 large cookies.

Note: Many variations work well with these cookies. Try other cereals instead of corn flakes. Substitute dried banana for raisins or use 1/4 cup applesauce to replace an equal part of the oil, use M&M candies in place of chips, add more raisins if desired and include seeds or other dried fruit for added flavor.

Auntie's House Bed and Breakfast is a 1912 Craftsman home that was built by the same man who constructed Amarillo's first elevator. The house served as officers' quarters for Amarillo Air Force Base during World War II, became an apartment house, and has survived a major fire.

Owners Skip and Corliss Burroughs remodeled the place themselves and opened as Auntie's House Bed and Breakfast in 1995. The basement commons room houses her collection of Civil War memorabilia and reflects his love for World War II airplanes.

AUNTIE'S HOUSE BED AND BREAKFAST
Everyday Cinnamon Rolls

3 CUPS COMMERCIAL BISCUIT MIX
I CUP MILK

TOPPING:

3 TO 4 TABLESPOONS BUTTER OR MAR-
    GARINE, MELTED
1/2 CUP SUGAR
4 TEASPOONS CINNAMON

FROSTING:

1-1/2 CUPS POWDERED SUGAR
1/2 TEASPOON VANILLA
8 TEASPOONS MILK

Wildorado

population 180

WHERE TO EAT:

JESSE'S CAFE

Combine biscuit mix with milk and stir to blend. Let stand a few minutes then roll out on a lightly floured surface to about 12 x 14 inches. Brush on butter and shake a mixture of sugar and cinnamon over dough. Roll from short side and cut into about 15 rolls. Lightly grease a 9 x 13 pan. Place rolls in pan. Bake in a 375° oven for 20 to 25 minutes. Combine sugar, vanilla and milk. Drizzle frosting over warm rolls. Serve while warm. About 15 cinnamon rolls.

GOOD FOOD IN WILDORADO:

Black-eyed peas are found in almost every Texas Panhandle garden. Wonderfully flavorful when picked and served fresh, the peas are almost as good when canned or frozen. This recipe is typical of the many good dishes served by local cooks. Of course, no family in Texas or Oklahoma can serve a New Year's Day meal without including black-eyed peas for good luck.

Black-eyed Peas and Ham

3-1/2 CUPS FRESH OR THAWED FROZEN
 BLACK-EYED PEAS

3 CUPS REGULAR OR LOW-SODIUM CHICKEN
 STOCK

4 OUNCES HAM, CHOPPED

1 SMALL ONION, FINELY CHOPPED

2 TABLESPOONS BALSAMIC VINEGAR

4 CLOVES GARLIC, MINCED

1 BAY LEAF

1/2 TEASPOON DRIED THYME

1/4 TEASPOON RED PEPPER

SALT AND PEPPER TO TASTE

Combine all ingredients in large saucepan. Bring to a boil then reduce heat to simmer and continue cooking until peas are tender, about 40 to 45 minutes. 6 to 8 servings.

COOKIN' WITH AMARILLO CORPORATE
COWBOYS, FROM MANSFIELD CATTLE
COMPANY, VEGA

Bob's Tenderloin

1 BEEF TENDERLOIN, ABOUT 5 TO 6
POUNDS, WELL TRIMMED

2/3 CUP SOY SAUCE

1 CUP ORANGE JUICE

SEVERAL SHAKES WORCESTERSHIRE SAUCE

4 TEASPOONS VINEGAR

JUICE OF ONE LEMON

PINCH OF SUGAR

GARLIC AND PEPPER TO TASTE

Combine and mix all marinade ingredients together. Marinate tenderloin for several hours, turning occasionally. Cook on charcoal grill over medium coals (about 6 inches above coals) for 30 to 45 minutes. Tenderloin should be mopped with marinade and turned about 3 times. About 15 servings.

Melba Rook's Buttermilk Biscuits

4 CUPS FLOUR

1 TEASPOON SALT

1/4 CUP BAKING POWDER

1/4 CUP SUGAR

2/3 CUP BUTTER

1-1/3 CUPS BUTTERMILK

Sift together the flour, salt, baking powder and sugar. Cut in the butter and add milk, forming a soft dough. Knead on a floured board. Roll out to 3/4 to 1 inch thick. Cut into 1-1/2 inch circles and place an inch apart on a greased sheet. Bake in a 400° oven for 10 to 12 minutes. 2 dozen biscuits.

Vega

population 850

A community proud of its farming and ranching heritage.

WHAT TO SEE:

BOYS RANCH Drive 20 miles north on Hwy. 385 to Cal Farley's Boy's Ranch, home to over 400 boys and girls. See Old Tascosa and Boot Hill Cemetery. This area was "Cowboy Capital of the Plains" at the turn of the century.

Landergin

A revitalized truck stop

WHAT TO SEE:

**ROUTE 66 ANTIQUES
AND VISITORS CENTER**
This once-abandoned Route
66 watering hole has come
back to life thanks to
George and Melba Rook
who proudly show off their
collection of authentic
Route 66 signs—the only
complete collection in exis-
tence.

Melba Rook's Quick Dinner Rolls

2 CUPS MILK

1/2 CUP SHORTENING

3/4 CUP SUGAR

3 TEASPOONS SALT

1/4 CUP YEAST

2/3 CUP LUKEWARM WATER

2 CUPS COLD WATER

12 CUPS FLOUR

Scald milk. Add shortening sugar, and salt.
Set aside to cool. Dissolve yeast in lukewarm
water. Add cold water to milk mixture. Stir in
yeast. Add flour and knead until dough is soft
and satiny. Spray 48 muffin tins with nonstick
spray. Pinch off dough and half fill each cup.
Cover lightly. Let rise until doubled. Bake in a
350° oven for 12 minutes. 4 dozen rolls.

*Alice Rice operates the Neon Soda Saloon
inside the Route 66 Antiques and Visitors Center
in Landergin. When she and Melba Rook began
planning the menu, they decided to include an
old-fashioned chocolate cake served by Ollie Lee
O'Conner at Ollie's Restaurant in Vega over fifty
years ago. Several of Ollie's family members stop by
regularly for a slice of the nostalgic cake.*

ROUTE 66 ANTIQUES AND VISITORS CENTER
Ollie's Chocolate Cake

2 CUPS FLOUR

2 CUPS SUGAR

2 TEASPOONS SODA

2 TABLESPOONS COCOA

3/4 CUP OIL

2 EGGS

1 CUP SOUR MILK

1 CUP BOILING WATER

FROSTING:

  1 CUP SUGAR

  1 TABLESPOON WHITE CORN SYRUP

  1 TABLESPOON COCOA

  1/4 CUP MILK OR CREAM

  1 STICK MARGARINE

  1 TEASPOON VANILLA

Sift dry ingredients together in large bowl. Add oil, eggs, and sour milk; beat well in mixer. Add boiling water and continue beating for 3 minutes. Pour into a greased and floured 9 x 13 inch pan. Batter will be thin. Bake at 350° 45 minutes. Cool and frost.

For frosting, combine all remaining ingredients except vanilla. Bring to a boil and boil for 2-1/2 minutes. Add vanilla and beat until icing begins to thicken. Spread on cake quickly as this sets up fast. Nuts may be added if desired. 12 servings.

GOOD FOOD IN ADRIAN:

At the exact geo-mathematical midpoint of Route 66, The Adrian Cafe is the oldest continuously operating eatery along Route 66 between Amarillo and Tucumcari. A sign in the front window proclaims: Midway Cafe, 1139 miles from Chicago and 1139 miles from Los Angeles. Fran Houser owns the eatery that is home to locals. She says this pie is close to the one prepared by Jesse Finch, who once owned the cafe and was a legendary Route 66 figure.

Adrian

population 225

W H A T   T O   S E E :

Adrian is the midpoint of old Route 66, halfway between Chicago and Santa Monica.

W H E R E   T O   E A T :

THE ADRIAN CAFE The oldest continuously operating eatery still in business between Amarillo and Tucumcari, a good place to eat as well!

BENT DOOR CAFE Historic stop recently reopened—there are many stories here.

THE ADRIAN CAFE
Coconut Cream Pie

2/3 CUP SUGAR

2-1/2 TABLESPOONS CORNSTARCH

1/2 TEASPOON SALT

1 TABLESPOON FLOUR

3 CUPS MILK

3 EGG YOLKS, BEATEN

1 TABLESPOON BUTTER

3/4 CUP COCONUT

1-1/2 TEASPOONS VANILLA

1 UNBAKED 9-INCH PIE SHELL

M E R I N G U E :

3 EGG WHITES

1/4 TEASPOON CREAM OF TARTER

1/2 TEASPOON VANILLA

Mix sugar, cornstarch, salt and flour well. Stir in milk gradually. Cook over medium heat, stirring constantly until mixture is hot; stir in beaten egg yolks. Cook until thick. Add butter, coconut, and vanilla. Pour into a 9-inch pie shell.

Combine meringue ingredients, beat until stiff and spread over the pie. Bake in 400° oven for 6 to 10 minutes until meringue is lightly browned. 6 slices.

Robert and Priscilla Jacobson farm near Adrian on the land Robert's family settled in 1909. Priscilla is a wonderful cook, making use of fresh garden products and taking advantage of her own family heritage of good food and her background in home economics.

Mustard Relish

I QUART GREEN TOMATOES, COARSELY
  GROUND
I QUART ONIONS, GROUND
I QUART CABBAGE, GROUND
I2 MEDIUM SOUR PICKLES, GROUND
9 LARGE SWEET PEPPERS, PREFERABLY 7
  GREEN AND 2 RED, GROUND
6 HOT PEPPERS, GROUND
I/2 CUP PICKLING SALT (SCANT)

Next, combine:
I-I/2 QUARTS VINEGAR
3 CUPS SUGAR (SCANT)
I CUP FLOUR
IO TABLESPOONS PREPARED MUSTARD
2 TABLESPOONS WHITE MUSTARD SEEDS
I TABLESPOON TUMERIC
2 TABLESPOONS CELERY SEED
SEVERAL WHOLE CLOVES

Combine green tomatoes, onions, cabbage,
pickles, peppers and salt in large kettle. Mix
and boil for 15 to 20 minutes. Pour into a
clean cloth and drain well. Set aside.

Combine remaining ingredients. Cook
mixture until thickened, stirring constantly,
then pour over vegetable mixture. Cook for 10
minutes. Pour into hot sterilized canning jars
and seal immediately. Approximately 9 pints.

Potato Cake

- 1 SCANT CUP BUTTER
- 2 CUPS SUGAR
- 1 CUP COOL MASHED POTATOES
- 4 EGGS
- 2 CUPS FLOUR
- 2 TEASPOONS BAKING POWDER
- 1 TO 2 TABLESPOONS COCOA OR CAROB POWDER
- 1/4 TEASPOON SALT
- 1/2 CUP MILK
- 1 TEASPOON VANILLA
- 1/2 CUP NUTS, OPTIONAL

FROSTING:

- 1 EGG, UNBEATEN
- 1-1/2 CUPS POWDERED SUGAR
- DASH OF SALT
- 1/3 CUP BUTTER, SOFTENED
- 2 TO 4 TABLESPOONS COCOA OR CAROB POWDER
- 1 TEASPOON VANILLA

Whip butter and add sugar and cooled potatoes. Add eggs and beat thoroughly. Combine dry ingredients and add alternately to the potato mixture with the milk and vanilla. Pour into two 8-inch greased cake pans. Bake in a 350° oven for 30 to 35 minutes or until cake tests done. Cool.

Combine frosting ingredients and beat until creamy and fluffy. Fill and frost cake. 8 slices.

Note: Three thin layers may be made instead of two. Double the frosting recipe if the extra layer is desired and cut the baking time by 5 minutes.

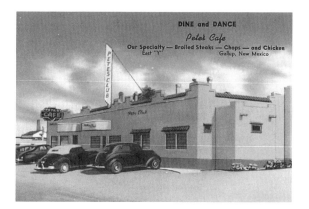

H ispanic and Native American cuisine reigns supreme in this spectacular state. Popularity has elevated this satisfying food to nationwide renown. Perhaps the most essential ingredient for any indigenous recipe is the chile pepper that grows in some 2,000 varieties. New Mexico chiles are served fresh, roasted, stewed, and fried. The "hotness" varies, depending on growing conditions and variety.

Many New Mexico recipes have a foundation in pinto beans, cheese, chile, and tortillas. Tortillas are the fastest growing segment of the baking industry. Salsa sales have overtaken ketchup. Strong multi-dimensional seasonings add zest and character to the food.

The official New Mexico state vegetables are chiles and pinto beans. The official state cookie is the bizcochito. Spectacular native dishes include sopaipillas, chorizo burritos, huevos rancheros, carne adovada, tamales, Navajo tacos, and piki bread. The New Mexico wine industry is more than three centuries old. Franciscan priests were producing wine here as early as 1602. Vine cuttings came by way of the Camino Real from Mexico where the fertile valley of the Rio Grande offers a fine climate for cultivation.

In New Mexico, travelers can spend the night where a stagecoach regularly stopped on the Camino Real. They can attend a Pinto Bean Fiesta or eat in an elegant colonial mansion where the constitution of New Mexico was signed. They may decide to experience a gourmet breakfast surrounded by the architecture of Bart Prince, or have breakfast at a hotel where movie stars have produced spectacular Hollywood westerns. Route 66 in New Mexico remains the Land of Enchantment!

Glenrio

(now abandoned)

WHAT TO SEE:

FIRST AND LAST
Decaying corpse of "First in Texas, Last in Texas" Motel and Cafe sign. Stand in the empty street by the wooden state line marker and put one foot in Deaf Smith County, Texas, the other in Quay County, New Mexico.

San Jon

population 300

WHAT TO SEE:

ORIGINAL 66 Take a 20-mile gravel stretch of original Route 66 between Glenrio and San Jon.

AMPHITHEATER A 1000-seat outdoor theater is located on the bluff of the Llano Estacado where the exploits of Billy the Kid are portrayed each summer. 10 miles south on NM 469.
(505) 461-1694

GOOD FOOD IN TUCUMCARI:

When Lillian Redman shared this custard bread pudding recipe with me, she also shared many of her highway memories, gathered from her days as a Harvey Girl and later as the operator of the Blue Swallow Motel. Always a friend to those along the highway, she symbolizes all that is good about the historic road.

Lillian Redman's Custard Pudding

2 CUPS BREAD OR CAKE CUBES

1 QUART WARM MILK

3 TABLESPOONS MARGARINE

2 EGGS

1/4 CUP SUGAR

1 TEASPOON VANILLA

1/4 TEASPOON NUTMEG

1/2 TEASPOON SALT

Sprinkle bread cubes in a greased 2-quart baking dish. Heat milk and add margarine. Continue heating until margarine has melted. Beat eggs well and add sugar, vanilla, nutmeg, and salt. Gradually pour egg mixture into the milk. Pour liquid over bread in baking dish. Set baking dish in pan of warm water and place in a 350° oven for 1 hour.

Serve custard pudding warm or cold. It is good with fruit sauce or whipped cream. Hot fudge sauce, butterscotch sauce, or crushed fruit also makes a nice topping. 8 servings.

Chorizo sausage came to America because of its popularity in Spain. The sausage is coarsely textured and very spicy. Widely used for cooking, it is also suitable for slicing and can be found in many specialty shops in western Route 66 communities. This frittata makes a great brunch.

Chorizo, Onion, and Potato Frittata

1/2 CUP OLIVE OIL OR VEGETABLE OIL

2 POUNDS RUSSET POTATOES, PEELED AND SLICED IN 1/4 INCH SLICES

2 ONIONS, SLICED IN 1/4 INCH SLICES

8 OUNCES CHORIZO SAUSAGE

12 EGGS

SALT AND PEPPER TO TASTE

Heat oil in a large heavy skillet. Add potatoes in batches and cook until tender and golden brown, about 8 minutes. Drain on paper towel.

Pour off all but 1 tablespoon of the oil. Add onions and sauté over medium low heat until translucent. Increase heat and add sausage, crumbling with back of spoon. Cook for 5 minutes. Transfer onions and sausage to a large bowl, and add potatoes. Mix and toss together.

Preheat broiler. Beat eggs to blend. Pour over potato mixture. Season with salt and pepper. Spray a 12-inch broilerproof skillet with nonstick spray. Pour egg-potato mixture into skillet. Reduce heat in broiler and cook frittata until eggs are set, about 10 minutes. Broil frittata until top is lightly browned, about 3 to 4 minutes. Slide out onto plate and

Tucumcari

population 6900

WHAT TO SEE:

BLUE SWALLOW MOTEL Lillian Redman, a former Harvey Girl, has run the Blue Swallow since 1958. The motel is now for sale. 815 E. Tucumcari Blvd.

TEPEE CURIOS Across the street from the Blue Swallow.

TUCUMCARI HISTORICAL MUSEUM 416 S. Adams

WHERE TO EAT:

DEL'S RESTAURANT Good food in Tucumcari since the early 1940s, 1202 E. Tucumcari Blvd.

EL TORO CAFE 107 S. 1st St.

LA CITA Eat under a Mexican sombrero! 812 S. 1st St.

Santa Rosa

population 2300

WHAT TO SEE:

BLUE HOLE This clear artesian spring is 87 feet deep. La Pradira Lane.

SCENIC DRIVE Take SR 91 10 miles south to Puerto de Luna where Coronado once camped.

HISTORIC CLUB CAFE Now closed.

SANTA ROSA LAKE STATE PARK Occasional eagle sightings, fishing. Drive seven miles north on NM 91.

OLD 66 TO SANTA FE To follow the original 1926 alignment of Route 66, turn north on Highway 84 to Dilla, Ribera, Rowe, and Santa Fe.

WHERE TO EAT:

JOSEPH'S RESTAURANT On Route 66 since 1956. 865 Will Rogers Dr.

COMET DRIVE-INN RESTAURANT 217 Parker. (505) 472-3663

cut into wedges. Serve while hot with salsa, guacamole, sour cream, fresh tomatoes, and homemade toast. 8 servings.

GOOD FOOD IN SANTA ROSA

Chef Ron Chavez of Club Cafe fame is no longer in business, but his reputation carries on. Ron and his family suggest travelers now try good New Mexico flavor at the Comet Drive Inn Restaurant and at Joseph's Restaurant. Chavez says that a New Mexico red chile is ranked the best in the world! And New Mexico chile is what makes authentic Mexican food outstanding! Olé! Enjoy! After a meal that is both flavorful and spicy, taste buds need a satisfying complement. In a recipe booklet Chavez put out several years ago, he included this recipe for Natillas, a soothing dessert.

Ron Chavez's Natilla

4-1/2 CUPS MILK

1/2 CUP WHITE FLOUR

2 EGGS, SEPARATED

1 CUP SUGAR

1 TEASPOON CINNAMON

1 TEASPOON NUTMEG

1 TEASPOON VANILLA

Warm 4 cups of the milk in a saucepan until it almost reaches the boiling point, but does not boil. (Small bubbles should form around the edge of the pan.) To the milk, add a mixture of beaten egg yolks, flour, sugar, and cinnamon blended with 1/2 cup cold milk. Boil mixture until thickened. A spoon should be coated with the custard when thick enough. Remove from heat and add vanilla and nutmeg. Fold in stiffly beaten egg whites. Serve the custard warm or cold. 8 servings.

GOOD FOOD IN SANTA FE:

Kathi Ackerman leads a busy life and thrives on all the activity. She operates the Bed and Breakfast of New Mexico Reservation Service and runs a bed and breakfast in her own home, "Adobe A."

Through The Bakery, her wholesale baking outlet, she also serves a number of regular clients including Off the Wall Gallery on Canyon Road and Dancing Ground of the Sun Bed and Breakfast.

Kathi bakes daily for her guests and prepares mouthwatering recipes like pannokuken, Santa Fe granola, piñon apricot scones, and star fruit juice. Most of her recipes come from her family but have been revised to incorporate Southwestern foods.

Here is a recipe that is popular in the region because of the use of piñon nuts. If piñon nuts aren't available, substitute slivered almonds. To roast piñon nuts, place on ungreased cookie sheet and bake at 350° until lightly browned, stirring often.

Kathi Ackerman's Piñon Pineapple Muffins

3 TABLESPOONS BUTTER
2 EGGS BEATEN LIGHTLY
3/4 CUP BROWN SUGAR, PACKED
1 CUP CRUSHED CANNED PINEAPPLE, INCLUDING LIQUID
1-3/4 CUP FLOUR
2 TEASPOONS BAKING POWDER
1/2 TEASPOON SALT
1/4 TEASPOON BAKING SODA
3/4 CUP ROASTED PIÑON NUTS

Santa Fe
population 65,000

WHAT TO SEE:

ART AND ARCHITECTURE A city filled with pueblo architecture and spectacular art. Galleries throughout the city but especially on Canyon Road.

MANY ATTRACTIONS The Plaza, churches, museums, and sculpture gardens.

SPANISH MARKET Spanish Market, last weekend each July. The largest market for traditional handmade Hispanic goods in the country.

WINTER MARKET Winter Market, each December. A smaller version of the summer Spanish Market.

INDIAN MARKET Indian Market, second weekend each August.

SANTA FE OPERA (505) 985-5900

WHERE TO EAT:

PINK ADOBE 406 Old Santa Fe Trail

LA TERTULIA 416 Agua Fria

LA CHOZA 905 Alarid

TIA SOFIA'S Especially for breakfast. 210 W. San Francisco.

WHERE TO STAY:

TOPPING:

1 TABLESPOON SUGAR
1/4 TEASPOON GROUND CINNAMON

In a bowl soften butter and add lightly beaten eggs and brown sugar. Mix well. Add the pineapple and liquid. Combine dry ingredients and add to the butter and pineapple mixture. Blend well. Stir in roasted piñon nuts.

Pour batter into greased muffin tins and bake in a 325° oven for 25 minutes.

Combine topping of sugar and cinnamon. Sprinkle on each muffin. 6 jumbo or 12 regular muffins.

The charm and mystery of Kachina deities can be felt at Four Kachinas Inn, built in 1992 by owners and art collectors, John Daw and Andrew Beckerman. Located just a half block from the state Capitol, the inn was designed with the pitched tin-roof style of turn-of-the-century northern New Mexico. Four rooms are named after Hopi Kachinas, the supernatural beings who live in the San Francisco Peaks. Behind the inn, an additional cottage houses another guest room with ten-foot ceilings and the original claw foot tub. A guest lounge/trading post filled with art, books, and maps makes a comfortable place to relax and enjoy refreshments.

Each morning, host John Daw delivers guests a gourmet continental breakfast including his freshly baked breads and pastries. This coconut pound cake took the "Best of Show" award at the 1992 Santa Fe County Fair.

FOUR KACHINAS INN

Coconut Pound Cake

2 CUPS SUGAR

2 CUPS FLOUR

1 SMALL CAN (5 OUNCES) EVAPORATED MILK
PLUS WATER TO MAKE 1 CUP

3/4 POUND (3 STICKS) BUTTER, MELTED

1 TEASPOON VANILLA EXTRACT

1 TEASPOON ALMOND EXTRACT

5 EGGS

1 CAN (3-1/2 OUNCES) ANGEL-FLAKE
COCONUT

Combine sugar and flour in large bowl.
Add evaporated milk and water, melted
butter, vanilla and almond extracts; mix
thoroughly until batter is smooth. Add eggs
one a time, beating well after each addition.
Fold in the coconut. Pour batter into four
greased and floured 3 x 5-1/2 x 2-1/2 loaf
pans. Bake in preheated 325° oven for 40 to
50 minutes. Cool in pans for 5 minutes then
turn out onto racks to cool.

To bake in a bundt pan, allow 1 hour, 15
minutes. Wrap and store overnight before
serving. This cake freezes well. 4 small loaves.

*Adobe Abode offers the ultimate in bed-and-
breakfast service. The unpretentious exterior
doesn't prepare one for the fresh, crisp southwestern
charm found inside. Built in 1907, the inn was
once officers' quarters for Ft. Marcy, but today
reflects Native American, Hispanic, and Anglo
cultures with no two rooms alike. Antiques from
Europe, Spanish Colonial furniture, folk art of
Oaxaca, puppets from Java, and items that owner
Pat Harbour has gathered from the Provence area
of France all blend tastefully to reflect a passion for
art and design.*

Three guest rooms are in the restored home and three more with private entrances and patios are in a walled courtyard behind the main house. All have amenities found in the finest country inns. Breakfast at the Adobe Abode can only be described as gourmet, with guests seated next to the open kitchen where Pat prepares and serves her savory meals.

ADOBE ABODE

Nancy's Butterscotch Coffee Cake

1 PACKAGE YELLOW CAKE MIX

1 PACKAGE (3 OUNCES) INSTANT BUTTER-
SCOTCH PUDDING MIX

1/2 CUP SOFT BUTTER

4 EGGS

1 CUP SOUR CREAM

1 TABLESPOON VANILLA

TOPPING:

1/2 CUP BROWN SUGAR

1-1/2 TEASPOONS CINNAMON

1/4 TEASPOON NUTMEG

1/2 CUP WALNUTS

1/2 CUP BUTTERSCOTCH CHIPS

Grease a bundt pan well. Mix up cake ingredients in a food processor. Combine topping ingredients in a small bowl. Layer two together alternately in the greased pan, then stir top slightly with a fork. Bake at 350° for 45 minutes. Do not overcook. Let sit in pan until cool, then turn upside down on a plate to serve. This cake is best if baked the day before serving. 12 servings.

ADOBE ABODE

Ginger Lime Honeydew Compote

RIND OF 1 LIME, REMOVED IN STRIPS WITH
  VEGETABLE PEELER
1/2 CUP FRESH LIME JUICE
1/2 CUP SUGAR
1 TABLESPOON GRATED PEELED FRESH
  GINGER ROOT
1/3 CUP WATER
1 HONEYDEW MELON SCOOPED INTO BALLS
SEVERAL FRESH MINT LEAVES

In a small heavy saucepan, combine rind, lime juice, sugar, ginger, and water. Bring mixture to a boil, stirring until sugar is dissolved. Boil for 3 minutes. Pour syrup through fine sieve into bowl and let cool. In serving bowl, toss the melon balls with the syrup and mint and chill, covered, for at least two hours or overnight.

Note: At the 5000-foot altitude of the city of Santa Fe, boil the mixture for 5 minutes instead of three.

Alexander's Inn is not the typical adobe design so many people equate with Santa Fe. Instead, this romantic bed and breakfast can be found in a 1903 Craftsman style home with a large front porch and lovely garden. Family antiques enhance the dormer windows, stained glass, and gleaming hardwood floors. Fresh flowers grace every room.

The Inn has won many awards including GLAMOUR MAGAZINE's "One of the most romantic inns of the Southwest." Breakfasts may include gourmet coffee, scrumptious muffins, homemade granola and fresh fruits, all served in the cozy kitchen or on the veranda surrounded with lilacs, wisteria and apricot trees.

Our Daily Granola

I LARGE BOX (42 OUNCES) OLD-FASHIONED
  OATMEAL
I/2 CUP WHEAT GERM
I/2 CUP OAT BRAN
I/2 CUP WHEAT BRAN
I TABLESPOON CINNAMON
I CUP EACH WALNUTS, PECANS, ALMONDS
I CUP CANOLA OIL
I CUP HONEY
I CUP MAPLE SYRUP
I CUP MOLASSES
3 TABLESPOONS VANILLA
2 TEASPOONS SALT
I CUP EACH COCONUT, CHOPPED DATES,
  DRIED CRANBERRIES, RAISINS, OR OTHER
  DRIED FRUIT TO TASTE

Preheat oven to 350°. In a large roasting
pan combine oatmeal, wheat germ, oat bran,
wheat bran, cinnamon, and salt. Stir in
chopped nuts. Then add oil, honey, syrup,
molasses, and vanilla until ingredients are
coated. Bake 30 minutes, stirring every 10
minutes. Remove from oven and add dried
fruit. Freezes well. 12 cups.

Apple Muffins

3 CUPS CHOPPED APPLES
I CUP WHITE SUGAR
I CUP BROWN SUGAR
I TEASPOON SALT
2 TEASPOONS SODA
I TABLESPOON CINNAMON
I CUP VEGETABLE OIL
3 EGGS
2 CUPS CHOPPED NUTS
2 TEASPOONS VANILLA
3-I/2 CUPS FLOUR

Preheat oven to 350°. Grease 24 muffin tins. Thoroughly combine apples and sugar, then add salt, soda, and cinnamon. Mix well. Stir in oil, eggs, nuts, and vanilla. Finally, stir in flour. The batter will be thick and gooey. Fill muffin tins 2/3 full. Bake 30 minutes. 24 muffins.

Preston House became the first bed and breakfast in Santa Fe when Signe Bergman opened the historic home in 1981. Her background in art and design is apparent in its cozy and romantic rooms. The home, built in 1886, is on the National Register of Historic Places. It remains the only known Queen Anne style structure in New Mexico besides the Montezuma Hotel near Las Vegas. George Cuyler Preston was a land speculator active in politics of territorial New Mexico.

Today there are six rooms in the main house, two garden cottages, and an adobe compound across the street in western architectural style. Preston House is featured in many guide books, travel articles, and as a "Great Country Inn" on the Discovery channel.

PRESTON HOUSE
Dill Bread

1 PACKAGE DRY YEAST

1/4 CUP WARM WATER

1 CUP LARGE CURD COTTAGE CHEESE

1 EGG, BEATEN

2 TABLESPOONS GRATED ONION

1 TABLESPOON MELTED BUTTER

1 TABLESPOON SUGAR

1 TABLESPOON DILL SEEDS

1 TEASPOON SALT

1/4 TEASPOON BAKING SODA

2-1/2 CUPS SIFTED FLOUR

MELTED BUTTER AND COARSE SALT

Algodones

population 175

WHAT TO SEE:

DESERT BEAUTY Halfway between Santa Fe and Albuquerque: high desert beauty including horseback riding, snow skiing, and golfing.

AMUSEUMENTS Nearby casino gambling and horse racing.

OLD 66 Follow pre-1938 Route 66 for 45 uninterrupted miles south on NM 313 into Albuquerque then NM 314 on to Los Lunas.

WHERE TO STAY:

HACIENDA VARGAS BED AND BREAKFAST INN P.O. Box 307, 1431 El Camino Real on Historic Route 66. Paul and Julia De Vargas . (505) 867-9115 or (800) 261-0006

Dissolve yeast in warm water and let stand about 10 minutes.

Heat cheese to lukewarm and combine with yeast, egg, onion, melted butter, sugar, dill seed, salt, and soda. Gradually add flour, beating thoroughly after each addition. Place dough in buttered bowl and let rise until doubled. Punch down, knead one minute and turn into a buttered 1-1/2 quart casserole. Cover and let rise 3 to 40 minutes. Bake in a 375° oven for 30 to 35 minutes. Brush top with butter and salt when done. 1 loaf.

GOOD FOOD IN ALGODONES:

Hacienda Vargas Bed and Breakfast Inn has been carefully restored and beautifully furnished by Paul and Julia Vargas to offer a peaceful retreat and the opportunity to experience pristine vistas and rich New Mexico ethnic traditions.

The original building was once a stagecoach stop on El Camino Real, an Indian trading center, and a U.S. post office. An early adobe chapel is perfectly preserved within the enclosed compound. Located on historic Route 66, Hacienda Vargas has five suites and two rooms artistically decorated to provide both comfort and privacy. Jacuzzis, kiva fireplaces, a courtyard that encloses a 200-year old tree, original adobe, and historic surroundings add to the magic in this Land of Enchantment historical hacienda.

To complete the experience, Frances Vargas prepares and serves gourmet southwestern breakfasts in the comfortable dining room.

HACIENDA VARGAS
Chorizo Roll

4 LINKS MEXICAN CHORIZO SAUSAGE

12 EGGS

1-1/2 CUPS MILK

2 CUPS CHEDDAR CHEESE

SALT AND PEPPER TO TASTE

2 CUPS CUBED FRENCH BREAD

8 OUNCES CREAM CHEESE

1 TABLESPOON DICED GREEN CHILE

Fry chorizo, chop into small pieces, and drain. Beat eggs and add all ingredients except cream cheese and green chile. Mix softened cream cheese with green chile and set aside. Spray a jelly roll pan with cooking spray. Line pan with foil, including sides and spray generously again. Spread egg mixture in pan. Bake 45 minutes in a 350° oven until eggs are firm. Allow eggs to cool, then turn out onto waxed paper, carefully peeling off foil using waxed paper to help. Spread cream cheese and green chile mixture over entire surface. Roll egg mixture into tight cylinder. Garnish with avocado and salsa recipe below. 6 servings.

HACIENDA VARGAS
Salsa

2 LARGE TOMATOES

1/2 CUP TOMATO SAUCE

2/3 CUP GREEN CHILE ROASTED OR 4
    JALAPEÑOS, PEELED AND CHOPPED

1/3 CUP YELLOW ONIONS

1 TABLESPOON FRESH CILANTRO, FINELY
    CHOPPED

2 TEASPOONS FRESH PARSLEY FINELY
    CHOPPED

2 TEASPOONS RED WINE VINEGAR

1 TEASPOON FRESHLY SQUEEZED LEMON
    JUICE

1 SMALL HOT DRIED RED PEPPER, CRUSHED

Combine all ingredients in a medium bowl, let salsa sit at room temperature for 1/2 hour then refrigerate. 3 cups

Savory Potato Pancakes

3 LARGE POTATOES, PEELED
2 TABLESPOONS FINELY GRATED ONION
3 EGGS
I TEASPOON SALT
PEPPER TO TASTE
FRESHLY GRATED NUTMEG TO TASTE
1/3 CUP ALL-PURPOSE FLOUR
OIL OR BUTTER FOR FRYING

TOPPING:

APPLESAUCE
SOUR CREAM

Grate the potatoes by hand or in a food processor, pressing out excess moisture between paper towels. Stir in the onion, eggs, salt, pepper, nutmeg, and flour. Heat a thin layer of oil or butter in a heavy skillet. Drop the potato mixture by heaping tablespoons into the oil, flattening each mound with a spatula. Fry the pancakes for about 3 to 4 minutes on each side, until uniformly crisp and golden brown. Drain on paper towels. Serve hot with applesauce and sour cream. 6 servings.

Jake Lovato, artist, gallery owner, and community supporter is the founder of the annual Cowboy Dutch Oven Cookoff. Used by pioneer cooks, chuck wagon operators, and cowboys across the West, Dutch ovens are heavy cast-iron pots with three short legs and a lid with a lip to hold coals on top. The Dutch oven is probably an ancestor to today's crock pots. Dutch oven heat is regulated by coals and Jake hopes to become the master. Those entering his contest must bring all their own ingredients, including the Dutch oven. Jake furnishes the coals. Prizes are awarded in several categories. Along the way, Jake has developed this great cornbread recipe, guaranteed to please.

Jake Lovato's Creamy Corn Bread

1 CUP BUTTER (AT ROOM TEMPERATURE)

3/4 CUP SUGAR

4 EGGS

HANDFUL OF REAL GREEN CHILE (TO TASTE)

1 CAN (15-1/2 OUNCES) CREAM-STYLE CORN

1/2 CUP GRATED MONTEREY JACK CHEESE

1 CUP FLOUR

1 CUP CORNMEAL

2 TABLESPOONS BAKING POWDER

1 TEASPOON SALT

Cream the butter, sugar, and eggs. Add remaining ingredients and pour into a Dutch oven. Bake until golden brown with most of the coals on the oven lid. Or wimp out and bake in a regular oven in a 9 x 9 greased pan for about 15 minutes at 350°. "But it's not as good," says Jake. (At lower altitude, bake at 375°.) 8 to 10 servings.

Bernalillo
population 6000

WHAT TO SEE:

ANNUAL NEW MEXICO WINE FESTIVAL Labor Day Weekend. Experience the flavor of 17 New Mexico wineries, good music, art, food, and other New Mexico agricultural products.

NEW MEXICO COWBOY DUTCH OVEN COOKOFF 1st weekend each June.

LAS FIESTAS DE SAN LORENZO 9th, 10th and 11th of August each year.

CORONADO STATE MONUMENT Includes a large Pueblo with 1,200 rooms excavated in the 1930s. 2 miles northwest on SR 44.

JEMEZ MOUNTAIN TRAIL DRIVE A day of spectacular beauty.

SILVA SALOON Open since 1933 and still operating with the third liquor license issued in New Mexico. Camino Del Pueblo (Old Route 66).

ROSE'S POTTERY HOUSE Between Silva Saloon and Range Cafe, Camino Del Pueblo (Old Route 66).

RUNNING BUFFALO ART GALLERY 168 Calle Don Francisco

WHERE TO EAT:

RANGE CAFE 925 Camino del Pueblo. (505) 867-1700

PRAIRIE STAR 1000 Jemez Canyon Dam Rd. (505) 867-3327

WHERE TO STAY:

LA HACIENDA GRANDE
21 Baros Lane, Bernalillo. (505) 867-1887 or (800) 353-1887

HACIENDA DE PLACITAS
491 Highway 165, Placitas. (505) 867-3775 or (888) 867-0082

La Hacienda Grande can be found in one of the oldest homes in New Mexico. Thought to have been built between 1711 and 1750, it was owned by several generations of the Gallegos/Montoya family until recently. The location was a terminal along El Camino Real, the famous highway from Mexico to Taos that predates 1595. Parts of the remaining structure once served as a wine cellar, granary, chapel, and stable.

Shoshona Zimmerman and her brother turned the historic hacienda into a bed and breakfast in 1993, retaining old world charm and adding amenities necessary for the comfort of today's travelers. Walls are two feet thick and until the recent renovation, most of the floors were dirt stained with ox blood. Ceilings were made of sod. "I was drawn to this part of the country for its profound spiritual quality," Shoshona explains. "There is a resonance to life here that is not found in most places."

In late 1995, La Hacienda Grande was selected by COUNTRY INNS *magazine as one of the year's Top Inn Buys.*

LA HACIENDA GRANDE
Amaretto Pancakes

I-3/4 CUPS FLOUR
I/4 CUP SUGAR
2 TABLESPOONS BAKING POWDER
4 TABLESPOONS CLARIFIED BUTTER
I EGG
I CUP MILK
I/4 CUP AMARETTO

Combine the dry ingredients and blend well. Add the liquids; stir only to blend and cook on a hot griddle, using clarified butter instead of oil. Serve with pure maple syrup. 10 to 12 pancakes.

Shoshona loves to prepare natural and healthful dishes for her guests. She says her method to clarify butter, "ghee," is the easy way, and doesn't require the careful monitoring necessary when doing this on the surface unit.

LA HACIENDA GRANDE
Clarified Butter

1 POUND BUTTER

Place one pound of butter in the oven at 300° and bake for one hour. Pour the liquid through a fine strainer and discard remaining solids. Use in place of vegetable oils to cook and bake.

At Hacienda de Placitas, guests revel in 100 year-old architecture, spectacular views, an on-site art gallery, and food recognized as some of the best in the country by BETTER HOMES AND GARDEN'S COUNTRY HOME magazine.

Carol Dinsmor, the innkeeper, is an artist specializing in jewelry, weavings, masks, and pottery. She is also a gourmet cook, having operated a cooking school and catering business before coming to New Mexico in 1992.

Hacienda de Placitas is known locally as "Windmill House." The original windmill that served the Santa Fe railway remains near the hacienda along with other portions dating to Spanish land grant days. The present 5,000 square foot hacienda includes a main reception room, three suites, kitchens, and an art gallery. Two guest houses, landscaped terraces, and a pool add to the 300 acres of high desert charm. This is a place not to miss!

66 KITSCH A giant collection of the velvet paintings, rattlesnake ashtrays, and rubber tomahawks that have lured motorists since 1934.

HACIENDA DE PLACITAS

Plum Flan with Walnut Quiche Crust

Substitute peaches, fresh-pitted cherries, or unpeeled apricots for plums in this creamy dish, or combine yellow plums and apricots for a mix of flavors. Pine nuts are a flavorful alternative to walnuts.

1-1/2 CUPS ALL-PURPOSE FLOUR

4 TEASPOONS GRANULATED SUGAR

1/4 TEASPOON SALT

1/4 TEASPOON BAKING POWDER

6 TABLESPOONS BUTTER

1/3 CUP GROUND WALNUTS

1-1/2 POUNDS SLIGHTLY FIRM PLUMS

1/2 CUP GRANULATED SUGAR

1/4 CUP PACKED BROWN SUGAR

3/4 TEASPOON GROUND CINNAMON

3 EGG YOLKS

1-1/4 CUPS DAIRY SOUR CREAM

In a large bowl stir together flour, 4 teaspoons granulated sugar, salt, and baking powder. Cut in the butter until the mixture resembles fine crumbs. Stir in the ground walnuts. Press the mixture into the bottom and up the sides of a 10-inch quiche dish. Quarter the plums and remove the pits. Arrange the plum pieces in a spoke fashion in the prepared crust. Combine 1/2 cup granulated sugar, the brown sugar, and cinnamon; sprinkle over plums.

Bake uncovered in a 400° oven for about 15 minutes. Combine the egg yolks and sour cream; pour over plums. Return quiche dish to oven and bake 25 to 30 minutes longer or until set. Cool on wire rack at least 20 minutes to set. 8 servings.

HACIENDA DE PLACITAS

Poached Pears in Burgundy Wine Sauce

For a fancier dessert, Carol sets the pears in vanilla custard then swirls some of the syrup through the custard with a spoon.

8 RIPE MEDIUM BOSC PEARS
1 CUP BURGUNDY WINE
1 CUP WATER
2 TABLESPOONS LEMON JUICE
2 TABLESPOONS SUGAR
1 PACKAGE (6 OUNCES) RASPBERRY GELATIN

Peel pears, leaving stems on. Place pears in a deep 3-quart casserole. In small saucepan bring wine and water to a boil. Add lemon juice, sugar and gelatin, stirring until dissolved.

Pour liquid over pears, turning pears to coat. Cover and bake in preheated 350° oven for 45 to 60 minutes or until pears are tender. Occasionally spoon liquid over pears to color evenly.

To serve, place pears upright in individual dishes. Pour syrup over each pear; serve warm. Garnish with edible flowers and fresh raspberries if desired. 8 servings.

GOOD FOOD FROM MORIARTY:

Pinto beans were first planted in the Estancia Valley nearly 100 years ago and for years the area was considered the pinto bean capital of the world. The city celebrates its heritage at the Annual Pinto Bean Fiesta and Cook-off held the second Saturday each October. Here are two recent winning recipes.

Moriarty

population 3000

WHAT TO SEE:

ANNUAL PINTO BEAN FIESTA Second Saturday each October. Parade, bean cookoff, food, music, and crafts. At the same time as the Albuquerque International Balloon Fiesta. Crossley Park.

WHERE TO EAT:

EL COMEDOR DE ANAYAS A long-time local favorite. West Route 66 Ave.

MAMMA ROSA'S RESTAURANT Good Italian food. E. Route 66 Ave.

STEER INN BAR B QUE W. Route 66 Ave.

Stuffed Chiles

1-1/2 CUPS COOKED PINTO BEANS

1/2 CUP COLBY JACK CHEESE, SHREDDED

1-1/2 CUPS SWISS CHEESE, SHREDDED

1 TEASPOON GARLIC POWDER

SALT AND PEPPER

12 WHOLE GREEN CHILES, ROASTED AND
  PEELED

4 EGGS

BREAD CRUMBS

VEGETABLE SHORTENING FOR FRYING

Mash beans. Add cheeses, garlic powder, salt and pepper, and blend well. Make a small slice in each whole chile to enable stuffing. Place about 4 tablespoons of bean mixture in each chile. Beat eggs until frothy. Dip chiles into egg and roll in bread crumbs. Pan fry until golden and cheese is melting. 6 servings.

Pinto Bean/Chocolate Chip Cookies

1/2 CUP VEGETABLE SHORTENING

1 CUP BROWN SUGAR, PACKED

1 EGG, WELL BEATEN

1 CUP PUREED COOKED PINTO BEANS

2 CUPS FLOUR

1 TEASPOON CINNAMON

1/2 TEASPOON SALT

1 TEASPOON SODA

1 CUP CHOCOLATE CHIPS

WALNUT PIECES

Cream together the shortening and brown sugar. Add egg and beans and mix well. Stir together the flour, cinnamon, salt, and soda. Add to the bean mixture and blend well. Stir in chocolate chips.

Drop by teaspoons on ungreased cookie sheet and top each cookie with a walnut piece. Bake in a 350° oven for 12 to 15 minutes. 24 to 36 cookies, depending on size.

GOOD FOOD IN ALBUQUERQUE:

Dating back to 1912, the Charles A. Bottger Mansion offers a startling reminder to Old Town visitors that residents before statehood did not always build in the traditional pueblo revival style. The graceful turn-of-the-century home was built by architect Edward Christy in the then-popular "American Foursquare" style. With the arrival of Route 66, Miquela Bottger began renting rooms to travelers.

The well-preserved house is included in the National Register of Historic Landmarks and is the only lodging accommodation located in Old Town proper. Guests will find a suite and six comfortable rooms with hospitality as a hallmark. Afternoon tea is often served where these delicious and popular bizcochitos are the most popular offering. Bizcochitos are the official state cookie of New Mexico.

Breakfasts at Bottger Mansion Bed and Breakfast includes foods from the Indian, Hispanic, and Anglo cultures.

Albuquerque

population 485,000

WHAT TO SEE:

CENTRAL AVENUE An 18-mile ode to Route 66 history that includes the Kimo Theater and the De Anza and El Vado Motels.

INTERNATIONAL BALLOON FESTIVAL 9 days each October.

OLD TOWN 2000 block of Central Avenue N.W., then 1 block north.

SANDIA PEAK AERIAL TRAMWAY 11704 Coronado N.E.

NEW MEXICO MUSEUM OF NATURAL HISTORY 1801 Mountain Rd. N.W.

INDIAN PUEBLO CULTURAL CENTER 2401 12th St. N.W.

GALLERIES AND MUSEUMS University of New Mexico and accompanying galleries and museums. 640-acre campus on Central Ave.

LUMINARIAS Luminarias at Christmas throughout the city.

VINEYARDS Anderson
Valley Vineyards, Gruet
Winery, Sandia Shadow
Winery, and Sabinal
Vineyards are part of the
oldest wine growing region
in the country. (800) 374-
3061.

WHERE TO EAT:

ROSA! RESTAURANT AND
BAR 1100 San Mateo N.E.

ARTICHOKE CAFE 424
Central S.E.

SCALO NORTHERN
ITALIAN GRILL 3500
Central S.E.

DURAN CENTRAL
PHARMACY Great food in
the back, a local favorite.
1815 Central N.W. (505)
243-3639

M & J RESTAURANT /
SANITARY TORTILLA
FACTORY A place not to
be missed! 403 2nd St. S.W.

MONTE VISTA FIRE
STATION 3201 Central Ave.
N.E.

MARIA TERESA'S 618 Rio
Grande N.W. in Old Town.

LE CAFE MICHE 1431
Wyoming N.E.

STEPHEN'S RESTAURANT
1311 Tijeras Ave. N.W.

DOUBLE RAINBOW 3416
Central N.E. Fantastic
desserts.

LOS QUATES 4901 Lomas

Bizcochitos
(Anise Seed Cookies)

2 CUPS BUTTER

1-1/2 CUPS SUGAR

1 TEASPOON ANISE SEEDS

2 EGGS

6 TO 7 CUPS SIFTED FLOUR

1-1/2 TEASPOONS BAKING POWDER

1/2 TEASPOON SALT

1/4 CUP MILK (WATER, BOURBON, OR
    SHERRY MAY BE SUBSTITUTED)

2 TABLESPOONS SUGAR

1 TEASPOON CINNAMON

Cream butter, sugar, and anise seeds in a large mixing bowl. Add eggs and beat well.

Combine flour, baking powder, and salt in another mixing bowl. Add to creamed mixture along with milk or other liquid to form a stiff dough.

Knead dough slightly and pat or roll to a 1/4 to 1/2 inch thickness. Cut dough into desired shapes with cookie cutter.

Combine sugar and cinnamon in a small bowl. Dust the top of each cookie with a small amount of the mixture.

Bake on greased cookie sheets in a 400° oven for about 10 minutes or until cookies are slightly browned. 6 dozen 2-1/2-inch cookies.

Becky Steele of Albuquerque prepares this delicious chile rellenos casserole for company. Chiles rellenos are good served with a green salad and fresh fruit.

Chiles Rellenos Casserole

6 EGGS, SEPARATED

1 TABLESPOON FLOUR

1/4 TEASPOON SALT

1/4 TEASPOON PEPPER

1 CAN (4 OUNCES) WHOLE GREEN CHILES

1/2 POUND SHREDDED CHEDDAR CHEESE

Lightly spray an 8 x 11 x 2 inch baking pan with nonstick spray. Beat egg whites until stiff. Combine flour, salt and pepper with egg yolks. Fold into whites and pour half of the mixture into baking pan. Slit chiles lengthwise and lay flat over egg mixture. Cover with grated cheese. Pour on remaining egg mixture. Bake in a 325° oven for 25 minutes. 4 servings.

Casas de Sueños Bed and Breakfast Inn offers a distinctive stay in a compound built in the 1930s by eccentric artist J.R. Willis who used the main building for his studio and added extra casitas for his artistic friends. Nineteen guest cottages are scattered among lush gardens, fountains, original works of art, winding paths, and secluded courtyard seating.

Hovering above the main entrance to the adobe compound is the mystical sculpture-like structure that was an early design by world famous architect Bart Prince. Dubbed "the snail," by lawyer/owner Robert Hanna, this "dream room" makes a spectacular architectural statement as it rises into the Albuquerque sky.

Each casita is tastefully decorated with tempting names like O'Keefe, Kachina, and Route 66. Several friendly on-staff innkeepers offer hors d'oeuvres each afternoon and sumptuous breakfasts

FRONTIER RESTAURANT A long-time Route 66 and university favorite. 2400 Central N.E.

LINDY'S Narke and Steve Vatoseow run this Route 66 eatery across from Kimo Theater. 500 Central S.W.

THE ROUTE 66 DINER 1405 Central Ave. S.E.

WHERE TO STAY:

BOTTGER MANSION BED AND BREAKFAST 110 San Felipe N.W. (505) 243-3639

CASAS DE SUENOS BED AND BREAKFAST INN 310 Rio Grande Blvd. S.W. (800) 242-8987

WILLIAM MAUGER ESTATE BED AND BREAKFAST 701 Roma N.W. (505) 243-3639 or (505) 242-8755

WHERE TO EAT:

LUNA MANSION Built in 1881, an elegant piece of New Mexico history, now an upscale restaurant.

WHAT TO DO:

HISTORIC ROUTE 66 Take NM 6, historic Route 66, for 33 miles to Correo. It is also 33 miles to Correo from Albuquerque west on I-40.

alone or in the sunny dining room or nearby patio. Casas de Sueños truly lives up to its name, "House of Dreams" (and memories) in New Mexico, The Land of Enchantment.

CASAS DE SUEÑOS
Sueños Chile Braid

8 OUNCES SAUSAGE

2 MEDIUM POTATOES, CUBED

1/2 CUP CHOPPED ONION

3 CLOVES GARLIC, MINCED

1/4 CUP CHOPPED GREEN PEPPER

1/4 CUP CHOPPED RED PEPPER

1/2 CUP CHOPPED GREEN CHILES

1 TABLESPOON CHOPPED FRESH CILANTRO

1 TEASPOON CUMIN

1 TEASPOON OREGANO

1 CUP GRATED CHEDDAR CHEESE

1 SHEET FROZEN PUFFED PASTRY

1 EGG, BEATEN

Sauté all the above ingredients except the cheese, pastry, and egg. Combine cheese with the sautéed mixture.

Prepare the sheet of frozen puffed pastry by rolling out to a 12 x 16 rectangle. Make diagonal 3-inch slices down each side about 1 inch apart. Spoon the sausage filling down the center of the pastry leaving strips free to fold over the center in a braid. Starting at the top, take a strip from each side and with moistened fingertips press the pastry strips together. Continue braiding strips from each side all the way to the bottom.

The filling should be completely enclosed inside the pastry. (For a little added interest, you can shape the pastry into the chile pepper shape and sprinkle with cayenne pepper.) Place on a greased baking sheet and brush with a beaten egg. Bake in a 400° oven for 30 minutes. Can be served with salsa and sour cream if desired. 8 to 10 servings.

Tortilla Soup has many variations. This one is particularly good. Adjust the spiciness to taste.

Tortilla Soup

2 TABLESPOONS CORN OIL

4 CORN TORTILLAS, CUT IN 1-INCH STRIPS

3 CLOVE GARLIC, MINCED

2 MEDIUM ONIONS, CHOPPED

4 TOMATOES, SKINNED AND CHOPPED

1 TABLESPOON GROUND CUMIN

1/2 TO 1 JALAPEÑO PEPPER (DEPENDING ON HEAT DESIRED)

8 CUPS CHICKEN STOCK

1/4 CUP FRESH CILANTRO

1 CUP DICED COOKED CHICKEN

SALT AND PEPPER TO TASTE

GARNISHES:

EXTRA CRISP FRIED STRIPS OF TORTILLA

GRATED CHEDDAR CHEESE

DICED AVOCADO

CHOPPED CILANTRO

Heat oil in 4-quart stockpot and fry tortilla strips. Add garlic and onions and cook until onions are soft. Add remaining ingredients except chicken, bring to a boil, then simmer in covered container for 20 minutes. Add chicken and continue simmering for 5 minutes more. Taste and add salt or pepper to taste. Serve with garnishes in separate bowls. 8 generous servings.

Grants

population 8900

WHAT TO SEE:

ICE CAVES AND BANDERA CRATER Twenty-five minutes southwest on SR 53.

EL MORRO NATIONAL MONUMENT Southwest on SR 53 another 15 minutes from Ice Caves.

EL MALPAIS NATIONAL MONUMENT South and Southwest on SR 53 and 117.

NEW MEXICO MUSEUM OF MINING Corner of Sante Fe and Irons. (505) 287-4802

MT. TAYLOR One of the Navajo's four sacred mountains. SR 547 north from Grants .

PUEBLO OF ACOMA Oldest continuously inhabited city in the United States. Twenty minutes east of Grants on I-40, take exit 102 south. (505) 470-4966

THE URANIUM CAFE AND THE MONTE CARLO RESTAURANT Part of Route 66 since the 1940s.

WHERE TO EAT:

GRANT'S STATION RESTAURANT 200 W. Santa Fe

GOOD FOOD IN GRANTS:

Fajitas first became popular in the southwest in the late 1980s. Ron Chavez of the fabled Club Cafe in Santa Rosa referred to fajitas as "the new rage of the age." Whatever the name, the mouthwatering aroma and sizzle as fajitas are presented hot from the kitchen make them an instant success. Here are two versions of the popular dish that are served frequently in Grants.

Sizzling Fajitas

3/4 CUP ITALIAN DRESSING
1 CAN (14 OUNCES) GREEN CHILES, DICED
1-1/2 POUNDS OF SKIRT OR FLANK STEAK
1 LARGE ONION, SLICED LENGTHWISE
1 BELL PEPPER
10 FLOUR TORTILLAS

TOPPINGS:

SLICED AVOCADO
SHREDDED CHEDDAR CHEESE
SOUR CREAM
JALAPEÑO PEPPER SLICES

Combine dressing and chiles in 9 x 13 pan. Add meat, turning to coat with the mixture. Cover and refrigerate several hours or overnight, turning occasionally. Grill or broil meat, onions, and pepper to desired doneness. Slice meat across the grain, 1/2 inch thick. Fill warm flour tortillas with meat, onion, pepper and any toppings desired. Serve while hot. 10 servings.

Santa Fe Fajitas

1/4 CUP SOY SAUCE

1/4 CUP PINEAPPLE JUICE

3 TEASPOONS COMMERCIAL FAJITA MIX

1 POUND FLANK, SIRLOIN, CUBE STEAK, OR BONELESS CHICKEN BREASTS, CUT IN THIN STRIPS

2 TABLESPOONS VEGETABLE OIL

1 MEDIUM ONION, THINLY SLICED

1 BELL PEPPER, THINLY SLICED

6 FLOUR TORTILLAS, WARMED

GARNISH OF SALSA, GUACAMOLE AND SOUR CREAM

Combine soy sauce, pineapple juice and fajita mix. Stir well and set aside. In a large skillet, brown meat in oil. Add onion and bell pepper and cook 5 minutes. Stir in fajita mixture and cook 5 minutes more. Pile fajitas in warm tortillas. Top with your favorite salsa, guacamole, and/or sour cream. Fold or roll tortilla. 6 servings.

GOOD FOOD IN GALLUP:

In the 3rd Annual Indian Country Dining Guide, published by CMA Advertising in Gallup, local residents were invited to share favorite Southwestern recipes with their neighbors. Salsa, Navajo fry bread, enchilada casseroles, sopaipillas, green chile stew, piñon cookies, guacamole, chile con queso, gazpacho, and a wide variety of other spicy favorites were included. Here are some delicious examples.

Continental Divide

WHERE TO STAY:

STAUDER'S NAVAJO LODGE BED AND BREAKFAST 3 miles west of Continental Divide at Coolidge, Exit 44, West Coolidge Rd. Sherwood and Roberta Stauder.

Ft. Wingate

WHERE TO EAT:

LOST OASIS CAFE Open for lunch and dinner, closed Sundays. Bear Springs Plaza.

Gallup

population 19,200

WHAT TO SEE:

NATIVE CULTURES Neighboring Navajo, Hopi, and Zuni Nations.

ANNUAL GALLUP INTER-TRIBAL INDIAN CEREMONIAL Red Rock State Park, 8 miles east of Gallup. Second week in August.

RICHARDSON'S TRADING POST

THE FINAL 16 MILES of The Main Street of America in New Mexico. Continue west from Gallup on NM 118 to Arizona.

WHERE TO EAT:

**EL RANCHO HOTEL
DINING ROOM** 1000 East
Highway 66

**EARL'S FAMILY
RESTAURANT** Serving
Route 66 customers since
1947. A good place to stop.
1400 E. Highway 66.

PANZ ALEGRA 1202 E.
Highway 66

THE BUTCHER SHOP
2003 W. Highway 66

EAGLE CAFE A historic
location! 220 W. Highway
66.

RANCH KITCHEN Over 40
years on Route 66. 3001 W.
Route 66.

**LA BARRACA FAMILY
RESTAURANT** 1303 E.
Highway 66

**PEDRO'S MEXICAN
RESTAURANT** Where many
locals eat. 107 Burke Drive

VIRGIE'S RESTAURANT
5800 W. Highway 66

"A-OK" CAFE Inside the
Shush Yaz Trading
Company. Where the locals
go for a great lunch. 214 W.
Aztec

WHERE TO
STAY:

EL RANCHO HOTEL
Opened in 1937, a favorite
Route 66 stop. A must see
location!

Mary Muller's Posole Stew

1 POUND LEAN PORK SHOULDER
2 POUNDS FROZEN POSOLE (HOMINY)
JUICE OF ONE LIME
2 TABLESPOONS COARSE RED CHILE
3 CLOVE GARLIC
1/4 TEASPOON DRIED OREGANO
SALT AND PEPPER TO TASTE

Cook the pork in a pressure cooker with water to cover for 20 minutes. Reduce pressure under cold water. Open pot and add posole, lime juice and chile. Add water, about twice as much as the amount of posole. Cook under pressure for 45 minutes. Reduce pressure again under cold water. Remove the pork and cut it into small pieces. Return to cooker. Add garlic, oregano and salt and pepper to taste. Continue to simmer without pressure for another hour or until hominy has burst but is not mushy. Serve as a main coarse or as a side dish. 6 to 8 servings.

Note: The times are set here for high altitude. At lower altitude, shorter cooking times will be needed.

Martha Joe's Navajo Fry Bread

3 CUPS FLOUR (ALL WHITE OR HALF WHOLE
   WHEAT)
1-1/2 TEASPOONS BAKING POWDER
1/2 TEASPOON SALT
1-1/3 CUPS WARM WATER
SHORTENING

Use either white or half whole wheat flour. Mix flour, baking powder, and salt. Add warm water to make a soft dough. Knead until smooth. Tear off a chunk of dough about the size of a small peach. Pat and stretch until it is thin. Poke a hole through the center and drop in sizzling hot deep fat (375°). Lard is the traditional shortening, but many use vegetable oil today. Brown on both sides. Drain and serve hot. Eat with honey or jam. 10 to 12 pieces.

Gazpacho New Mexico

A delectable and cooling "liquid salad" from Spain with a special New Mexico touch.

2 POUNDS TOMATOES

1 CUCUMBER

1 LARGE ONION

1/2 GREEN PEPPER

1/4 CUP OLIVE OIL

1 CUP TOMATO JUICE

1 CAN (4 OUNCES) DICED GREEN CHILE

2 LARGE CLOVES GARLIC, MINCED

1 TABLESPOON VINEGAR

SALT AND PEPPER TO TASTE

Dice half the tomatoes, cucumber, onion, and green pepper and set aside in a bowl. Combine the remaining vegetables and green chiles in a blender or food processor. Add the tomato juice, garlic, olive oil, and vinegar. Blend until smooth. Pour over bowl of chopped vegetables. Stir well and season to taste. Cover and chill thoroughly. Serve while very cold with garlic croutons or hot garlic bread. 8 servings.

There are several versions of Mexican Wedding Cookies. This one, using real butter and cake flour, is exceptionally good. After baking, there is a small hole in the center of each cookie. This is a recipe where substitutions don't work. Use real butter and cake flour.

Mexican Wedding Cookies

2/3 CUP PECANS

1-3/4 CUPS POWDERED SUGAR

1 STICK (8 TABLESPOONS) BUTTER, SOFT-
ENED AND CUT INTO SEVERAL PIECES

3/4 CUP SOFT VEGETABLE SHORTENING

1 TEASPOON VANILLA

2-1/2 CUPS CAKE FLOUR

1/4 TEASPOON SALT

ADDITIONAL POWDERED SUGAR

Chop pecans and stir into 1/2 cup of the powdered sugar. Set aside. Cream the butter and shortening until fluffy, then blend in vanilla.

Add remaining powdered sugar to the creamed mixture and beat until smooth. Add flour and salt, stirring just to combine. Stir in the nuts and sugar.

Form dough into 1/2 inch balls and place 1 inch apart on two lightly buttered cookie sheets. Bake in 350° oven for 12 to 15 minutes. Cookies should not be browned. Cool on rack, then sift a light coating of powdered sugar over cookies. 5 1/2 dozen cookies.

A   R   I   Z   O   N   A

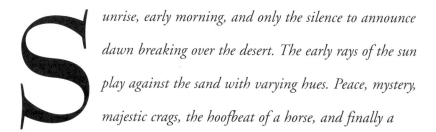

687 PAINTED DESERT, FROM HIGHWAY 66, ARIZONA

*S*unrise, early morning, and only the silence to announce dawn breaking over the desert. The early rays of the sun play against the sand with varying hues. Peace, mystery, majestic crags, the hoofbeat of a horse, and finally a cowboy's song. Arizona offers a 20th-century frontier adventure.

When travelers embrace Route 66 in Arizona, they step into a different time and space. Ancient traditions and values provide a rich perspective of life and there is a feeling of renewed strength. Rugged individuals, strong people who love life, welcome all who want the experience.

Food in Arizona is flavorful, dynamic, satisfying, yet simple. No pretense is tolerated. Travelers to Arizona will find the real thing at cafes like Joe and Aggies in Holbrook. One Easterner boasted he had never found chile too hot for his taste. Aggie brought out her best and when he could finally talk again, he admitted to having met his match.

Arizona offers experiences found nowhere else: the last Valentine Diners, gourmet dishes from El Tovar, ghostly experiences at the famous Museum Club, a bed and breakfast in an 1897 bordello, superb Chinese food, Angel Delgadillo's Snow Cap, Navajo tacos, and the unexpected surprise of Oatman, revitalized and greedy for every tourist dollar.

Arizona enhances Route 66 like no other state!

Chambers

population 450

NATIONAL MONUMENTS
24 miles west is the Petrified Forest National Park and Painted Desert. Take Exit 311 off I-40.

Holbrook

population 5,900

WHAT TO SEE:

NAVAJO COUNTY COURT HOUSE AND MUSEUM
On the National Register of Historic Places. 100 E. Arizona St.

THE BLEVINS HOUSE AND BUCKET OF BLOOD SALOON

SYDNEY SAPP HOUSE
Call the Chamber of Commerce at (800) 524-2459 for information on these Holbrook events:

OLD WEST CELEBRATION
First weekend in June.

NATIVE AMERICAN INDIAN DANCES June through August.

GATHERING OF EAGLES ART SHOW Each July.

SOUTHWEST QUILT FESTIVAL Each August.

GOOD FOOD IN HOLBROOK:

The Holbrook Summer Indian Dance Program includes this popular recipe for Navajo Tacos, shared by the Holbrook Chamber of Commerce. This popular southwestern dish is the Navajo version of a Mexican tostada. Instead of Mexican-style tortillas, Navajo fry bread forms the base for these tacos.

HOLBROOK
Navajo Tacos

TO MAKE FRY BREAD:

4 CUPS WHITE FLOUR
8 TEASPOONS BAKING POWDER
1 CUP POWDERED MILK
1 TEASPOON SALT (OPTIONAL)
WARM WATER AS NEEDED

Mix flour, baking powder, milk, and salt. Slowly add warm water to mixture to make a medium stiff dough, soft enough to easily shape, but not sticky. Hand knead to form a ball about 4 inches in diameter. Shape into 4 flat rounds about 8 inches in diameter. The dough should be about 1/4 inch thick. Use of a rolling pin is not recommended. Add a small amount of flour if the dough becomes too sticky to handle.

Deep fry in hot oil, (375°). When a large bubble forms, pop it with a fork. When the sides begin to brown, turn and finish frying on other side.

Serve while hot, topped with pinto beans, ground beef or other diced meat, diced lettuce, tomato, onion, and grated cheese. Add other toppings like guacamole, sour cream, or hot salsa if desired. 4 servings.

This pizza makes a delicious casual meal that is unusual because of the tortilla crust topped with a delicious combination of seasoned beef and chopped vegetables.

HOLBROOK
Mexican Pizza

6 OUNCES GROUND BEEF

1/2 PACKAGE (1.25 OUNCES) TACO SEASON-
   ING MIX

2 FLOUR TORTILLAS (10-INCH SIZE)

1 CUP GRATED CHEDDAR CHEESE

1 CUP GRATED MONTEREY JACK CHEESE

1 CUP CHOPPED TOMATOES, DRAINED

1/3 CUP SLICED GREEN ONION

1/4 CUP DICED BLACK OLIVES

2 TABLESPOONS MINCED GREEN PEPPER

1-1/2 TABLESPOONS SLICED PICKLED
   JALAPEÑO PEPPERS

Cook beef and taco seasoning in heavy skillet until brown, crumbling with fork until separated. Remove and cool.

In same skillet, add a tortilla and cook until crisp, about 2 minutes, turning once. Remove and cook second tortilla until crisp. Leave this tortilla in skillet and reduce heat to medium low. Sprinkle Cheddar cheese over tortilla. Top with second tortilla. Heat until cheese melts, pressing with a spatula, about 2 minutes. Preheat broiler. Transfer tortillas to a pizza pan. Top with cooked beef, sprinkle with tomato, onion, olives and green pepper. Top with Monterey Jack cheese. Broil until cheese melts, about 3 minutes. Cut into wedges and serve. 2 servings, or 6 appetizers.

Take US 180 southeast from Holbrook for the south entrance to the Petrified Forest National Park

WHERE TO EAT:

JOE AND AGGIE'S Oldest restaurant in Holbrook still in business. A lot of history here! 120 W. Hopi Dr.

BUTTERFIELD STAGE COMPANY 609 W. Hopi Dr.

WHERE TO STAY:

WIGWAM VILLAGE MOTEL Elinor Lewis, manager, is daughter of Chester Lewis who built the motel in 1950. (602) 524-3048

Joseph City

population 900

WHAT TO SEE:

JACK RABBIT TRADING
POST

Winslow

population 8,400

WHAT TO SEE:

LA POSADA The future of
this great Harvey House
remains in question. 401 E.
2nd St.

OLD TRAILS MUSEUM
One of the best regional
museums. Janice Griffith
will greet you. 212 Kingsley
Ave.

**WINSLOW CHRISTMAS
PARADE** A classic for over
50 years, includes food and
craft booths. Weekend
before Thanksgiving.

**HOMOLOVI RUINS STATE
PARK** 3 miles east to I-40.
(520) 289-4106

**LITTLE PAINTED DESERT
COUNTY PARK** Northeast
off SR 87

**SOUTH MOGOLLON RIM
DRIVE** Spectacular views!
South on highway 87 or 99.

METEOR CRATER 22 miles
west off I-40. (520) 289-
2362

*Here it is! Those giant yellow signs with the
Route 66 rabbit still entice travelers for miles.
Then all at once, here it really is! Just when you're
ready for a cold cherry cider, a new board game for
the kids, and a perfect photo opportunity, the really
big jack rabbit appears. How can anyone pass up
an opportunity like this?*

*Jack Rabbit Trading Post is the perfect place
to make today's memories. Antonio and Cindy
Jaquez keep a bit of history alive and share this
hearty corn dish.*

JACK RABBIT TRADING POST
Cindy's Corn Dish

I CAN (15-1/2 OUNCES) CREAMED-STYLE
  CORN
1/3 CUP YELLOW CORNMEAL
I CUP EVAPORATED MILK
I CUP GRATED CHEESE
I CAN (4 OUNCES) DICED GREEN CHILES
I TABLESPOON SUGAR
1/2 TEASPOON SALT

Spray an 8-inch square pan with vegetable
spray. Mix all ingredients in a large bowl.
Pour into prepared pan and bake in a 350°
oven for 35 to 45 minutes. Serve as a side dish
with diced tomatoes. 5 to 6 servings.

GOOD FOOD IN WINSLOW:

*The Falcon Restaurant has been a local
favorite since it was opened on Route 66 back in
1955. Owners Jim, George, and Pete Kretsedemas
have provided fine home-style meals to thousands
of Route 66 travelers and to generations of local
families. Their banquet room hosts local civic clubs*

and area businessmen meet there for morning coffee. Located between 2nd and 3rd streets, The Falcon Restaurant is strategically placed to accommodate one-way traffic from both directions. Winslows residents' driving habits were changed years ago when city traffic also carried cross-country travelers through town. The new interstate quarantined the city, returning most of the traffic to local residents. Pete says the city route is actually shorter than I-40 that circles north of town.

Jim, George, and Pete are among the few original restaurant owners along Route 66. The Falcon Restaurant remains a classic stop, offering the best of both worlds.

FALCON RESTAURANT
Boston Clam Chowder

2 MEDIUM ONIONS, DICED

2 CUPS SLICED CELERY

1/2 CUP DICED GREEN BELL PEPPER

1/4 CUP DICED LEEK

1 SMALL CARROT, SHREDDED

1/2 CUP SOYBEAN OIL

2 TEASPOONS WORCESTERSHIRE SAUCE

1/3 TEASPOON THYME

1/3 TEASPOON OREGANO

2 TEASPOONS ROSEMARY

1 TEASPOON SALT, OR TO TASTE

1/3 TEASPOON PEPPER

1/4 TEASPOON CAYENNE PEPPER

1/2 CUP FLOUR

2-1/2 CUPS POTATOES, DICED

2 CUPS BOILING WATER

4 CUPS WARM MILK

1 CAN CHOPPED CLAMS

Combine onion, celery, pepper, leek, and carrot in saucepan with oil. Cook slowly until tender. Add spices and flour to form a paste.

WHERE TO EAT:

FALCON RESTAURANT A Route 66 classic, and the Kretsedemas brothers will make you feel welcome! A must stop! 1113 East 3rd.

IRENE'S Across from La Posada. Eat in one of the last remaining Valentine diners and reminisce about history! 400 E. 2nd.

CAPTAIN TONY'S For pizza and other Italian food. 2217 North Park Dr.

ONE SPOT GRILL Another Valentine diner but it may be closed. On the site of the first house in Winslow. 114 E. 3rd St.

Flagstaff

population 52,000

WHAT TO SEE:

MUSEUM CLUB
Depression-era roadhouse, not to be missed! 3404 E. Route 66.

RIORDAN MANSION STATE HISTORIC PARK
1300 Riordan Ranch St.

LOWELL OBSERVATORY
Pluto was discovered here in 1930. 1400 W. Mars Hill Rd.

MUSEUM OF NORTHERN ARIZONA Native American art and artifacts, contemporary art, geology and science exhibits, nature trail. Traditional Native American summer festivals and sale exhibits. Call (520) 774-5213 for dates. Located on N. Fort Valley Rd. enroute to Grand Canyon.

ARIZONA SNOWBOWL SKI AREA AND SKYRIDE
Coconino National Forest, 14 miles north. (520) 779-1951

OAK CREEK CANYON / SEDONA Take Highway 89A south from Flagstaff to Sedona for a spectacular 16-mile drive then visit to the art center of Sedona.

Add hot water and milk. Stir to blend. Add potatoes and cook until potatoes are tender. Remove from heat and do not reheat. Heat clams separately and add to the soup. Serve and enjoy! Approximately 10 servings.

GOOD FOOD IN FLAGSTAFF:

Birch Tree Inn is a 1917 restored farmhouse with five guest rooms on the second floor. The home features a large side-wrapped porch. Owned by onetime mayor and sheriff Joseph Waldhaus for 40 years, the home became a Northeastern Arizona University fraternity house in 1969. A series of owners followed before lifelong friends Donna and Roger Pettinger and Sandy and Ed Znetko refurbished the house as Birch Tree Inn in 1989. They provide a warm welcome and wonderful food to their many guests. Sanders and Donna offer many of their favorite recipes in the BIRCH TREE INN COOKBOOK. *The book is divided into seasonal sections and offers recipes to match the climate and many activities offered in the area.*

BIRCH TREE INN

Stuffed French Toast with Praline Sauce

12 TO 14 SLICES CINNAMON RAISIN BREAD, CRUSTS REMOVED

4 OUNCES CREAM CHEESE AT ROOM TEMPERATURE

1/2 CUP CRUSHED PINEAPPLE, LIGHTLY DRAINED

2 TABLESPOONS GRATED ORANGE RIND (OPTIONAL)

5 EGGS, BEATEN

2-1/2 CUPS MILK

1 TEASPOON ALMOND FLAVORING

1 TEASPOON CINNAMON

Spray a 9 x 13 baking pan with nonstick spray. Place a layer of cinnamon raisin bread evenly in bottom, cutting pieces to fit if necessary. Spread cream cheese evenly over each piece of bread in the pan.

Spoon crushed pineapple evenly over cream cheese covered bread. Sprinkle with orange rind, then place a second layer of bread evenly on top, sandwich style.

Blend eggs, milk, almond flavoring, and cinnamon together in mixing bowl and pour carefully over bread. Cover baking pan with foil and let stand at least 30 minutes, or refrigerate overnight.

Bake in 350° oven for 40 to 50 minutes, removing foil the last 15 minutes. Serve with warm praline sauce. 8 servings.

BIRCH TREE INN
Praline Sauce

1/2 CUP BUTTER
1-1/2 CUPS BROWN SUGAR
1/2 CUP MAPLE SYRUP
1/2 CUP WHIPPING CREAM
1/2 CUP CHOPPED PECANS

Melt butter in a saucepan over low heat, blend in brown sugar until syrupy. Simmer over low heat for 5 minutes. Stir in maple syrup.

Blend in whipping cream until smooth, add chopped pecans and serve while warm. 3 cups.

Sally and Howard Krueger moved to Flagstaff from Chicago to purchase The Inn at 410 in 1993. They say it "matches our personality perfectly." This must certainly be the case, because they have won numerous awards for operating one of Arizona's best bed-and-breakfast locations.

WHERE TO EAT:

HISTORIC LOCATIONS:
GRAND CANYON CAFE Since the 1940s at 110 E. Route 66.

MIZ ZIP'S Since the 1950s at 2924 E. Route 66.

GRANNY'S CLOSET Formerly the Lumberjack Cafe. 218 S. Milton Rd.

OTHER LOCAL FAVORITES:

BEAVER STREET BREWERY & WHISTLE STOP CAFE 11 S. Beaver St.

LA BELLAVIA Breakfast and lunch. 18 S. Beaver St.

BRANDY'S RESTAURANT AND BAKERY 1500 E. Cedar Ave., #40

PASTO ITALIAN DINING For dinner. 19 E. Aspen St.

CHEZ MARC BISTRO 503 Humphrey's St.

MARC'S CAFE AMERICAN 801 S. Milton

WHERE TO STAY:

BIRCH TREE INN 824 W. Birch Ave. (520) 774-4209

INN AT FOUR TEN 410 N. Leroux St. (520) 774-0088

The Inn at 410 was built in 1894, then sold in 1907 to a wealthy Flagstaff banker, businessman, and rancher who renovated it into Craftsman style for his bride.

Today there are four suites and five rooms, all with private baths. The Kruegers prepare elegant gourmet breakfasts that emphasize a healthy lifestyle and they welcome afternoon arrivals with an array of tempting treats.

Sally says her Hash Brown Pie is a "satisfying and homey" dish she learned to prepare while honing her skills in a class on brunch food. She developed the blueberry muffin recipe from several favorites and thinks the Hopi blue cornmeal gives a bit of added flavor typical of the southwest.

The Kruegers have recently published their own cookbook, MOUNTAIN MORNINGS, BREAKFAST AND OTHER RECIPES FROM THE INN AT 410 B & B. It is filled with delightfully healthful treats that make staying in their bed and breakfast one of those especially memorable experiences.

THE INN AT 410 BED AND BREAKFAST

Hash Brown Pie

1 PACKAGE (12 OUNCES) FROZEN HASH
    BROWN POTATOES, THAWED
1/4 CUP MARGARINE, MELTED
1 BAG (10 OUNCES) FROZEN SPINACH,
    THAWED
1 TABLESPOON MARGARINE
1 SMALL ONION, CHOPPED
1/2 TEASPOON GROUND NUTMEG
3/4 CUP SHREDDED LOW-FAT CHEDDAR
    CHEESE
3/4 CUP SHREDDED LOW-FAT MONTEREY
    JACK CHEESE
1 CUP SKIM MILK

4 LARGE EGGS
1/2 TEASPOON BEAU MONDE SEASONING
1/4 TEASPOON GROUND WHITE PEPPER
6 CHERRY TOMATOES
CHOPPED FRESH PARSLEY FOR GARNISH

Preheat oven to 425°. Spray a 9-inch round pie plate with nonstick cooking spray. Press thawed potatoes between paper towels to absorb moisture. This should be done several times. Make a crust by firmly pressing potatoes along bottom and sides of pie plate. Brush with 1/4 cup melted margarine. Bake 20 minutes or until golden. Cool.

Meanwhile, using clean hands, squeeze excess moisture from thawed spinach. In a small skillet, over medium heat, melt one tablespoon margarine. Sauté chopped onion until translucent, about 5 minutes. Crumble dry spinach into pan and stir in nutmeg. Remove from heat and cool to room temperature.

Spread spinach mixture evenly over potato crust. Spread the shredded cheeses evenly over the spinach. Cover with foil and refrigerate.

The next morning, preheat oven to 350°. In the bowl of an electric mixer, beat the milk, eggs, Beau Monde, and white pepper together until thoroughly blended. Pour over the cheese. Bake 30 to 35 minutes or until puffed and cooked through.

Remove pie from oven and allow to stand five minutes to firm. Serve while hot with a garnish of cherry tomatoes and a sprinkling of chopped parsley. 6 generous slices.

Note: The hash brown "crust" is unique and delicious. The key to a crisp crust is to press as much moisture from the potatoes as possible.

Bluecorn Blueberry Muffins

1 CUP BLUE CORNMEAL

1/2 CUP ALL-PURPOSE FLOUR

1/2 CUP WHOLE WHEAT FLOUR

1/3 CUP SUGAR

1-1/4 TEASPOONS BAKING POWDER

1/4 TEASPOON SALT

4 TABLESPOONS DRY BUTTERMILK POWDER

1 CUP FRESH OR FROZEN BLUEBERRIES,
  UNTHAWED IF FROZEN

1 LARGE EGG

1 CUP PLUS 2 TABLESPOONS WATER

1/4 CUP CANOLA OIL

2 TABLESPOONS APPLESAUCE

Preheat oven to 400°. Spray 12 muffin cups with nonstick spray.

Measure cornmeal, flours, sugar, baking powder, salt, and dry buttermilk into a large bowl. Stir to combine thoroughly. Carefully fold in blueberries.

Measure egg, water, oil, and applesauce into a medium bowl. Whisk to combine. Mix wet ingredients into dry ingredients, stirring just until mixed. Do not over mix. Batter will be thin.

Use an ice cream scoop to fill prepared muffin cups. Bake muffins 20 to 25 minutes or until toothpick inserted into the center of a muffin comes out clean.

Cool in pan for 5 minutes then turn out to serve. 12 muffins.

Ed Wojciak wandered west from New Jersey in 1976 when Flagstaff had only about 50 restaurants. He and his new wife, Brandy, soon opened La Bellavia in the old downtown section of the city where a pizza parlor, Chicken Delight and sub shop had once served nearby college students.

La Bellavia is a comfortable place that serves quality food, a favorite of local residents, and a great stop for breakfast. La Bellavia is open from 6:30 a.m. to 2:30 p.m. daily.

LA BELLAVIA
Zucchini Quiche

1 BAKED 10-INCH CRUST
12 OUNCES ZUCCHINI, GRATED
1 SMALL ONION, DICED
1 TABLESPOON COOKING OIL
7 EGGS
2 CUPS MILK
SALT AND PEPPER TO TASTE
10 OUNCES SWISS CHEESE, GRATED
1/4 TEASPOON NUTMEG

Sauté grated zucchini and onion in cooking oil until onion is golden. Meanwhile, beat the eggs and add milk, salt and pepper to taste. Add the cheese and the zucchini mixture to the eggs. Pour into a baked 10-inch pie pan and sprinkle lightly with nutmeg. Place pie pan on a cookie sheet and bake the quiche in a 350° oven for 1 hour. Allow to stand 5 to 10 minutes before slicing. 6 large or 8 medium servings.

Brandy Wojciak met her husband in Flagstaff. Soon after their marriage they founded La Bellavia in central Flagstaff. Their culinary skills soon attracted a large breakfast crowd. Brandy soon began a successful catering business and when the opportunity arose to expand into a second location, she opened Brandy's Restaurant and Bakery. The restaurant at Cedar Hills Center is not on the regular tourist route but draws a large crowd of regulars from hometown neighbors. Have lunch at Brandy's or pick up some of her wonderful pastries. I guarantee a memorable treat!

Lemon-Blueberry Muffins

1-3/4 CUPS ALL-PURPOSE FLOUR

1/2 CUP SUGAR

2 TEASPOONS BAKING POWDER

1/4 TEASPOON SALT

1/2 CUP CHOPPED WALNUTS

1 TEASPOON GRATED LEMON PEEL

1 EGG

1 CUP MILK

4 TABLESPOONS MELTED MARGARINE

1 TEASPOON VANILLA

1-1/2 CUPS BLUEBERRIES

Preheat oven to 400°. Grease or line with cupcake papers a 12-cup muffin tin. In a large bowl combine flour, sugar, baking powder, and salt. Stir in walnuts and lemon peel.

In a small bowl beat together the egg, milk, margarine, and vanilla. Pour egg mixture into dry ingredients and stir just until flour is moistened. Batter will be lumpy. Fold in blueberries. Spoon into muffin cups and bake for 20 to 22 minutes or until tops are golden. 12 muffins.

When I inquired about good cooks in the Flagstaff area, the first person mentioned was Roabie Johnson, who works at the Flagstaff Library. Roabie grew up in Albuquerque and moved to Flagstaff to attend college. She loves the outdoors and worked for several years as a river guide. This potato recipe was a great favorite on trips. Even though it is a large recipe and is given with outdoor directions, it can be easily adapted for the oven.

Roabie Johnson's
Wild and Scenic Dutch Oven Cowboy Spuds

1 POUND BACON, CHOPPED

5 POUNDS POTATOES, WASHED AND CUT IN
LARGE CHUNKS

2 ONIONS, EACH SLICED IN 6 TO 8 PIECES

3 CANS BEER

2 ENVELOPES (1.15 OUNCES EACH) ONION
SOUP MIX

1 POUND LONGHORN OR JACK CHEESE,
GRATED

Fry the bacon in a Dutch oven until brown. Pour off most of the grease. Add potatoes, onions, beer and soup mix. Cook over the fire, on a grill, or on the ground with coals on the top and bottom of the Dutch oven. Add more coals to the top if the oven cools too much. You should be able to hold your hands about 10 inches above the Dutch oven lid. Stir occasionally. Add more beer if needed. The potatoes should cook in about 1-1/2 hours. When the liquid is thick and the potatoes are done, place cheese on top. Heat until melted.

The potatoes are good for breakfast with eggs if there are any leftovers. Bake these potatoes in your oven at home when you aren't cooking outdoors. 15 to 20 servings.

Roabie Johnson says her mother is a wonderful Southern cook who blended her culinary roots with her western environment. This bread recipe is an adaptation from her mother.

Roabie Johnson's Heirloom Bread

3 CUPS WHITE FLOUR

1 CUP WHOLE WHEAT FLOUR

2 TEASPOONS BAKING POWDER

1-1/2 TEASPOONS BAKING SODA

1/2 TEASPOON SALT

2 TEASPOONS CINNAMON

1/2 TEASPOON NUTMEG

1/2 TEASPOON GROUND CLOVES

1 CUP MARGARINE

1-1/2 CUPS SUGAR

4 EGGS

2 TEASPOONS VANILLA

2 CUPS APPLESAUCE

2 CUPS CHOPPED PECANS

1 CUP CURRANTS

Combine flours, baking powder and soda and spices in large bowl; set aside. Cream margarine and sugar. Add eggs, vanilla, and applesauce. Add to dry mixture and blend until smooth. Stir in pecans and currants. Grease two 9 x 5 x 3 loaf pans. Bake in 350° oven for 1 hour or until bread tests done with a toothpick inserted into the center. 2 loaves.

Longtime Flagstaff resident Peggy Harris was born near Springfield, Missouri, another Route 66 community. She and her husband have five children and eight grandchildren. Two of her sons are professional chefs. Peggy never wanted to be a ho-hum cook so she did a lot of experimenting. Her friends rave about her mulligatawny soup. For years she didn't have a recipe but prepared it by using a pinch of this and that. Finally, friends insisted she write the recipe. Peggy says this soup is one that requires tasting to adjust flavors for individual preferences.

Peggy Harris's Mulligatawny Soup

1 ONION

1 LARGE OR 2 SMALL CARROTS

3 STALKS CELERY

4 TABLESPOONS FLOUR

4 TABLESPOONS BUTTER OR MARGARINE

4 CUPS CHICKEN STOCK

2 CUPS CHOPPED COOKED CHICKEN

2 TART COOKING APPLES, CHOPPED

2 CUPS COOKED RICE

2 TEASPOONS CURRY POWDER

1 TEASPOON (APPROXIMATELY) OF EACH OF
THE FOLLOWING: TUMERIC, CARDAMON,
CORIANDER, GARLIC AND SALT

1/2 TEASPOON PEPPER

2 CUPS CREAM

Chop onion, carrots and celery finely by hand or in the food processor. Melt the butter or margarine and sauté vegetables in heavy skillet until tender. Add enough flour to make a roux. More margarine may be necessary.

In a stock pot, heat the chicken stock and chicken. Add the apples and rice. Stir in the vegetables and seasonings, adjusting quantity to your individual taste. Stir in the cream just before serving. Approximately 10 cups.

Beaver Street Brewery and Whistle Stop Cafe is on the corner of Phoenix and Beaver Streets, just south of the railroad tracks and historic downtown Flagstaff. The original building, home to several businesses through the years, was constructed in 1938 of Malpais rock collected from surrounding volcanic beds.

Beaver Street Brewery and Whistle Stop Cafe opened in March of 1994, featuring handcrafted brews by owner and brewmaster Evan Hanseth and an award winning "American Fresh" menu created by Chef Kate Chadwick and her staff. The brewery has become one of Flagstaff's "hotspots," for both locals and tourists.

This rib-sticking chile is a favorite that is bound to satisfy!

BEAVER STREET BREWERY AND WHISTLE STOP CAFE

Hart Prairie Chile

Brown together in a large skillet:

2 TABLESPOONS CANOLA OIL

2-1/2 POUNDS OF BEEF CHUCK ROAST, TRIMMED AND CUT INTO 1/4 INCH CUBES

1-1/2 POUNDS OF BEEF CHUCK ROAST, TRIMMED AND COARSELY GROUND

1 RED BELL PEPPER, DICED IN 1/2 INCH PIECES

1 FRESH POBLANO CHILE, DICED IN 1/2 INCH PIECES

1 RED ONION, CUT IN STRIPS

1 TABLESPOON FRESH GARLIC, MINCED

When vegetables become translucent, add:

1/2 CUP CHILE POWDER

2 TABLESPOONS CUMIN

1 TABLESPOON GARLIC POWDER

1 TABLESPOON ONION POWDER

1 TEASPOON CAYENNE PEPPER

1 TABLESPOON KOSHER SALT

1 TABLESPOON OREGANO

ADD:

1 CUP BITTER ALE OR OTHER MILD BEER

4 CUPS CHICKEN BROTH

4 CUPS DICED CANNED TOMATOES IN JUICE

Simmer for 20 minutes then add:

2 CUPS BLACK BEANS, COOKED AND
DRAINED

2 CUPS KIDNEY BEANS, COOKED AND
DRAINED

2 CUPS PINTO BEANS, COOKED AND
DRAINED

Continue simmering until meat is tender and chile is hot. Serve immediately to a large crowd or cover tightly and store in refrigerator briefly or freeze. 20 servings.

G O O D   F O O D   I N   W I L L I A M S :

Terry Ranch Bed and Breakfast is hosted by Sheryl and Del Terry. They built the comfortable two-story log home themselves and opened in 1995. Sheryl's parents owned a bed and breakfast in Mesa, Arizona, and Del was a building consultant so they were able to apply their experience in designing the best in comfort for their guests. The Terry's offer four beautifully appointed rooms with private baths, all on the first floor. An inviting wrap-around porch, complete with rockers, is an added bonus for relaxing in this superb mountain atmosphere. Sheryl has a collection of favorite family recipes to choose from and prepares gourmet breakfasts for guests.

Williams

population 2500

W H A T   T O   S E E :

GRAND CANYON
NATIONAL PARK SOUTH
RIM

GRAND CANYON
RAILROAD Call (800) THE-
TRAIN

MEMORY LANE
MUSEUM, GIFT SHOP,
AND INFORMATION
CENTER 326 W. Route 66

W H E R E   T O   E A T :

ROD'S STEAK HOUSE
301 E. Bill Williams

OLD SMOKY'S PANCAKE
HOUSE AND
RESTAURANT 624 W.Bill
Williams

OLD 66 COFFEE HOUSE
Formerly the Little Fat Lady
Cafe. 246 E. Bill Williams

TWISTERS, A 50'S SODA
FOUNTAIN 417 E. Bill
Williams

W H E R E   T O
S T A Y :

THE RED GARTER BED
AND BAKERY 137 W.
Railroad Ave. (520) 635-
1484 or (800) 328-1484

TERRY RANCH BED AND
BREAKFAST 701 Quarter-
horse. (520) 635-4171 or
(800)210-5908

CANYON COUNTRY INN
442 W. Bill Williams Ave.
(520) 635-2349 or (800)
643-1020

GRAND CANYON
NATIONAL PARK LODGES
Fred Harvey Hospitality
since 1876 (520) 638-2401
for accommodations.

TERRY RANCH

Strawberry Muffins

2 CUPS FLOUR

1 CUP SUGAR

1 TEASPOON BAKING SODA

1 TEASPOON CINNAMON

1 TEASPOON NUTMEG

1/2 TEASPOON SALT

2 EGGS, BEATEN

1/2 CUP VEGETABLE OIL

1/2 CUP BUTTERMILK

1/2 CUP STRAWBERRY JAM

In a large mixing bowl, stir together the flour, sugar, baking soda, cinnamon, nutmeg, and salt. Make a well in the center. Combine the eggs, oil, and buttermilk and pour all at once into the well.

Stir until dry ingredients are moistened. Do not overmix. Gently fold in the jam. Place batter in well-greased or paper lined muffin tins. Bake in 375° oven for 20 minutes. 18 muffins.

TERRY RANCH

Hot Spiced Percolator Punch

4 CUPS APPLE CIDER

1 CUP ORANGE JUICE

2 CUPS CRANBERRY JUICE

3/4 CUP LEMON JUICE

1 CUP SUGAR

1 TABLESPOON ALLSPICE

1 TEASPOON WHOLE CLOVES

3 CINNAMON STICKS

Place juices in percolator. Place sugar and spices in percolator basket. Allow beverage to perk. Serve guests while drink is very hot. 10 servings, about 3/4 cup each.

Located on Whiskey Row in downtown Williams, The Red Garter Bed and Bakery offers a memorable stay in a fully restored 1897 bordello. John Holst, the innkeeper, is a former Williams building inspector who has carefully renovated the historic building at 137 Railroad Avenue. He opened The Red Garter Bed and Bakery in 1994. There is a honeymoon suite with a view of the steam train to the Grand Canyon, the Madam's room at the top of the stairs, and two rooms formerly called cribs. A full service bakery and coffee shop is located in the downstairs turn-of-the-century saloon. Holst has many historic photographs and a wealth of stories to share.

RED GARTER BED AND BAKERY
Gingerbran Muffins

1/2 CUP OIL

2/3 CUP MOLASSES

2 EGGS

1/4 CUP MILK

2 CUPS FLOUR

1-1/2 TEASPOONS BAKING POWDER

1 TEASPOON GROUND GINGER

1/2 TEASPOON CINNAMON

1/2 TEASPOON NUTMEG

1/4 TEASPOON GROUND CLOVES

1/4 CUP WHEAT BRAN

Grease 8 to 10 2-inch muffin tins. Combine oil, molasses, eggs and milk. Mix well. Stir flour with baking soda and spices. Add to liquid mixture but do not overmix. Pour muffin batter into tins. Sprinkle tops with wheat bran. Bake in 350° oven for 20 minutes or until browned. 8 to 10 muffins.

Blueberry Cinnamon Rolls

1/2 CUP SUGAR

1 PACKAGE ACTIVE DRY YEAST

1/2 TEASPOON SALT

1 CUP FLOUR

1 CUP MILK

1/4 POUND BUTTER

2 EGGS

3 CUPS FLOUR

FILLING:

2 TABLESPOONS MELTED BUTTER

2 TABLESPOONS BROWN SUGAR

DASH OF CINNAMON

1 GENEROUS CUP THAWED BLUEBERRIES

FROSTING:

1 CUP POWDERED SUGAR

1/4 TEASPOON VANILLA EXTRACT

2 TABLESPOONS MILK

Combine sugar, yeast, salt and 1 cup flour in mixing bowl. Heat milk and butter to 120° microwave oven. Add to dry mixture, then stir in eggs and 3 cups flour, one cup at a time. Mix well until a soft dough is formed. Knead several minutes until dough is smooth and satin-soft but not sticky. Form into a ball and cover. Allow dough to rise until double in size, 45 minutes to 1 hour. Roll dough into a 12 x 15 rectangle.

Spread filling ingredients over dough. Roll from 15-inch side and cut into 8 rolls. Place on greased cookie sheet. Allow rolls to rise again for another 45 minutes to 1 hour. Bake in preheated 350° oven for 20 to 25 minutes or until browned.

Combine frosting ingredients, pour over warm rolls and serve. 8 very large rolls.

Joyce Sullivant, proprietor at the Canyon Country Inn, offers what she calls "flavor of country" rooms at the inn she bought in 1994. Homemade continental breakfasts await guests who take their meals back to their rooms to relax. The inn was built in 1989 and offers the privacy of a motel with the decorating warmth of a country inn, a "Beary" nice combination according to Joyce.

CANYON COUNTRY INN
Lemon Bread

1 CUP MARGARINE

1-1/2 CUPS SUGAR

4 EGGS

4 CUPS ALL-PURPOSE FLOUR

1/2 TEASPOON SALT

1 TEASPOON BAKING SODA

1 CUP BUTTERMILK

1 TABLESPOON GRATED LEMON RIND

1 CUP CHOPPED NUTS

GLAZE:

3/4 CUP LEMON JUICE

1 CUP POWDERED SUGAR

Beat margarine until fluffy, then slowly add sugar and continue beating until mixture is light and airy. Add eggs one at a time and blend well. In a separate container combine flour, salt, and baking soda. Alternately pour flour mixture and buttermilk into the whipped margarine and sugar. Combine well, then stir in lemon rind and nuts. Pour bread into two 9 x 5 x 3 greased bread pans. Bake bread in 300° oven for 1-1/2 hours or until toothpick inserted in center comes out clean. Cool bread in pans for 15 minutes then turn out on rack to continue to cool. If you like a glaze, combine lemon juice and sugar and beat until blended. Pour over warm bread. 2 loaves.

Ash Fork

WHAT TO SEE:

FLAGSTONE CAPITOL OF THE COUNTRY Nearby stone quarries produce native sandstone in shades of buff, buckskin, red, and purple.

Begin west of here to drive 178 miles of uninterrupted Route 66, all the way to Topock.

El Tovar at Grand Canyon opened for business in 1905, just 50 feet from the edge of the South Rim at Grand Canyon. Mary Colter, the Fred Harvey Company's resident architect, designed El Tovar in partnership with the Santa Fe Railroad as the finest Harvey House in the country. Today it remains an oasis of Victorian-era luxury and northern Arizona's premier restaurant.

In the spacious dining room, food is served on a grand scale. Many feel the most spectacular meal is breakfast. As the sun rises, guests feast on gourmet dishes such as cornmeal and blackberry waffles, sour cream and banana pancakes, and savory breakfast fry bread tacos.

The lunch menu may include the famous El Tovar chile. At the dinner hour, fennel-crusted trout is often on the menu. Coffee, made with water piped from the North Rim of the canyon, is legendary.

John Kingsmore, executive chef for the Grand Canyon National Park Lodges shares the recipes.

GRAND CANYON NATIONAL PARK LODGES
Fennel-Crusted Trout

4 BONELESS TROUT (8 OUNCES EACH)
1 CUP DRIED FENNEL SEEDS, GROUND FINE
1/3 CUP FLOUR
1 TEASPOON SALT
1 TEASPOON WHITE PEPPER
1/2 CUP EGG WASH
OIL

Mix together the fennel, flour, and seasonings. Brush trout with egg wash then coat with fennel mixture. Sauté quickly in just enough oil to coat bottom of pan. Serve with lemon or your favorite compound butter.

Recommended wine selection is sauvignon blanc or chardonnay. 4 portions.

GRAND CANYON NATIONAL PARK LODGES
El Tovar Chile

1-1/2 POUNDS DICED FILET MIGNON

1 POUND DICED PORK LOIN

1 WHITE ONION, DICED FINE

1 JALAPEÑO PEPPER, CHOPPED FINE

1 TABLESPOON FRESH GARLIC

3 CANS (12 OUNCES EACH) BEER

3 TABLESPOONS CHILE POWDER

1 TABLESPOON PAPRIKA

1 TABLESPOON CUMIN

1 TABLESPOON TABASCO SAUCE

1/2 CUP DICED TOMATOES

1/2 CUP TOMATO SAUCE

SALT AND PEPPER TO TASTE

1/2 CUP GRATED MONTEREY JACK CHEESE

Sauté the filet mignon, pork loin, onion, and jalapeño pepper. Add remaining ingredients. Add salt and pepper and simmer for 2 to 3 hours on low heat.

To serve, put a serving of chile into ovenproof bowl, top with Jack cheese, and put under broiler for a few moments until cheese is melted and slightly brown. Serve with blue corn chips and a slice of cornbread. 4 portions.

GOOD FOOD IN SELIGMAN:

Angel Delgadillo is the driving force behind the Historic Route 66 Association of Arizona. He operates his barber shop just a few doors from his brother Juan Delgadillo's Snow Cap. Both establishments are "must see" stops for Route 66 travelers. Angel and Juan are interviewed regularly for specials about Route 66 that are shown around the world. Stop, too, at the grocery store next to the barber shop. Juan and Angel's brother Joe operated it until his retirement. It's still a friendly place with a good deli.

Seligman
population 1000

WHAT TO SEE:

ANGEL DELGADILLO'S BARBER SHOP Angel has done more than almost anyone else to promote and save Route 66.

ROUTE 66 FUN RUN WEEKENDS Last weekend of each April, between Ash Fork and Golden Shores with most activities centered in Seligman.

WHERE TO EAT:

JUAN DELGADILLO'S SNOW CAP

COPPER CART RESTAURANT Louise Brown, hostess.

259

Peach Springs

WHAT TO SEE:

BURMA SHAVE STYLE SIGNS Recreated by American Safety Razor Company/Reminisce.

Angel's wife, Vilma, shares these favorite family recipes.

Vilma Delgadillo's Brown Rice Casserole

1/4 CUP BUTTER

1 CUP CHOPPED ONION

1 CLOVE GARLIC, MINCED

1/2 POUND FRESH MUSHROOMS, QUARTERED

1/8 TEASPOON THYME

1 CUP BROWN RICE

1 CUP SLICED CARROTS

2 CUPS CHICKEN BROTH

SALT AND PEPPER TO TASTE

2 CUPS SLICED ZUCCHINI

1/2 CUP SHREDDED SWISS CHEESE

1/4 CUP TOASTED SUNFLOWER SEEDS

SALT AND PEPPER TO TASTE

Preheat oven to 350°. In a flameproof casserole, melt the butter and sauté the onions and garlic for about 5 minutes. Add mushrooms and thyme and cook 2 minutes more. Stir in the rice, carrots, broth, salt and pepper. Bring mixture to a boil. Cover and bake in oven for 30 minutes. Remove and stir in zucchini and cheese and bake an additional 30 minutes. Sprinkle with toasted sunflower seeds before serving. 6 to 8 servings.

Martha Delgadillo's Impossible Quesadillo Pie

2 CANS (4 OUNCES EACH) CHOPPED GREEN CHILES

4 CUPS SHREDDED CHEESE (ABOUT 1 POUND)

2 CUPS MILK

1 CUP BAKING MIX

4 EGGS

Preheat oven to 425°. Grease a 10-inch pie plate. Sprinkle chiles and cheese in plate. Blend milk, baking mix and eggs until smooth in a blender, food processor, or with hand beater for at least a minute. Pour mixture into pie plate. Bake 25 to 30 minutes or until knife inserted in the center comes out clean. Let stand 10 minutes before cutting. 8 slices.

Vilma Delgadillo's Chiles Rellenos Casserole

1 POUND GROUND BEEF

1/2 CUP CHOPPED ONION

1/2 TEASPOON SALT

1/4 TEASPOON PEPPER

2 CANS (4 OUNCES EACH) GREEN CHILES,
    SEEDED, CUT IN HALF LENGTHWISE

SEVERAL DASHES HOT SAUCE

1-1/2 CUPS SHREDDED LONGHORN CHEESE

1-1/2 CUPS MILK

1/4 CUP FLOUR

1/2 TEASPOON SALT

DASH OF PEPPER

4 EGGS

In a skillet, brown beef and onions. Drain fat. Sprinkle meat with salt and pepper. Spread half the chiles in a 10 x 6 baking dish. Sprinkle with cheese and top with meat mixture. Arrange remaining chiles over meat. Beat egg whites until foamy. Combine egg yolks with milk, flour, salt and pepper. Fold into whites and pour over meat. Bake in a 350° oven until knife comes out clean when inserted in center. 6 servings.

Truxton

population 125

WHERE TO EAT:

FRONTIER CAFE Mildred Barker operates the cafe and motel and has a great story about how the cafe originated.

WHERE TO STAY:

FRONTIER MOTEL

FRONTIER CAFE
Old-Fashioned Banana Pudding

2-1/2 CUPS EVAPORATED MILK
4 EGGS, SEPARATED
2/3 CUP SUGAR
6 TABLESPOONS CORNSTARCH
1 TABLESPOON BUTTER
1/2 TEASPOON VANILLA
PINCH OF SALT
VANILLA WAFER COOKIES
2 TO 3 BANANAS

Scald the milk and stir in beaten egg yolks. Combine sugar and cornstarch, and stir into egg mixture. Add butter and continue stirring until mixture has thickened. Add vanilla and pinch of salt.

Line a 2-quart dish with cookies. Slice bananas over the cookies. Pour pudding mixture over bananas and allow to cool. If desired, whip egg whites and add 1/2 cup sugar. Spread over pudding and place in 400° oven for oven for 5 minutes to brown. 8 servings.

Hackberry

WHAT TO SEE:

OLD ROUTE 66 VISITOR CENTER Authentic roadside homestead operated by artist, historian, naturalist, and enthusiastic Route 66 supporter Robert Waldmire. A must see location!

Kingman

population 17,000

WHAT TO SEE:

POWERHOUSE TOURISM, VISITORS CENTER, AND ROUTE 66 MUSEUM. Across from Locomotive Park. (520) 753-5001

HUALAPAI MOUNTAIN PARK 12 miles southeast

MOHAVE MUSEUM OF ART AND HISTORY 400 W. Beale

GOOD FOOD IN KINGMAN:

This crisp salad tasted especially good in the high desert climate when we had dinner with friends while attending the October Air Show.

Spinach and Strawberries

2 POUNDS FRESH SPINACH, WASHED AND STEMMED
1 PINT RIPE STRAWBERRIES, SLICED
2 TABLESPOONS DICED GREEN ONION TOPS

DRESSING:

2 TABLESPOONS SESAME SEEDS

1/2 CUP SUGAR

1/4 TEASPOON PAPRIKA

1/4 TEASPOON WORCESTERSHIRE SAUCE

1/3 CUP VEGETABLE OIL

1/4 CUP CIDER VINEGAR

1 TABLESPOON POPPY SEEDS

SALT AND PEPPER TO TASTE

Arrange spinach, strawberries and green onion on individual serving plates. Toast sesame seeds in shallow tray in 350° oven for 10 minutes or until golden and set aside.

Combine all dressing ingredients except sesame and poppy seeds in a blender or food processor, mixing until thickened. Stir in sesame and poppy seeds. Drizzle dressing over spinach and berries. Serve immediately. This dressing makes more than will be needed for one recipe of salad. Keep remainder in refrigerator to use another time.

Note: Mixed salad greens may be substituted for spinach if desired. 8 servings.

GOOD FOOD IN OATMAN:

Jackie Rowland is a transplanted Okie who runs Fast Fanny's Place in Oatman. She has watched this tiny forgotten mining town come to life again because tourists have rediscovered mountain life above the hairpin turns that were necessary for years in order to proceed along Route 66. Here is Jackie's favorite breakfast recipe. She keeps tortillas and chorizo in the freezer so she can prepare the dish for "Roadies" who often drop by for a visit. Add a couple more eggs and another tortilla or two to stretch the recipe when more folks show up than expected. The salsa recipe is a prize winner, served at a local chile cook-off.

KINGMAN AIR AND AUTO SHOW Around the first weekend in October each year.

ANNUAL PRCA RODEO, DANCE AND PARADE Second weekend in October each year.

WHERE TO EAT:

HOUSE OF CHAN Some of the best Chinese food along Route 66. 960 W. Beal.

WHERE TO STAY:

QUALITY INN AND ROUTE 66 DISTILLERY On Historic Route 66. Outstanding collection of memorabilia. Many rooms are named for famous guests.

Oatman

population 100

WHAT TO SEE:

OATMAN HOTEL Clark Gable and Carol Lombard spent their wedding night here.

THE OATMAN HOTEL RAGGEDY ASS MINERS BAR Decorated with hundreds of dollar bills fastened to the ceilings and walls.

STREET LIFE
"Panhandling" burros along the street. Live gunfights on weekends and holidays and the "Jezebels Sashay" on weekend afternoons.

MAIN STREET Bed races down Main St. in January.

INTERNATIONAL BURRO BISCUIT TOSS Each September.

SIDEWALK EGG FRY COMPETITION Each 4th of July.

Plenty of shops for every taste.

WHERE TO EAT:

THE MINING COMPANY Former Silver Creek Saloon & Steak House. Good Italian and American food served here along with great atmosphere.

OATMAN HOTEL Where the menu is written on old paper sacks!

CENTRAL PALACE A great place for garlic "stinken burgers."

CASTER JOES Indian tacos are a favorite here

Jackie's Mexi Breakfast

1/2 POUND BEEF OR PORK CHORIZO
  (MEXICAN SAUSAGE)
4 TABLESPOONS MARGARINE
12 TO 14 CORN TORTILLAS
6 TO 8 EGGS, BEATEN
1 CUP DICED TOMATOES, DRAINED
1 MEDIUM BELL PEPPER, DICED
1 SMALL ONION, DICED
1 CUP SHREDDED CHEDDAR CHEESE
SOUR CREAM
GUACAMOLE
WARM SALSA

In a large skillet brown the chorizo, then remove. Add margarine and the tortillas torn in 1-inch pieces. Warm to soften. Add chorizo to egg mixture and fold in diced vegetables. Pour over tortillas and cook in skillet, stirring occasionally until eggs are set. Sprinkle with cheese and cover until melted. Serve with sour cream, guacamole, and salsa. 4 servings.

Linda Ellithorpe's Jail House Salsa

2 CANS (15-1/2 OUNCES EACH) TOMATOES,
  MASHED
1 CAN (8 OUNCES) TOMATO SAUCE
1 CUP MINCED ONION
1 CUP MINCED BELL PEPPER
2 CANS (4-1/2 OUNCES EACH) CHOPPED
  MILD CHILES
GARLIC POWDER, OREGANO, CILANTRO,
  SALT AND PEPPER TO TASTE

Mix well and serve with tortilla chips. About 6 cups.

"Uncle Charlie Hicks" is another Okie who has retired to Oatman. Uncle Charlie bartends at the Oatman Hotel, is the head gunfighter with the Ghostrider Gunfighters every weekend, and as "Reverend Uncle Charlie Hicks," is the local marrying and burying preacher.

Uncle Charlie collected this stew recipe while doing a stint as a gold prospector. His cornbread just naturally goes along with it. Be sure to look him up when in Oatman.

Golden Shores /Topock

population 350

W H A T   T O   S E E :

OLD ROUTE 66 BRIDGE ACROSS THE COLORADO RIVER

Uncle Charlie Hicks's Beer Stew with Drop Dumplings

2 POUNDS LEAN BEEF, CUT INTO CHUNKS

1 LARGE ONION, COARSELY CHOPPED

1 CAN (15-1/2 OUNCES) BEEF BROTH

1 CAN BEER

1 BAY LEAF

3 TABLESPOONS BROWN SUGAR

1/4 CUP RED WINE VINEGAR

D R O P   D U M P L I N G S :

1 CUP FLOUR

1 TEASPOON SALT

1/2 TEASPOON BAKING SODA

MILK TO MAKE A STIFF, STICKY BATTER

Brown beef and onions together in a large stew pot. Add broth beer, bay leaf, sugar and vinegar. Cover and simmer until meat is tender.

Mix dry ingredients for dumplings. Add milk slowly. Drop by spoonfuls into bubbling stew. Cover and steam for twenty minutes. Add a little water if stew gets too thick. 6 servings.

Uncle Charlie Hicks's Cornbread

1 CUP FLOUR

1 CUP CORNMEAL

1/4 CUP SUGAR

4 TEASPOONS BAKING POWDER

3/4 TEASPOON SALT

1 CUP MILK

1/4 CUP OIL

2 EGG WHITES

Combine dry ingredients in a small bowl. Add milk, oil and egg whites and stir to blend. Pour into a 9 x 9 pan and bake in a 425° oven for 20 minutes. 6 to 8 servings.

PHOTO BY "DICK" WHITTINGTON

L ike a magnet, California draws millions of visitors annually to a land of contrasting flavors, casual ambiance, and urban sophistication. Today's visitors will find good food and incredibly fresh produce in abundance all along the legendary highway.

Choices have exploded and a healthy lifestyle is now vitally important to many nutrition-conscious residents. Tomatillos, pesto, Caribbean spices, artichokes, and jícama are commonplace. The California wine culture is older than statehood and began in the Route 66 community of Rancho Cucamonga. This is the state where roasted garlic first became popular, offbeat fruits abound, eating healthy is the popular "in" thing to do, and fruits and vegetables are served ripe and tasty. Yet old favorites and classic stops remain. Casa del Desierto has experienced new life, the Claremont Inn surrounds history with new flair, and The Derby continues to serve good food to Santa Anita customers.

And a new generation of eateries have appeared. Dive! a Deep See Experience has burst forth from the front of a Century City Mall and Thunder Roadhouse promotes "Live to Ride, Ride to Eat!" At the pier in Santa Monica, just a few blocks from the point where Santa Monica

Boulevard intersects with Ocean Avenue, Rusty's Surf Ranch entices customers with the exciting new contemporary world of fusion cuisine.

Route 66 in California still offers a firm anchor and new opportunity to those headed westward. The Main Street of America can never be captured and held to one time!

Needles

population 5,300

WHAT TO SEE:

EL GARCES An abandoned Harvey House and Depot that may soon come to life again.

NEEDLES REGIONAL MUSEUM Across the street from El Garces at 929 Front St.

LAUGHLIN AND HAVASU CITY

EAST MOJAVE NATIONAL SCENIC AREA A 1.5-million-acre preserve bordered by I-15 on the north, I-40 on the south and the Nevada line to the east. Includes wildlife, native flowers, Mitchell Caverns, the Providence Mountains, Kelso Dunes and desert space! Tours begin at Essex Rd. (760) 389-2281

GOOD FOOD IN NEEDLES:

The Old Trails Inn Bed-and-Breakfast is located on the site of the early 1930s Palms Motel. In 1991 the Wilde family began extensive renovation on the remaining cabin court structures so that travelers can experience the nostalgia of an earlier generation with the amenities of today. The feel of a simpler time remains.

Each "cabin" forms part of a circle around a common landscaped court. Rooms are decorated with antiques reminiscent of the 1930s and the commons room is filled with local bits of history and memorabilia.

OLD TRAILS INN BED-AND-BREAKFAST

Potato Cake

1 CUP SHORTENING

2 CUPS SUGAR

3 EGGS

1 CUP COLD MASHED POTATOES

2 TABLESPOONS COCOA

1 TEASPOON CINNAMON

2 TEASPOONS BAKING SODA

2 CUPS FLOUR

1/2 CUP SOUR MILK

In a medium sized mixing bowl whip the shortening and blend in sugar. Combine thoroughly then add eggs and mashed potatoes. Combine dry ingredients and add to egg mixture along with the sour milk. Mix only until blended. Pour batter into an two 8-inch cake pans that have been sprayed with nonstick spray. Bake in a 350° oven for 30 minutes. Use your favorite frosting or serve warm without frosting. 12 servings.

GOOD FOOD IN BARSTOW:

At the Idle Spurs Steak House guests will find attractive western decor and enclosed patio dining. The popular restaurant was built in the 1950s as a home. When the location evolved into a restaurant, the original hand-laid flagstone flooring remained and can be found in the bar and patio. Comfortable and casual, Idle Spurs is noted for good steaks and equally good service. The desert atmosphere blends perfectly here with the good food. Idle Spurs is open for lunch and dinner.

IDLE SPURS STEAK HOUSE
Black Bean Salsa

I CAN (15 OUNCES) BLACK BEANS, DRAINED AND RINSED

1-1/2 CUPS COOKED FRESH CORN KERNELS

2 MEDIUM TOMATOES, CUT AND DICED

I GREEN BELL PEPPER, CUT AND DICED

1/2 CUP RED ONION, FINELY DICED

I TO 2 FRESH GREEN SERRANO OR JALAPEÑO PEPPERS, THINLY SLICED, INCLUDING SEEDS

1/3 CUP FRESH LIME JUICE

1/3 CUP EXTRA-VIRGIN OLIVE OIL

1/3 CUP CHOPPED FRESH CORIANDER

I TEASPOON SALT

1/2 TEASPOON GROUND CUMIN

1/2 TEASPOON PURE GROUND RED CHILE (NOT CHILE POWDER) OR A PINCH OF CAYENNE PEPPER

WHERE TO EAT:

66 BURGER HUT Formerly Irene's, a long-time 66 eatery. 701 W. Broadway.

HUNGRY BEAR A Route 66 stop since 1965. 1906 W. Broadway

WHERE TO STAY:

OLD TRAILS INN BED AND BREAKFAST The 1930s Palms Motel has been restored. 304 Broadway. (760) 326-3523

Amboy

population 14

WHERE TO EAT:

ROY'S CAFE AND MOTEL Don Meyers and Walt Wilson lease this ultimate Route 66 stop. At last check, the whole town was still for sale.

Ludlow

population 400

WHERE TO EAT:

LUDLOW COFFEE SHOP Operated by the Knoll family for over 30 years.

Newberry Springs

population 1000

WHERE TO EAT:

BAGDAD CAFE (AKA SIDEWINDER CAFE) Stop in and visit with owner Andrea Pruett and relive memories of the 1989 movie *Baghdad Cafe,* which was filmed here. 46548 National Trails Highway.

Barstow

population 20,000

WHAT TO SEE:

CASA DEL DESIERTO Once a Fred Harvey Hotel and now the train and bus depot, seen by crossing the Old Iron Bridge.

BARSTOW STATION Many gift shops including a McDonald's built entirely from railroad passenger cars.

ANTIQUE MALL 8000-square foot antique mall in the center of town.

CALICO EARLY MAN ARCHEOLOGICAL SITE 15 miles northeast on I-15. (760) 256-5102

RAINBOW BASIN NATIONAL NATURAL LANDMARK 8 miles north on SR 58. (760) 255- 8760

Combine all ingredients in a large bowl. Mix well. Set aside to let the flavors blend until ready to serve. 4 1/2 cups.

GOOD FOOD IN VICTORVILLE:

These nachos make wonderful appetizers and the spice can be adjusted for personal taste.

Jalapeño and Chicken Nachos

1-1/2 CUP COOKED, DICED CHICKEN BREAST

12 OUNCES CREAM CHEESE, AT ROOM TEMPERATURE

1 JALAPEÑO PEPPER, SEEDED AND MINCED

1/4 CUP FINELY CHOPPED RED ONION

3 CLOVES GARLIC, MINCED

1 TEASPOON GROUND CUMIN

1 TEASPOON CHILE POWDER

1-1/2 CUPS GRATED MONTEREY JACK CHEESE

SALT AND FRESHLY GROUND BLACK PEPPER TO TASTE

12 MEDIUM-SIZED FLOUR TORTILLAS

Preheat the oven to 375°. Combine all ingredients except the tortillas in a large mixing bowl. Beat until well blended. Taste and season with salt and pepper.

Melt oil in skillet on medium high heat. Brown each tortilla for about 1 minute. Spread 6 of the tortillas with a generous amount of filling. Cover with remaining tortillas. Place on cookie sheets and bake until bubbling, about 5 to 7 minutes. Cut into wedges and serve as appetizers in a napkin lined basket. 72 bite-sized nachos.

GOOD FOOD IN SAN BERNADINO:

At Le Rendezvous French Restaurant a warm and pleasant country atmosphere has been created by Chef Jean Pierre Sene and his wife, Isabelle, who acts as hostess. Enjoy entrees prepared with the utmost care and relax with a glass of wine from their distinguished list.

LE RENDEZVOUS
Seafood Mornay

1/4 CUP CHICKEN BROTH
PINCH OF SALT AND CAYENNE PEPPER
1/2 POUND SCALLOPS
3/4 POUND SEA BASS, CUT IN CUBES
3/4 POUND SHRIMP, PEELED, DEVEINED
  AND COOKED
1 CUP SLICED MUSHROOMS
2 TABLESPOONS BUTTER
1/2 CUP FLOUR
1/3 CUP DRY WHITE WINE
1/2 CUP CREAM
2 OUNCES GRATED CHEESE

Place chicken broth and salt and pepper in saucepan and bring to boil. Add scallops, then sea bass and poach for a few minutes. Remove from heat and add shrimp. Strain, saving the broth. Place fish in a dish with mushrooms.

In the same saucepan, melt butter and mix with flour. Add wine and the strained broth, mixing with a whip. Bring mixture to boil then remove from heat and add cream. Pour sauce over seafood to serve. Sprinkle with grated cheese then put plate in hot oven for about 10 minutes, until golden brown.

Serve with rice. Accompany with a dry white wine, such as a chardonnay, or white bordeaux. 4 servings.

CALICO GHOST TOWN
11 miles northeast on I-15.
(760) 254-2122

WHERE TO EAT:

IDLE SPURS STEAK
HOUSE 29557 Highway 58

EL RANCHO CAFE A long-time Route 66 eatery. 112 E. Main St.

Victorville
population 41,000

WHAT TO SEE:

CALIFORNIA ROUTE 66
MUSEUM An important California stop, sponsored by the California Historic Route 66 Association and The National Route 66 Federation. 6th and D Streets.

ROY ROGERS-DALE
EVANS MUSEUM 15650 Seneca Rd. (760) 243-4547

WHERE TO EAT:

LA FONDA MEXICAN
RESTAURANT Good food near the Route 66 Museum. 15556 6th St.

HOLLANDBURGER CAFE
Breakfast and lunch, home cooking. 17143 D Street, on Route 66.

SUMMIT INN On Route 66 since 1952. Off I-15, Cajon Pass. Exit Oak Hill Rd.

San Bernardino

Population 131,000

WHAT TO SEE:

RIM OF THE WORLD DRIVE

SAN BERNARDINO NATIONAL FOREST

LAKE ARROWHEAD AND BIG BEAR LAKE

ROUTE 66 RENDEZVOUS Third weekend of September each year. More than 1,200 cars on display on or near E Street downtown.

NATIONAL ORANGE SHOW Occurs in May.

WHERE TO EAT:

LE RENDEZVOUS FRENCH RESTAURANT 4775 N. Sierra Way

MITLA CAFE A long-time Mexican favorite on old Route 66, 602 N. Mt. Vernon.

LE RENDEZVOUS

Crêpes Suzette

CRÊPE BATTER:

2 LARGE OR 3 SMALL EGGS
1/2 CUP MILK
1 CUP SIFTED FLOUR
1 TEASPOON OIL
PINCH OF SALT

You will need a small crêpe frying pan, 5- to 6-inch size. Beat the eggs, add milk, flour, oil and salt. Beat well. Heat frying pan with a little oil. Pour in 1/8 of batter and rotate quickly to spread. Cook for 30 seconds on each side.

FILLING:

1 TABLESPOON BUTTER
3 TABLESPOONS SUGAR
1/2 A JUICY ORANGE
1/2 A JUICY LEMON
2 OUNCES BRANDY
2 OUNCES GRAND MARNIER

Place crêpe pan over medium heat, add butter and sugar in center of pan. When sugar turns golden brown, squeeze juice of half an orange and lemon and add brandy. Rotate the pan and stir slowly until caramel is all melted.

Place crêpes, one at a time, in the syrup. Turn them over then sprinkle with Grand Marnier, then fold and pour more Grand Marnier over each. Flame and serve. 4 servings, with 2 crêpes for each person.

Lifelong San Bernardino residents Mike and Maria Austin have winning ways with chile! They started competitive cooking on the International Chile Society circuit in 1989 and through their combined efforts won several championships before deciding to form separate teams to double their winning opportunities. The gamble paid off. Mike was International Chile Society Arizona State Champion in 1991, California State Champion in 1993 and 1995, and 5th in the 1993 World Championship. Maria won the Nevada State Championship in 1991 and placed 11th in the World Championship. Both Mike and Maria have a passion for good times, good chile, and travel, which includes many trips along Route 66!

Fontana

population 20,000

WHAT TO SEE:

ROUTE 66 ORANGE JUICE STAND Old Route 66 orange juice stand in Wal-Mart parking lot.

BONO'S RESTAURANT For over 50 years, Mrs. Bono presided over the highway at 15395 Foothill. Her Italian eatery may still be empty and seeking a new owner.

Mike Austin's Bun Burner Chile Shack

5 POUNDS TRI-TIP OR TOP SIRLOIN, CUT IN SMALL CUBES

1 LARGE SWEET ONION, FINELY CHOPPED (ABOUT 1 CUP)

6 CLOVES GARLIC, FINELY CHOPPED

4 CANS (14-1/2 OUNCES EACH) CHICKEN BROTH

1 CAN (15 OUNCES) TOMATO SAUCE

10 TABLESPOONS PURE CALIFORNIA CHILE POWDER

6 TABLESPOONS GROUND CUMIN

3 TABLESPOONS EXTRA-HOT NEW MEXICO CHILE POWDER

1 TABLESPOON PASILLA CHILE POWDER

2 TEASPOONS GARLIC POWDER

SALT TO TASTE

In a large nonstick skillet, cook meat over medium heat one pound at a time, removing meat and setting aside when it is no longer pink.

Meanwhile, in a large chile pot, combine all remaining ingredients and simmer for 1 hour.

Add meat to sauce and cook for 2 more hours, keeping covered as much as possible. If you want hotter chile, add more New Mexico chile powder. 10 servings.

Maria Austin's
Fam-Lee Affair Chile

4 1/2 POUNDS TRI-TIP OR TOP SIRLOIN, CUT IN SMALL CUBES

1 WHITE ONION, FINELY CHOPPED (ABOUT 3/4 CUP)

1/2 CUP CALIFORNIA CHILE POWDER

5 TABLESPOONS GROUND CUMIN

1/4 CUP PURE HOT NEW MEXICO CHILE POWDER

2 CANNED GREEN CHILES, SEEDED, STEMMED AND FINELY CHOPPED

3 CANS (14-1/2 OUNCES EACH) CHICKEN BROTH

1 CAN (8 OUNCES) TOMATO SAUCE

10 CLOVES GARLIC, FINELY CHOPPED

SALT TO TASTE

In a large nonstick skillet cook meat over medium heat until no longer pink. Drain off fat and set meat aside.

Meanwhile, in a large chile pot, combine remaining ingredients and simmer for 1 hour. Add meat to sauce and simmer an additional 2 hours.

Adjust seasonings. For hotter results, add more New Mexico chile powder or cayenne. Be careful! Say a prayer! 10 servings.

Jay and Janice Ilsley brought their wonderful old home back to life and opened for their first guests at Christmastime in 1984. Gala yuletide gatherings had been a tradition at the home. The many windows of red and green stained glass helped the Ilsleys decide to continue the name Christmas House.

The lavish home was constructed for shipbuilder H.D. Cousins in 1904. His Victorian Queen Anne mansion was surrounded by 80 acres of citrus groves and grape vineyards. The Cousins raised thoroughbred horses and entertained lavishly. The house features an elegant staircase with hibiscus flowers carved into the newel posts, seven fireplaces, and much of the original grandeur.

Jay and Janice offer special activities and opportunities that make a visit to Christmas House a truly memorable experience.

CHRISTMAS HOUSE
German Apple Pancakes

APPLE FILLING:

- I TABLESPOON BUTTER
- 3 APPLES, PEELED, CORED AND SLICED
- I TABLESPOON SUGAR
- I TEASPOON CINNAMON
- I/3 CUP RAISINS
- I/4 CUP BRANDY OR APPLE JUICE, OPTIONAL

Melt butter in skillet. Add apples and cook slowly in the butter. Add remaining ingredients and cook until apples are tender, about 3 to 4 minutes.

Rancho Cucamonga
population 102,000

WHAT TO SEE:

ROUTE 66 TERRITORY MUSEUM Bob Lundy, director. 7965 Vineyard Avenue, #F5.

RAINS HOUSE (CASA DE RANCHO) Oldest fired brick house in San Bernardino County. Vineyard Ave. at Hemlock. (909) 798-8570

THE CUCAMONGA RANCHO WINERY (THOMAS VINEYARDS) Thomas Winery was the oldest in California, established in 1839, the second winery in the United States. Now part of a shopping center. Corner of Foothill and Vineyard.

RANCHO CUCAMONGA GRAPE HARVEST FESTIVAL 1st weekend in October each year.

AREA WINERIES Visit Philippi Vintage Co., San Antonio Winery, or Galleano Winery.

WHERE TO EAT:

MAGIC LAMP INN 8189 Foothill Blvd.

SYCAMORE INN 8318 Foothill Blvd.

PANCAKES:

3 EGGS

1-1/2 CUPS MILK

1-1/2 CUPS FLOUR

1/2 TEASPOON SALT

2 TABLESPOONS BUTTER

1/4 CUP POWDERED SUGAR

Preheat oven to 425°. Use an ovenproof 10-inch skillet, preheating it while batter is prepared. Beat the eggs lightly; add milk, flour and salt. Beat vigorously for 2 minutes. Add butter to the hot skillet, swirling it to cover surface evenly. Transfer batter to the skillet; place apple filling in the center of the batter. Bake 30 to 40 minutes or until pancake is puffed, lightly browned and firm to touch. Sprinkle with sifted powdered sugar and serve while hot. 4 to 5 servings.

CHRISTMAS HOUSE
Berry Filled Custard Crêpes

CRÊPES:

5 EGGS

1 1/3 CUP FLOUR

1 TABLESPOON OIL

2 CUPS MILK

Mix batter in blender and refrigerate. Butter a crêpe pan then swirl with batter for 2 minutes, turn over for 30 seconds. Makes 30 crêpes.

FILLING:

- 4 OUNCES NATURAL CREAM CHEESE, SOFTENED
- 2 TABLESPOONS HEAVY WHIPPING CREAM
- 2 EGG YOLKS
- 2 TEASPOONS SUGAR
- 2 CUPS FRESH STRAWBERRIES OR BLUEBERRIES

Beat cream cheese until smooth and add whipping cream, egg yolks, and sugar. Beat until smooth. Carefully fold in fresh berries with a spatula. Ladle a generous 1/4 cup of this mixture down the center of each crêpe and place seam down in ovenproof dish. Spoon wine sauce over each crêpe.

WINE SAUCE:

- 1/2 CUP BERRY JAM
- 1/3 CUP SHERRY
- 1/3 CUP WATER

Bring jam, wine, and water to a boil and stir for about 2 minutes or until slightly thickened. Pour over crêpes. Bake for 11 to 15 minutes in 325° oven. Serve hot, garnished with more fresh berries and mint leaves. 10 servings, 3 small crêpes each.

Upland

WHERE TO EAT:

BUFFALO INN A favorite for students from nearby Claremont. Real buffalo burgers and homemade potato chips called "buffalo chips" are always on the menu. 1814 W. Foothill Blvd.

Rancho Cucamonga is home to the Cucamonga Rancho Winery (Thomas Vineyards) at the corner of Foothill and Vineyard. Thomas Winery is the oldest in California, established in 1839, the second winery in the United States, and now part of a shopping center.

To toast the city and the California wine industry, try this champagne punch that makes a delightful addition for any special occasion. The mock champagne that follows makes an excellent choice for those who don't want the real thing.

RANCHO CUCAMONGA
Champagne Punch

2 BOTTLES CHAMPAGNE OR ASTI SPUMANTE (750 ML EACH)
1 CUP CRÈME DE CASSIS (BLACK CURRANT LIQUEUR)
28 OUNCES OF CARBONATED WATER

Combine all ingredients. 22 four-ounce servings.

RANCHO CUCAMONGA
Mock Champagne

5 POUNDS GRANULATED SUGAR
2 OUNCES VANILLA EXTRACT
2 OUNCES ALMOND EXTRACT
4 TEASPOONS LEMON JUICE
4 CUPS WATER
GINGER ALE AS NEEDED

Combine sugar, extracts, lemon juice and water. Bring to boil just long enough to dissolve sugar, 2 to 3 minutes. Store syrup in refrigerator. When ready to serve, combine the 1/2 cup syrup with each liter of ginger ale. 1-1/2 gallons; 50 four-ounce servings.

The Claremont Inn has historic ties with Route 66. Called Griswold's Claremont Inn until 1995, it now has new owners who have polished and renewed the glamour of the historic location, yet managed to save the history. Here is a delicious bread that is served regularly.

THE CLAREMONT INN
Pumpkin Bread

2/3 CUP SHORTENING

2 CUPS SUGAR

4 EGGS

2 CUPS CANNED PUMPKIN

2/3 CUP WATER

3-1/3 CUPS ALL-PURPOSE FLOUR

2 TEASPOONS BAKING SODA

3/4 TEASPOON SALT

1/2 TEASPOON BAKING POWDER

1 TEASPOON CINNAMON

1 TEASPOON GROUND CLOVES

2/3 CUP WALNUTS

2/3 CUP RAISINS

Cream shortening. Add sugar and beat well. Add eggs then stir in pumpkin and water. Combine flour with baking soda, salt, baking powder, cinnamon, and cloves. Add to creamed mixture, then fold in nuts and raisins. Pour batter into two 9 x 5 x 3 greased loaf pans. Bake in 350° oven for 1 hour. 2 loaves.

Historic Griswold's Claremont Inn was noted for outstanding Coconut Macaroons and the tradition continues. However, the chef was unable to satisfactorily size-down proportions for the popular cookies. So this easy chocolate macaroon recipe is a substitute, not from the inn, but still a scrumptious favorite. Be sure to use a Teflon cookie sheet.

Claremont
population 33,000

WHAT TO SEE:

EDUCATIONAL INSTITUTIONS Ivy League center of the West—Claremont Colleges: Pomona, Pitzer, Harvey Mudd, Scripps, Claremont McKenna College, and Claremont Graduate School.

GUIDED WALKING TOURS Call (909) 624-1681

MT. BALDY DRIVE North on Mills Avenue

THE VILLAGE Historical downtown center.

THE OLD SCHOOLHOUSE Specialty shops and restaurants in an old school building. 415 W. Foothill Blvd.

RANCHO SANTA ANA BOTANIC GARDENS 1500 N. College Ave. (909) 625-7767

WHERE TO EAT:

THE CLAREMONT INN 555 W. Foothill Blvd.

DON SALSA 415 West Foothill Blvd.

HARVARD SQUARE CAFE 206 W. Bonita (in The Village).

Chocolate Coconut Macaroons

1 CUP SWEETENED CONDENSED MILK

4 CUPS ANGEL FLAKE COCONUT

2/3 CUP MINI SEMI-SWEET CHOCOLATE BITS

1 TEASPOON VANILLA EXTRACT

1/2 TEASPOON ALMOND EXTRACT

Preheat oven to 325°. Combine milk and coconut. Mix by hand; mixture will be sticky. Add chocolate bits, vanilla and almond extracts. Stir to blend ingredients well.

Lightly spray a nonstick (Teflon coated) cookie sheet with cooking spray. Drop cookies by teaspoons onto cookie sheet, one inch apart. Bake 12 minutes or until cookies are lightly browned on top. Remove from pan with a Teflon coated spatula; cool thoroughly. Store in airtight containers or freezer bags. The cookies freeze well. 50 to 55 cookies.

At Don Salsa, award-winning chef and owner Nick Montoya serves outstanding Mexican food in Claremont's historic old schoolhouse!

DON SALSA

Special Salsa Fresca

3 CHOPPED FRESH TOMATOES

1 CHOPPED FRESH ONION

3 CLOVES CRUSHED FRESH GARLIC

1 MINCED YELLOW CHILE

2 TEASPOONS CHOPPED FRESH CILANTRO

1/2 CUP TOMATO JUICE

SALT AND PEPPER TO TASTE

Combine all ingredients and serve with chips. Keeps 3 to 4 days in the refrigerator. For best results, chill tomato juice before adding to salsa. 1-1/2 cups salsa.

Note: Try this on burgers or steaks and you'll never use ketchup again!

Claremont's Harvard Square Cafe in The Village is a trendy stop, popular with students, tourists, and the locals. The cafe features a large patio for dining under the stars as well as romantic indoor dining. You can listen to live jazz most evenings.

HARVARD SQUARE CAFE
Warm Chicken Oriental Salad

STRIPS OF CHICKEN BREAST
FOR SAUTÉEING: SESAME OIL, GARLIC,
    FRESH GINGER, CARROTS, SNOW PEAS,
    GREEN ONION
ORANGE HONEY
JAPANESE RICE WINE VINEGAR
FOR SALAD: LETTUCE, NAPA CABBAGE,
    CRISPY NOODLES, BLACK SESAME SEED

Sauté strips of chicken breast in hot sesame oil until golden brown. Add freshly chopped garlic and ginger, plus thinly sliced carrots. Add orange honey and cook until colored; add snow peas and green onion. Finally add Japanese rice wine vinegar and bring back to a boil. Serve over beds of crispy baby lettuce with shredded Napa cabbage. Top plates with crispy noodles and black sesame seeds.

GOOD FOOD FROM LA VERNE:

Most Americans think of California as the primary source of fruits, vegetables, nuts, and wines. Like most proud producers of quality products, California Grape Producers often print creative recipe booklets for their customers. Here is a wonderfully light salad that a friend in La Verne shared. She adapted it from one of the many booklets advertising California grapes and almonds.

La Verne
population 33,000

WHAT TO SEE:

OLD TOWN CENTER
Many shops and restaurants.

WHERE TO EAT:

CAFE ALLEGRO 2124 Third Street, Old Town.

VILLAGE INN COFFEE SHOP 2326 D Street, Old Town.

San Dimas
population 34,000

WHAT TO SEE:

FARMERS MARKET Every Wednesday, in center of town.

Glendora

population 55,000

WHAT TO SEE:

CENTER OF THE CITY
Route 66 was always on
Alosta through here. City's
center on Glendora Avenue
features orderly trees and
old buildings, carefully revitalized.

**TASTE OF GLENDORA
FESTIVAL** January each
year.

WHERE TO EAT:

FENDERBENDERS
Foothill Blvd. at Glendora
Ave.

THE DERBY A favorite
since 1946. 545 W. Alosta
Ave.

..

Almond Chicken Salad with Purple Grapes

2-1/2 CUPS COOKED DICED CHICKEN

1-1/2 CUPS SLICED SEEDLESS PURPLE GRAPES

1 CUP DICED CELERY

1/2 CUP SLIVERED, TOASTED ALMONDS

2 TABLESPOONS FRESH, MINCED PARSLEY

1/2 TEASPOON SALT

1 TEASPOON CURRY POWDER

1 CLOVE GARLIC, MINCED

1/4 CUP MAYONNAISE

1/2 CUP PLAIN YOGURT

ADDITIONAL GRAPES FOR GARNISH

Combine chicken with grapes, celery,
almonds, and parsley. Add salt, curry powder,
garlic, and mayonnaise to the yogurt. Blend
well; carefully stir into chicken mixture. Chill
salad before serving and garnish with
additional grapes. 6 to 8 servings.

GOOD FOOD FROM GLENDORA:

*NOT JUST A COOKBOOK BUT A GLENDORA
COMMUNITY TREASURE was published by the
Kiwanianne Club of Glendora in 1994. The
collection features favorite recipes from many
Glendora residents. Here are some of their good
dishes featuring the best of California's prolific
produce.*

Reverend Doug Hodson's Broccoli Salad

DRESSING:

I CUP MAYONNAISE

1/3 CUP SUGAR

2 TABLESPOONS VINEGAR

SALAD:

I-1/2 BUNCHES BROCCOLI

1/2 POUND BACON

I CUP RAISINS

1/2 RED ONION, CHOPPED

1/2 CUP DRY-ROASTED SUNFLOWER SEEDS

Combine dressing ingredients and chill for at least an hour before using.

Cut broccoli into small pieces. Brown bacon and drain well then break up into bite-sized pieces. Soak raisins in hot water to swell and moisten, then drain and pat dry. Combine broccoli, raisins, and onion in large bowl. Just before serving, add bacon pieces and sunflower seeds. Add dressing and serve immediately. 8 servings.

Diana Walburn's Curried Spinach Salad

2 CHICKEN BREASTS, BONED AND CUT INTO STRIPS

2 TABLESPOONS OIL

2 TABLESPOONS SOY SAUCE

6 CUPS FRESH, WASHED SPINACH

I CUP CHOPPED APPLE

1/4 CUP SPANISH PEANUTS

1/4 CUP RAISINS

2/3 CUP OIL

1/2 CUP MAPLE SYRUP

1/4 CUP CIDER VINEGAR

1/4 TEASPOON SALT

1 TABLESPOON INSTANT MINCED ONION

1 TEASPOON CURRY POWDER

1 TEASPOON DRY MUSTARD

Sauté chicken in oil and soy sauce over medium heat until cooked. Mix all dressing ingredients together. Toss salad with dressing and serve. 6 servings.

Audrey McAfee's Company Carrots

2 TO 3 CUPS FRESH CARROTS, CUT INTO
   JULIENNE STRIPS

2 TABLESPOONS BUTTER

FRESHLY GROUND PEPPER

PINCH OF DILL WEED

1/3 TO 1/2 CUP WHITE WINE

Sauté strips of julienne carrots in butter for 3 to 4 minutes. Be careful not to let them brown. Grind fresh pepper over carrots while they cook. Season with dill to taste. Add salt if desired. Lower heat and add wine. Cover and simmer until carrots are done, as long as 30 minutes. 4 to 5 servings.

Pamela Vermon's Blueberry Muffins

I STICK SWEET BUTTER

1-1/4 CUPS SUGAR

2 EGGS

1/2 CUP MILK

2 CUPS FLOUR

2 TEASPOONS BAKING POWDER

1/2 TEASPOON SALT

2 CUPS FRESH OR FROZEN BLUEBERRIES

Cream butter and sugar until fluffy. Add eggs one at a time. Add flour, baking powder, and salt with milk. Stir in berries and blend only until evenly mixed. Fill a 12-cup muffin tin and sprinkle with sugar if desired. Bake in 375° oven for 25 to 30 minutes. Cool in pan before removing. Serve warm or cold. 12 muffins.

GOOD FOOD IN AZUZA:

El Encanto, meaning charming place, has been a fine dining restaurant in Azusa since 1930. The Peppered New York Steak has proven to be one of the most popular entrees on the menu. The steak is pounded with cracked coarse pepper and broiled to the guest's taste, then sautéed with onions, bell peppers, garlic, and mushrooms.

While the recipe for their famous corn fritters dipped in syrup is never shared, the delicacy is regularly served as an accompaniment to such outstanding entrees as Roast Prime Rib au Jus, Australian Lobster Tails, and Broiled King White Shrimp.

Here is a recipe for corn fritters, not from El Encanto, but similar to their hallmark dish.

Azusa

population 41,500

Incorporated as a city in 1898. The city motto: "We have everything from A to Z."

WHAT TO SEE:

CANYON ROAD The San Gabriel Canyon Road offers a beautiful drive.

WHERE TO EAT:

EL ENCANTO INN 100 E. Old San Gabriel Canyon Rd.

COSTANZA COFFEE Corner of Alosta and Citrus

Corn Fritters

3/4 CUP WHOLE CORN

2 CUPS FLOUR

1 HEAPING TEASPOON BAKING POWDER

1 TEASPOON SUGAR

PINCH OF SALT

2 EGGS, BEATEN TOGETHER

1 CUP MILK

1/4 CUP VEGETABLE OIL

Combine all ingredients and blend thoroughly. Drop by tablespoons into hot (350°) oil and cook until browned on both sides. Drain and place in oven to keep warm. Sprinkle with powdered sugar if desired. Serve warm with honey or maple syrup. 6 servings.

TREASURED RECIPES, the Azuza Woman's Club Cookbook, combines a collection of tasty dishes selected from favorite recipes of local residents. Here are some of the fine examples.

Roberta Behrens's Fritz Squash

1 BUTTERNUT SQUASH, UNPEELED, SEEDED AND SLICED INTO THICK STICKS

OIL FOR DEEP FRYING

1/2 TEASPOON SALT

DIPPING SAUCE:

1 CUP BOTTLED CHILE SAUCE

2 TABLESPOONS ORANGE MARMALADE

Soak squash sticks in cold water for about 30 minutes, then dry thoroughly with a towel. Deep-fry until sticks are browned. Sprinkle with salt. Combine chile sauce and marmalade. Serve squash sticks with sauce. 4 to 6 servings.

Flo Flo Peck's
Salad Algerienne

4 MEDIUM-SIZE RIPE, BUT FIRM TOMATOES

1 RED ONION

1 MEDIUM-SIZE CUCUMBER

1 MEDIUM-SIZE BELL PEPPER

DRESSING:

2 TABLESPOONS OIL

3/4 TABLESPOON TARRAGON VINEGAR

ZEST OF ONE LEMON

PINCH OF FRESH OREGANO

12 BLACK OLIVES.

Dice all salad ingredients. Combine dressing and toss with salad. 6 servings.

Anne Moritz's
Snowballs

3/4 CUP BUTTER

1/3 CUP SUGAR

1 TEASPOON VANILLA

1 TABLESPOON WATER

2 CUPS CAKE FLOUR

PINCH OF SALT

1 CUP CHOCOLATE CHIPS

1 CUP CHOPPED NUTS

1/4 CUP POWDERED SUGAR

Cream butter and add sugar, vanilla and water. Stir in flour, salt, chocolate chips and nuts. Roll into balls 1 inch in diameter. Bake in 300° oven for 30 minutes. Sprinkle with powdered sugar before serving. 40 to 45 cookies.

Duarte

population 17,000

WHAT TO SEE:

DUARTE HISTORICAL MUSEUM 777 Encanto Parkway

CITY OF HOPE Health research center.

WHERE TO EAT:

THE TRAILS RESTAURANT Family owned since 1952. 2519 E. Huntington Dr.

WHERE TO STAY:

WHITE HORSE ESTATE BED AND BREAKFAST 330 Las Lomas Rd. (800) 653-8886 or (818) 568-8172

GOOD FOOD FROM DUARTE:

Situated in the foothills, just five minutes from the city, the White Horse Inn Estate offers all the charm and history that bed and breakfast guests have grown to expect. Junious Arthur and Agnes Mary Maddock built their Queen Anne ranch house on 40 acres of citrus property in 1900. Their Canadian background was evident in the stone foundation, shiplap siding and fish-scale shingles, all crowned with a corner turret.

But life was hard. Junious died in 1903 and his orchard overseer died six years later. A son, Gordon, managed the orchards into the 1940s. Developers soon took over much of the property but the home itself was saved.

New owners Stephen and Christine Pittard opened White Horse Inn Estate Bed-and-Breakfast in 1996. The home was restored and redecorated with the help of prestigious interior designers. Now there are four graceful rooms with a suite nestled in the tower.

California wines welcome guests in the evening and breakfast is served on the veranda or in the formal dining room. This favorite coffee cake is often served in front of a toasty fire on rainy afternoons.

WHITE HORSE INN ESTATE BED-AND-BREAKFAST

Apple Walnut Coffee Cake

1 MEDIUM RED APPLE, HALF SLICED AND
HALF CHOPPED

2/3 CUP SUGAR

1/2 CUP BUTTERMILK

1/3 CUP VEGETABLE OIL

1 EGG

1-1/4 CUPS ALL-PURPOSE FLOUR

1/2 TEASPOON SODA

1/2 TEASPOON NUTMEG

1/4 TEASPOON SALT

Preheat oven to 350°. Line a 9-inch round pan with waxed paper and grease the paper. Arrange apple slices in a spoke design on the paper.

Using a fork, beat sugar, buttermilk, oil and egg together in a medium bowl. Add remaining ingredients, including chopped apple, and stir until moistened. Spread in pan and bake for approximately 45 minutes.

TOPPING:

1/4 CUP BROWN SUGAR

1/4 CUP WALNUTS

1 TABLESPOON BUTTER, SOFTENED

Mix together with a fork until crumbly. Sprinkle mixture over the top and slice the coffeecake.

Note: Peaches, blueberries, or cranberries may replace apples. 8 servings.

Monrovia

population 36,000

WHAT TO SEE:

AZTEC HOTEL The only example of Mayan architecture along Route 66. 311 W. Foothill Blvd.

OLD TOWN Old Town and surrounding shops and restaurants.

OLD TOWN FAMILY FESTIVAL Every Friday night from 5:00 to 9:00 p.m. Myrtle St. between Olive and Palm .

WHERE TO EAT:

LA PARISIENNE RESTAURANT Outstanding French cuisine! 1101 E. Huntington Dr.

THE HAM SHOP 305 W. Huntington Dr.

THE BRASS ELEPHANT Architecture at this 1925 hotel shouldn't be missed! Aztec Hotel, 311 W. Foothill Blvd.

GOOD FOOD IN MONROVIA:

Each year the Monrovia Library sponsors a cookie contest in conjunction with their children's summer reading program. For the 1995 tenth anniversary contest, the pamphlet that included entrants recipes had the theme Wild About Cookies which tied in with the theme of Reading Safari. Children submitted favorite recipes under special categories. Here is a hearty selection from the Oatmeal Outpost Division.

Clark and Tyler Bravo's Oatmeal-Crispy Cookies

2 CUPS BUTTER, SOFTENED

2 CUPS BROWN SUGAR

2 CUPS SUGAR

4 EGGS

2 TEASPOONS VANILLA

4 CUPS FLOUR

2 TEASPOONS BAKING SODA

I TEASPOON BAKING POWDER

2 CUPS OATS

2 CUPS CRISPY RICE CEREAL

I CUP SHREDDED COCONUT

I PACKAGE (12 OUNCES) CHOCOLATE CHIPS

I CUP CHOPPED NUTS

Place first five ingredients in a large bowl and mix well. Add the flour, soda, and baking powder and continue stirring to blend well. Add remaining ingredients and stir with heavy spoon to blend. Drop by tablespoons, two inches apart, on ungreased cookie sheets. Bake in 350° oven until lightly browned, about 15 minutes. 9 to 10 dozen cookies.

Peggy Anderson, owner of The Ham Shop, shared these personal favorites. The Raisin Sauce is is the perfect accompaniment to flavorful ham.

THE HAM SHOP
Raisin Sauce

1-1/2 CUPS FIRMLY PACKED BROWN SUGAR

1-1/2 TABLESPOONS ALL-PURPOSE FLOUR

1-1/2 TEASPOONS DRY MUSTARD

1-1/2 CUPS WATER

1/2 CUP GOLDEN RAISINS

Combine all ingredients and stir well. Cook over low heat, stirring constantly until thick. Serve warm over ham. 2-1/3 cups sauce.

Peggy Anderson's Baked Pineapple

1 CUP SUGAR

2 TABLESPOONS FLOUR

2 CANS (15-1/4 OUNCES EACH) CHUNK
   PINEAPPLE, DRAINED

1-1/2 CUPS GRATED CHEDDAR CHEESE

1 CUP CRUSHED RITZ CRACKERS

1 STICK BUTTER

Mix sugar and flour. Place pineapple in a baking dish and cover with sugar and flour mixture. Add grated cheese and crackers. Melt butter and pour over all. Sprinkle some of the cheese on top. Bake at 350° for 40 minutes. 6 to 8 servings.

Arcadia

population 49,000

WHAT TO SEE:

SANTA ANITA RACE TRACK. (818) 449-6943

ST. ANTHONY'S GREEK FESTIVAL 3rd weekend in September each year.

WHERE TO EAT:

THE DERBY Established in 1922. 233 E. Huntington Dr.

ROD'S GRILL 41 W. Huntington Dr.

Pasadena

population 133,000

WHAT TO SEE:

PARADES Rose Bowl Game and Tournament of Roses Parade.

NORTON SIMON MUSEUM OF ART 411 W. Colorado. (818) 449-6840

OLD TOWN SECTION OF PASADENA Many shops and restaurants. Bounded by Union, Raymond, Green and Pasadena Avenues.

CULTURAL ATTRACTIONS Huntington Library and Botanical Gardens, Mission San Gabriel, Pacific Asia Museum, and Pasadena Historical Museum.

GAMBLE HOUSE 4 Westmorland Pl. (818) 793-3334

GOOD FOOD IN ARCADIA:

The Derby Restaurant first came into being in 1922. Racing indirectly built this famous stop for the rich and famous. It was the creation of the late George Woolf, one of the all-time masters of the saddle, who died in a riding accident in 1946. In 1951 Murph and Slugger Sturniolo took over both the Glendora and Arcadia Derby Restaurants and have continued to make them gathering places for those who love horse racing and good food.

THE DERBY'S BRASHOLI

Thinly slice sirloin steak. Make bread crumbs that include garlic, herbs, cheese, and butter. Pound the breadcrumb mixture into the sirloin. Fill with additional breading that includes Italian herbs and cheese and roll. Charbroil until done and serve with brown sauce.

GOOD FOOD IN PASADENA:

The Artists' Inn Bed-and-Breakfast in Pasadena is located in an 1895 farmhouse built in the Midwestern Victorian style of the time. In 1989, interior designer Janet Marango began restoration while pursuing her dream of a bed and breakfast. The big yellow inn opened in 1993, with five bedrooms, each depicting a different artist.

The Artists' Inn
Baked Apple Pancake

2 Granny Smith apples, peeled, cored
   and sliced
2 teaspoons ground cinnamon
1/2 cup sugar
1/2 cup brown sugar
2 tablespoons butter
1/4 teaspoon salt

Batter:

6 eggs, beaten lightly
1 cup milk
1 cup flour
2 teaspoons sugar
1/4 teaspoon salt
3 tablespoons melted butter

Sauté apple slices in cinnamon, sugar, brown sugar, and butter. Pour apples into the bottom of 6 ramekin dishes lightly sprayed with nonstick spray.

Mix batter, leaving it slightly lumpy and pour over apple mixture. Bake in 450° oven for 18 minutes, then reduce heat to 350° and bake 10 minutes longer. Pancakes will be puffed and golden brown. No syrup is necessary. 6 servings.

Sally Gilmore works full time but also enjoys sharing her home as a bed-and-breakfast stop. Gourmet cooking is a hobby and many of Sally's dishes begin with interesting recipes from her wide assortment of cookbooks, finishing up with her own special touches before serving. Breakfasts in her home are exceptional.

PASADENA PLAYHOUSE
39 S. El Molino Ave. (818) 356-7529

TRADER JOE'S IN SOUTH
PASADENA   The first location for this excellent food specialty chain. 613 Mission. (818) 441-6263

MISSION WEST ANTIQUE
AND GIFT DISTRICT

WHERE TO EAT:
IN OLD TOWN:

TWIN PALMS

DOMENICO'S ITALINA
RESTAURANT

CAFE BREEZEWAY

MCMURPHY'S IRISH
RESTAURANT

YOSHIZ JAPANESE FOOD

BILLY'S DUGOUT

THE RAYMOND   On the grounds of the bygone Raymond Hotel 1250 S. Fair Oaks.

WHERE TO
STAY:

THE ARTISTS' INN BED
AND BREAKFAST   1038 Magnolia St., South Pasadena. (818) 799-5668

OLD TOWN PASADENA
HOTEL BED AND
BREAKFAST   Twelve rooms, convenient to all of the activities in Old Town. 76 North Fair Oaks Ave. (818) 793-9313

Los Angeles

population 3,750,000

Route 66 was Figueroa and Ceasar E. Chavez Ave.

WHAT TO SEE:

SITCOMS Want to see a sitcom? Try Audiences Unlimited at **(818) 753-3483.**

SHOPPING Try Melrose Ave. between Fairfax and La Brea for hip shopping.

STAR TOURS See Los Angeles on star tours Starline Tours **(213) 463-3131** or Grave Line Tours (213) 469-4149 (for an unusual approach).

GRIFFITH PARK ZOO AND OBSERVATORY The best place to behold the city! 2800 E. Observatory Rd.

MUSEUMS Tour the Miracle Mile Museums:

LA COUNTY MUSEUM OF ART 5905 Wilshire

PAGE MUSEUM Behind La Brea Tar Pits 5801 Wilshire

HOLLYWOOD BOWL July through September for the best in concerts. 2301 N. Highland Ave. **(213) 850-2000**

Sally Gilmore's Balboa Brunch

3 TABLESPOONS BUTTER
2 CUPS SLICED LEEKS, WHITE PART ONLY
1 CUP FRESH MUSHROOMS SLICED
12 SLICES BREAD
1 POUND COOKED SMALL SHRIMP
1 POUND SWISS CHEESE, GRATED
3 TABLESPOONS CHOPPED FRESH DILL
5 EGGS
2-1/2 CUPS MILK
SALT AND PEPPER TO TASTE

Butter a 9 x 13 glass casserole dish. In a large skillet, melt the butter and sauté the leeks and mushrooms until tender. Remove bread crusts. Layer half the bread, half the leek and mushroom mixture, half the shrimp, half the cheese and half of the dill. Repeat.

Beat the eggs with the milk, adding salt and pepper to taste. Pour over the brunch mixture, cover, and refrigerate overnight. The next morning, uncover and bake in a 350° oven for 55 to 60 minutes. Note: Artichoke hearts may be added for variety. 8 generous servings.

GOOD FOOD IN WEST HOLLYWOOD & CENTURY CITY:

Thunder Roadhouse celebrates freedom of the open road where motorcycles are almost as important as the food. Open since 1993, celebrity investors include iron horse riders Peter Fonda, Dennis Hopper, and Dwight Yoakam. In the main dining room a teal 1932 Harley VL takes center stage and half a cycle is mounted on the wall. In the 1940s-style diner patrons can mount motorcycle-seat barstools. Those choosing the patio deck are positioned to gaze at more hogs or do some people watching along Sunset Strip. The Thunder

Road complex includes a 6,000 square foot Harley and Indian showroom specializing in $12,000 to $30,000 models. There is also a parts shop, vintage bike collection, and clothing boutique.

Good food is diverse enough to satisfy all comers. Executive Chef Brian Burt sticks to a Hollywood-meets-the-west theme, offering an outstanding home-style menu to get the motor running.

THUNDER ROADHOUSE
Kick-Ass Vegetarian Chile

1 CUP OLIVE OIL
5 POUNDS MEDIUM DICED ONION
1-1/2 CUPS MINCED GARLIC
4 POUNDS DICED RED BELL PEPPER
8 POUNDS POBLANO CHILE
2 POUNDS TOMATO PASTE
15 TABLESPOONS GROUND CUMIN
4 TABLESPOONS CAYENNE PEPPER
10 TABLESPOONS CHILE POWDER
4 TABLESPOONS WHITE PEPPER
12 TABLESPOONS SALT
5 BAY LEAVES
3 #10 CANS DICED TOMATOES
10 1/2-GALLON CANS VEGETABLE STOCK
8 POUNDS UNCOOKED KIDNEY BEANS
8 POUNDS UNCOOKED BLACK-EYED PEAS
8 POUNDS UNCOOKED PINTO BEANS

Preheat large stock pot over high heat and add oil, heating for 5 minutes. Add onion and garlic, stir and cook 5 minutes then add bell peppers. Stir and cook five minutes then add poblanos, tomato paste and seasonings. Stir well to release spice essence. Add tomatoes, vegetable stock, and beans. Cover and bring to a boil, stirring every 20 to 30 minutes for 4 to 4-1/2 hours. About 80 servings.

West Hollywood, Century City
Hollywood population 166,000

WHAT TO SEE:

UNIVERSAL STUDIOS
(818) 622-3801

WARNER BROTHERS VIP TOUR (818) 954-TOUR

Amble along the Hollywood Walk of Fame. Take in a new blockbuster movie at Mann's Chinese Theatre, 6925 Hollywood Blvd. (310) 289-MANN. Or try El Capitan Theatre, Hollywood at Orange. (213) 467-7674

HOLLYWOOD ENTERTAINMENT MUSEUM Memorabilia, education and fun. 7021 Hollywood Blvd . (213) 469-9151

SHOPPING Rodeo Drive between Wilshire and Santa Monica Blvd. for shopping at its pinnacle.

WHERE TO EAT:

THUNDER ROADHOUSE "Live to Ride, Ride to Eat!" 8371 Sunset Blvd., West Hollywood.

BARNEY'S BEANERY Long-time bikers' favorite, not soon forgotten. 8447 Santa Monica Blvd., West Hollywood.

Californians are noted for great salads. This version of spinach salad was served by friends in Century City on a warm summer evening. Our hostess grilled sea bass, served corn that was roasted in the coals, added this spinach salad, and topped the evening with an elegant strawberry Bavarian dessert.

Spinach Salad with Sweet and Sour Dressing

DRESSING:

  1/4 CUP OLIVE OIL

  2 TABLESPOONS RED WINE VINEGAR

  1 TABLESPOON SUGAR

  1/2 TEASPOON SALT

  1 TABLESPOON KETCHUP

SALAD:

  10 OUNCES FRESH SPINACH, WASHED AND
  TORN

  1 CUP SLICED MUSHROOMS

  2 LARGE FRESH TOMATOES, CUT IN WEDGES

  2 HARD-COOKED EGGS

  1/2 CUP BROKEN PECANS OR WALNUTS

  4 SLICES BACON, CRISPLY COOKED AND
  CRUMBLED

In a pint jar, combine olive oil, vinegar, sugar, salt and ketchup. Cover and shake well until blended. Combine spinach, mushrooms and tomatoes in large salad bowl. Pour dressing over salad and toss lightly. Garnish salad with eggs, nuts, and bacon. Serve immediately. 6 servings.

Dive!, Deep See Experience is located in the Century City Shopping Center at 10250 Santa Monica Boulevard. Dive! offers a unique experience reminiscent of the glory days of Route 66 when giant snakes coiled above the road and orange juice was dispensed from bigger-than-life fruit. The exterior of Dive is the nose cone of a life-size submarine, including periscope, and radar. Inside, visitors experience an original undersea voyage while dining on a theme menu including hot and cold gourmet submarine sandwiches, wood-roasted entrees, salads, and creative desserts. The two-story 11,000-square-foot restaurant is part of the Levy Restaurant group and includes partners Steven Spielberg and Jeffrey Katzenberg. Dive! opened in May of 1994.

DIVE!
Carrot Chips

4 LARGE CARROTS
6 CUPS CANOLA OIL
1/2 TEASPOON GRANULATED SUGAR
1 PINCH OF CINNAMON

Peel the carrots and slice them as thin as possible, preferably using a food processor. Set the carrot chips aside while heating the canola oil to a temperature of 275°. Carefully place the carrot chips into the hot oil for approximately 4 minutes, always turning.

When the chips are cooked, turn them onto a paper towel to drain, then sprinkle with sugar and cinnamon. The chips can also be eaten plain or used with a favorite dip.

Santa Monica

population 90,000

WHAT TO SEE:

SANTA MONICA PIER
West end of Colorado Ave.
Shops and restaurants, fishing, games, an antique carousel, and ocean excitement!

**WILL ROGERS STATE
HISTORIC PARK** 1501 Will
Rogers State Park Road
Pacific Palisades.

**CALIFORNIA HERITAGE
MUSEUM** 2612 Main St.
(310) 392-8537

PALISADES PARK Clifftops
overlooking the beachfront.

MUSEUM OF FLYING At
Clover Field, 2772 Donald
Douglas Loop N. (310)392-
8822

**SANTA MONICA
MOUNTAINS NATIONAL
RECREATION AREA**
Hiking, camping, horseback
riding, picnics, nature walks,
and breathtaking views.
(818) 597-9192, ext. 201

WHERE TO EAT:

Over 400 eateries await.
Many of the country's top
chefs, world cuisine, and
eclectic choices. Enjoy!

RUSTY'S SURF RANCH
256 Santa Monica Pier

TAVERN ON MAIN 2907
Main St.

DIVE!
Vegetable Sandwich

FOR EACH SANDWICH USE:

1 OUNCE BLACK OLIVE SPREAD
1 OUNCE GOAT CHEESE
2 OUNCES ROASTED RED BELL PEPPER
1 OUNCE THINLY SLICED RED ONION MARINATED IN BALSAMIC VINEGAR
1 OUNCE CLEANED SPINACH LEAVES
4 SLICES ROMA TOMATOES
6 INCH PIECE OF CRUSTY FRENCH BREAD

Spread the goat cheese and olive spread on opposite sides of the bread then arrange the remaining ingredients on the bread.

Note: Other vegetables may be substituted. 1 delicious, healthy sandwich.

GOOD FOOD IN SANTA MONICA:

Ye Old King's Head British Pub has been located on the last block of Route 66 in Santa Monica since 1974. Known for good traditional English fare, great decor, and a shoppe for English goods of all sorts, this stop is a traveler's delight.

Steak and kidney pie is a national favorite that has been popular since the Middle Ages. Oysters would have been added to the dish when they were cheap and plentiful, but mushrooms are more common today.

YE OLD KING'S HEAD BRITISH PUB

Steak and Kidney Pie

1-1/2 POUNDS RUMP OR STEWING STEAK

6 OUNCES KIDNEY

2 OUNCES BUTTER

2 MEDIUM ONIONS, FINELY CHOPPED

2 TABLESPOONS SEASONED FLOUR

2 CUPS BEEF STOCK OR STOCK MIXED WITH
RED WINE

1/4 POUND MUSHROOMS

1 PACKAGE (14 OUNCES) FROZEN PUFF PAS-
TRY, DEFROSTED

SALT AND PEPPER

BEATEN EGG FOR GLAZING

Trim steak and cut into bite-sized cubes.
Core and dice kidney. Heat half the butter in a
skillet and add onions. Cook for 5 minutes or
until softened. Remove onions. Roll the steak
in half the flour and add to the hot butter in
batches, adding more butter if necessary. Cook
until browned. Remove and brown kidney the
same way.

Return all the meat and onions to the
skillet along with any juices that have
accumulated. Sprinkle remaining flour over
meat and stir in. Gradually add stock, bring to
a boil, then turn down heat, cover, and
simmer for 1-1/2 hours or until meat is
tender.

Slice mushrooms and add to meat and
gravy. Allow to cool. Spoon the meat and
mushrooms into a 1-1/2-pint pie dish, piling
it in the center or inserting a funnel to hold
the pastry up. Add 1/2 cup of the gravy.

On a floured work surface, roll out the
pastry to at least 1 inch larger than pie dish.
Cut a circle, using the dish as a guide.
Moisten the rim of the dish and cut a strip
from the edge of the pastry to cover the rim.

GILLILAND'S 2424 Main St.

YE OLD KING'S HEAD
BRITISH PUB 116 Santa
Monica Blvd.

BOATHOUSE 301 Santa
Monica Pier

CAFE ATHENS 1000
Wilshire Blvd.

WHERE TO
STAY:

CHANNEL ROAD INN 219
W. Channel Rd. (310) 459-
1920

Moisten the pastry strip and place on the rim. Then moisten pastry on the rim and place the lid over the meat. Seal, trim and flute the edges.

Glaze the pie with beaten egg. Decorate the top with leaves cut from the pastry trimming and glaze those, too.

Place in a 425° oven and bake for 15 minutes, then lower heat and bake for another 30 minutes or until well risen and golden brown. Serve the rest of the gravy separately. 6 servings.

Channel Road Inn was originally the home of Thomas McCall, a pioneering Santa Monica businessman. The house was moved from a hilltop site in 1977 to its current location tucked into Santa Monica Canyon just a block from the beach. Built in 1910 in colonial revival style, the house is sheathed in blue shingles. Inside, carefully milled moldings and baseboards have been preserved to maintain historical accuracy. Owner Susan Zolla has collected "a few of my favorite things," that enrich living, to decorate the 14 guest rooms.

McCall came to America in 1879 and made his fortune with sheep and cattle in West Texas. When he moved to Santa Monica, he became an avid golfer and was a founder of the Brentwood Country Club. Innkeepers today pamper guests with afternoon refreshments and lavish breakfasts. Many other amenities make a stay at Channel Road Inn a relaxing and memorable experience.

CHANNEL ROAD INN

Vanilla Streusel Coffee Cake

3 CUPS ALL-PURPOSE FLOUR

1-1/2 TEASPOONS BAKING POWDER

1-1/2 TEASPOONS BAKING SODA

1/4 TEASPOON SALT

1-1/2 CUPS SOFTENED BUTTER

1-1/2 CUPS SUGAR

3 EGGS

1-1/2 CUPS SOUR CREAM

1-1/2 TEASPOONS VANILLA

3/4 CUP FIRMLY PACKED BROWN SUGAR

3/4 CUP CHOPPED NUTS

1-1/2 TEASPOONS CINNAMON

2 TABLESPOONS VANILLA MIXED WITH 2
    TABLESPOONS WATER

Sift together the flour, baking powder, baking soda, and salt and set aside. Combine butter and sugar in large bowl and beat until fluffy. Add eggs one at a time, beating well after each addition. Blend in the sour cream and vanilla. Gradually add sifted dry ingredients and beat well. Combine brown sugar, nuts and cinnamon in a separate bowl. Turn one-third of the batter into a buttered 10-inch tube pan and sprinkle with half the nut mixture. Repeat. Add remaining batter and spoon diluted vanilla over top. Bake 60 to 70 minutes in a 325° oven. Cool completely before removing from pan. 10 to 12 servings.

Baked Apple French Toast

1/2 CUP BUTTER

1/2 CUP BROWN SUGAR

1 TABLESPOON WATER

3 TO 4 LARGE GREEN APPLES (GRANNY
   SMITH ARE GOOD)

8 EGGS

3 CUPS MILK

2 TABLESPOONS VANILLA

6 TO 12 SLICES BREAD (WHITE, WHOLE
   WHEAT, FRENCH, SOURDOUGH OR YOUR
   FAVORITE)

CINNAMON

Melt butter and add sugar and water. Slice apples, leaving the skin on, and simmer in butter mixture for 1 to 2 minutes. Pour apples in bottom of a 9 x 13 pan and allow to cool. Beat together the eggs, milk and vanilla.

Slice bread in halves and layer over apples to cover whole dish. Pour egg mixture over all. Be sure bread is wet. Sprinkle with cinnamon. Bake in 350° oven for 40 to 45 minutes or until golden brown and puffy. This recipe may be made up the night before then baked in the morning. 10 to 12 servings.

Buttery Scones

2 CUPS FLOUR

1/2 TEASPOON SALT

2 TEASPOONS BAKING POWDER

1/2 TEASPOON BAKING SODA

4 TABLESPOONS SUGAR

1/2 CUP COLD BUTTER, CUT INTO 8 PIECES

3/4 CUP BUTTERMILK

1/2 CUP GOLDEN RAISINS

In a large bowl of an electric mixer, beat together the first six ingredients until butter is the size of small peas. Beat in the buttermilk until dry ingredients are blended. Do not overbeat. Stir in the raisins.

Spread mixture evenly into a greased 10-inch springform pan. Cut through dough to form 8 wedges. Bake in 425° oven for 20 to 25 minutes or until top is golden brown. Serve while warm with butter and honey or strawberry jam. 8 wedges.

Santa Monica Pier, the historic unofficial western terminus of Route 66, has been a magnet for visitors since it first opened in 1909. Perfect for watching sunsets, the pier is also a gathering place for those who crave the sand and sea. The 1922 Looff Carousel with 44 prancing handcarved steeds is the sprite-like center of this year-round playground. And don't forget the Ferris wheel that offers an unparalleled view for people watchers.

One of the many Pier stops that delights visitors is Rusty's Surf Ranch, next to the famous carousel. Often called "the ultimate beach hangout," Rusty's offers lunch and dinner daily, live entertainment, and dancing. This must-see attraction features a large life-like mural, museum quality displays of vintage surf boards, a great gift shop, historic photos of the Pier, and such eclectic items as Pamela Anderson Lee's Baywatch swimsuit. (The television series is often filmed on the beach nearby.) Barbecue has long been a staple in the area and Pacific seafood is famous worldwide. These two Route 66 traditions have found a perfect home at Rusty's Surf Ranch. Owners Russell Barnard and Mitch Cohen, enthusiastic supporters of Route 66 preservation, selected these two popular recipes from their menu.

Shrimp and Lobster Bisque

1 CUP WHITE WINE

3 CUPS WATER

1/2 POUND SHRIMP

1-1/2 POUNDS PACIFIC LOBSTER

1/4 POUND BUTTER

1/2 CUP DICED CARROTS

1 MEDIUM ONION, DICED

1 CLOVE GARLIC, CHOPPED

1/2 CUP FLOUR

1 TABLESPOON PARSLEY

2 BAY LEAVES

6 CUPS MILK

3 TABLESPOONS TOMATO PASTE

1 OUNCE SHERRY

Combine white wine and water and bring to a boil. Steam shrimp and lobster over wine broth for 7 to 8 minutes. Remove the shellfish and pull the meat from the shell.

Return the shells to the broth and reduce to 2 cups liquid. Strain the broth and chop the lobster and shrimp. Hold separately.

Melt butter in a soup pot. Add vegetables and sauté on medium heat for 4 to 5 minutes. Add the flour and herbs and mix well. Add milk and lobster broth and bring to a boil. Reduce heat and simmer for 30 minutes.

Strain the soup into another pot and add the lobster and shrimp meat, tomato paste and sherry. Heat over medium flame and serve. 8 servings.

Wrapped Salmon

1/2 MEDIUM CARROT

1/4 BELL PEPPER

1/4 CUP GREEN OR YELLOW SQUASH

1 SALMON FILLET (8 OUNCES)

1 TABLESPOON WHITE WINE

1 TEASPOON BUTTER

DASH OF LEMON JUICE

1/4 CUP CHOPPED TOMATO

1 TEASPOON MINCED FRESH BASIL

DASH OF BLACK PEPPER

Julienne the carrot, bell pepper and squash. Cut a 12 x 12 sheet of heavy-duty aluminum foil. Place the salmon at the center of the foil and cover with other ingredients. Fold the foil in half over the combined ingredients and starting at one end, fold over the foil on itself to form a tight seal. Continue this all the way around until a tight pouch is made. Preheat oven to 375°. Place foil on a cookie sheet or flat pan and bake for 12 to 14 minutes. Open at the table and enjoy the aroma before eating. 1 large or 2 smaller servings.

Just a few blocks to the north, where Santa Monica Boulevard touches Ocean Avenue, is a small stone, set in the grass beneath tall palms. The inscription is memorable:

WILL ROGERS HIGHWAY DEDICATED IN 1952 TO WILL ROGERS, HUMORIST, WORLD TRAVELER, GOOD NEIGHBOR. THIS MAIN STREET OF AMERICA, HIGHWAY 66, WAS THE FIRST ROAD HE TRAVELED IN A CAREER THAT LED HIM STRAIGHT TO THE HEARTS OF HIS COUNTRYMEN.

Alexander Elementary, 1994-1995, *Alexander Elementary Cookbook.* Commerce, Oklahoma: Self-published, 1995.

Bethesda Hospital, *With Hands and Heart Cookbook.* 6344 Forsyth, St. Louis, Missouri: Self-published, 1990.

Brewer, Agnes and Baker, Donna, *Potatoes and More!* 611 West Tenth Street, Stroud, Oklahoma: Self-published, 1995.

Clark, Marian, *The Route 66 Cookbook.* Tulsa: Council Oak Books, 1993.

Descendants of William E. and Ethel Short King, *Dining with Kings.* St. Clair, Missouri: Self-published, 1996.

Divernon Centennial Cookbook Committee, *Centennial Cookbook, Divernon, Illinois, 1900-2000.* 215 S. State, Divernon, Ilinois: Self-published, 1996.

Edwardsville Garden Club, *Recipes Old and New.* Edwardsville, Illinois:, Self-published, 1994.

Fine Arts Division of Amarillo College, Art Force, *Cookin' with Amarillo's Corporate Cowboys.* Amarillo, Texas: Self-published, 1987.

First National Bank and Trust Company of Miami, Oklahoma, *The Banker's Best Home Cookin'.* 2 North Main, Miami, Oklahoma: Self-published, 1992.

First United Methodist Church, *Cooking With Love.* 400 Elm, Yukon, Oklahoma: Self-published, 1996.

Flagstaff City-Coconino County Public Library, *Recipes Renewed.* 300 West Aspen, Flagstaff, Arizona: Self-published, 1993.

Former Lehn and Fink Employees, *Lasting Memories Cookbook.* Lincoln, Illinois: Self-published, 1996.

Fox Developmental Center, *Fox Center Cookbook, 1965-1990.* 134 West Main Street, Dwight, Illinois: Self-published, 1990.

Friends of St. Louis Children's Hospital, *Gateways.* 1 Children's Place, St. Louis, Missouri 63110: Self-published, 1990. $24.50.

James S. McDonnell USO Lambert-St. Louis International Airport, *USO's Salute to the Troops Cookbook.* P.O. Box 10367, St. Louis, Missouri: Self-published.

Jewish Hospital Auxiliary in Support of Barnes Jewish Hospital, *Cooking in Clover II.* 216 Kingshighway, St. Louis, Missouri 63110: Self-published. $12.50 plus postage.

Junior League of Springfield, Missouri, Inc., *Sassafras!* 2574 East Bennett, Springfield, Missouri 65804: Self-published, 1985-1994.

Kiwanianne Club of Glendora, *Not Just a Cookbook but a Glendora Community Treasure.* 535 E. Sierra Madre, Glendora, CA 91741: Self-published, 1994.

Krause, Helen, *Helen's Southwest*

Specialties. PO Box 704, Kellyville, Oklahoma, 74039: Self-published, 1994.

Krueger, Sally and Howard, Mountain Mornings, *Breakfasts and other Recipes from The Inn at 410.* Winters Publishing, 1996.

Mayor's Office of Special Events, City of Chicago, *Taste of Chicago Cookbook,* 1990.

Miller, Rickey, *Kitchen Memories from my Childhood.* PO Box 327, Hamel, Ilinois, 62046: Self-published, 1994.

Montgomery, Lora G. and Hyde, Faye, *Treasure Chest of Oklahoma's Wildlife Recipes.* Route 9, Box 563, Claremore, Oklahoma 74017: Self-published, 1995.

North, Margie Snowden, *A Honey of a Cookbook.* Rt. 1, Box 80, Erick, Oklahoma 73645: Self-published, 1996.

Northwestern Memorial Hospital, *First There Must Be Food.* Chicago, Illinois: Self-published, 1990.

Potts, Leanna K., *From Seed to Serve.* 717 Glenview, Joplin, Missouri 64801: Self-published, 1986.

Potts, Leanna K. and Evangela, *Thyme for Kids.* 717 Glenview, Joplin, Missouri 64801: Self-published, 1990.

St. Francis Hospital Auxiliary, *A Taste of St. Francis.* 1215 East Union, Litchfield, Illinois 62056: Self-published, 1994.

United Methodist Women, McLean, Texas, *Crusine Down Old Route 66.* Second and Gray, McLean, Texas, 79057: Self-published, 1990.

United Methodist Women, *United Methodist Cookbook, 1993.* 720 West Country Club, Elk City, Oklahoma: Self-published, 1993.

United Methodist Women, *Come Grow With Us.* 802 N. 4th, Sayre, Oklahoma, 73662: Self-published, 1994.

Winters, Tracy and Phyllis, *Be Our Guest, Cooking with Missouri's Innkeepers.* Self-published, 1993.

Znetko, Sandy and Ed and Pettinger, Donna and Roger, *The Birch Tree Inn Cookbook.* 824 West Birch, Flagstaff, Arizona, 86001: Self-published, 1989.

C

𝒟

E

F

G

7

People and Places

M

N

R

S

Y

Z